LAND OF GIANTS

LAND OF GIANTS

Where No Good Deed
Goes Unpunished

Steve Lopez

Camino Books, Inc.
Philadelphia

1 2 3 4 5   98 97 96 95

Library of Congress Cataloging-in-Publication Data

Lopez, Steve.
    Land of giants / by Steve Lopez
        p.   cm.
    ISBN 0-940159-30-9 (trade: alk. paper)
    1. Philadelphia (Pa.)—Politics and government—1865-
2. Philadelphia (Pa.)—Social conditions.   I. Title.
    F158.52.L67 1995
    974.8'11—dc20   95-9628

This book is available at a special discount on bulk purchases
for promotional, business, and educational use. For information write to:

Publisher
Camino Books, Inc.
P.O. Box 59026
Philadelphia, PA 19102

CONTENTS

INTRODUCTION

It was a simple plan. California boy goes to Philadelphia, snoops around for a couple of years, then goes back home.

That was March of 1985. Who knew?

Even before I could unpack, a bomb was dropped out of a helicopter, the city hired a deadbeat to repair the damage, voters re-elected the mayor anyway, and I knew two years wouldn't do it. I'd fallen in love with Philadelphia.

There is not a better place I know of to write a newspaper column for a living, and it's not a bad place to live, either. I've tried a few places. I considered a few others. Nothing compares.

Part of it is that you can get from the nightmare to the dream in 20 minutes and see everything along the way, and part of it is that Philadelphia is a city without pretense in a state without shame—the Land of Giants.

Somewhere in there lies both the frustration and the charm, and the essence of the column I write in The Philadelphia Inquirer, a 10-year sampling of which makes up this book.

H.L. Mencken once described his mission as a journalist this way: Comfort the afflicted, afflict the comfortable.

Obviously, my goal hasn't been that noble, or even close to it. Sometimes the idea was just to tell a story, or have some fun. But the Mencken line has been something of a guiding principle for me. So has the idea that a column can be a tool against ignorance and hypocrisy, whether written from a street corner in Philadelphia, the halls of Congress, or a battlefield in Bosnia. Part of what a column should do, it seems to me, is hold people up to their potential. To remind them not just what is, but what can be.

Which is why, on occasion, I have smacked people around a little bit. And none of that would have been possible, over the years, without help from a lot of people.

So here, a decade into my two-year stay, I'd like to thank the judges and roofers, the politicians and pretenders, the wiseguys and wannabes, the saviors and stiffs, the heroes and hacks.

It's a festival, this place.

I'd especially like to thank those of you who dimed out friend and foe alike, tipping me on stories big and small. And I assure you that as long as there are stories to be told, and nobody runs me out of town, the Hack Hotline will be open.

Steve Lopez

ACKNOWLEDGMENTS

I'd like to thank those at The Inquirer who have given me the opportunity to do a job I truly love, including Maxwell King, Gene Foreman, Jim Naughton (the editor who brought me to Philadelphia), Steve Lovelady, Steve Seplow, Fran Dauth, Bob Rosenthal, Butch Ward, Bill Marimow, David Tucker, and Gene Roberts. I am also indebted to the editing staff headed by John McQuiggan for cleaning up the hundreds of daily columns and coming up with years of great headlines. Special thanks to Ken Bookman for helping to compile this collection, gleaned from more than 1,000 columns since 1985, and to Bob Greenberg, Lois Wark, and Edward Jutkowitz for their generous assistance.

But I owe the biggest debt of thanks to The Inquirer's reporting staff, whose work is often the foundation for mine. It's risky to name any names at all, because I could cite dozens and still miss many. But four pros who set the highest standards for themselves and for the rest of us, and who have been helpful and inspirational to me, are Vernon Loeb, Emilie Lounsberry, Dale Mezzacappa, and Tommy Gibbons.

MOVERS
AND
SHAKERS

TRUE CONFESSIONS

December 24, 1989

Call it intuition. Call it instinct. When the city was embarrassed two weeks ago in the famous Snow Bowl at Veterans Stadium, something told me a local politician had to have had a hand in it.

Think about it, folks. A nationally televised debacle. A complete and total lack of class.

Use your head.

And so, before 65,000 fans file into nonalcoholic Veterans Stadium today to watch the Eagles play the Cardinals, I'd like to tell you one more story about the famous Eagles-Cowboys Snow Bowl.

Have you guessed the politician?

Using telepathy, I count 478,000 votes for Councilman Fran Rafferty.

Wrong.

Hey, I was disappointed too.

All right, I'm going to turn the story over to Eric Brosz, a paving contractor and a season ticket holder from Worcester, Montgomery County. He was sitting in Row 2600 level north side, 50-yard line.

"At the start of the game, well, there's four guys in front of us, they came in drunk, they each had cans of Budweiser, and during the moment of silence for Doug Scovil [the Eagles coach who died], they started spelling out EAGLES."

The hooligans mocked the national anthem. They insulted everyone who walked by. One of them puked before halftime. And in the fourth quarter they started throwing snowballs.

No. They weren't politicians.

The politician was on their left, wearing a powder blue ski cap that said Finland on it. Brosz heard the hooligans refer to him once or twice as Ed. He looked closer.

Ed Rendell.

You know him. Former district attorney, perennial candidate. Ran for governor. Ran for mayor.

Brosz says the snowball throwing got nastier. One of the four rowdies hit No. 15 for the Cowboys.

"Right between the shoulder blades," says Brosz, who started looking around for security guards.

He couldn't find anybody. But he thought Rendell, the city's former chief law enforcement official, might take action.

He did.

3

"Rendell says to this one guy, 'I'll bet you $20 you can't reach the field.' I couldn't believe it."

So the guy loads a good one. He winds up, lets it rip. A howitzer.

"It lands at the feet of the back judge—the same referee who got hit in the head earlier," Brosz says.

"Rendell pulls out his wallet, rips out a 20, and pays the guy."

I called Rendell.

Were you at the game? Yes. First row, 600 level? Yes. Wearing a powder blue Finland cap? Yes.

Did you bet a guy $20 he couldn't reach the field with a snowball?

"No."

No such thing?

"No. I was trying to talk guys out of throwing snowballs."

Rendell said I could ask the guy he was with. Attorney Cliff Haines.

I left a message for Haines, but I pretty much gave up on the story. Somebody was lying, but how could I know who?

An hour later the phone rang.

"Steve, Ed Rendell again."

He just called to say he'd lied.

I swallowed some teeth, but maintained my composure.

He said he got to thinking. He felt like a hypocrite. He had to call.

"I'm sorry I didn't tell you the truth originally."

Hey, no harm done. I mean it. Rendell said he thought if the guy got $20, he might stop throwing snowballs.

Maybe it's good he isn't mayor or governor. Can you imagine him in contract negotiations?

"What I did was stupid. To say 'I bet you can't reach the field,' maybe in some small way, encouraged them."

Former D.A. Ran for governor.

Rendell asked whether I'd talked to Haines. No, I said.

"If he calls you back, I'm sure he'll lie for me. He's the finest lawyer in Philadelphia. No way you'll get him to tell you the truth."

I'm not making this up. We said goodbye. The phone rang. Cliff Haines.

This is easier than opening Christmas presents.

Were you at the game, Cliff? Yes. The 600 level with Ed Rendell? Yes. Did Ed bet some guy $20 he couldn't reach the field with a snowball?

"No."

OK, pop quiz. Was former D.A. Ed Rendell's worst mistake to (A) bet a drunken hooligan he couldn't reach the field, (B) lie about it, (C) confess, or (D) take his friend down with him?

My vote is C. Too honest. Why do you think he can't win an election?

I said it before. I'll say it again.

Is this a great city or what?

CONVERSATIONS WITH DIANE

February 16, 1987

Diane Beloff called me last week.

She wanted to comment on my column about her husband, Councilman Lee Beloff.

Beloff and aide Bobby Rego are charged with consorting with the mob in a try to extort $1 million from the biggest developer in town. Beloff also is charged with extorting the use of an apartment for a woman other than his wife. Both Lee and Diane are charged with voter fraud.

I had wondered if Lee was laughing about supporters contributing $74,000 to his re-election cause despite his trouble. Diane said the Beloffs see nothing funny about their situation.

It was nice of her to clear that up. I asked if she wanted to keep talking.

We met the next day.

She talked about Lee's association with mobsters, his contacts with old girlfriends (including the one in the apartment) and ex-wives, his habit of running up major league bar and restaurant tabs.

Lee is a soft touch, she said.

She called City Council "a bunch of little children" playing ego and power games and said that "Lee plays the game as well as the next one."

She said the feds put Lee and Rego in separate rooms and offered them a chance to fink on each other.

She gave an account of what happened in the doomed $1 million extortion caper, and it smelled like a sneak preview of Beloff's defense.

The Beloffs' South Philadelphia rowhouse is ordinary outside, showroom stylish inside. A copy of Money magazine is on the coffee table.

Diane, a young 28, is look-again pretty, willowy, all wrapped up in feathery dark hair. Lee first saw her 13 years ago at a pool in Atlantic City.

She was 15. He was 32.

They had dinner that night. They started dating when she turned 16. The kids are 7 and 4 now, the marriage is eight, and the woman in the apartment gave it a test.

Diane got some of the details of that little arrangement in the newspaper, rather than from Lee. I'll get to that later.

Diane said I had been tough on Lee even before the feds lowered the noose. I said I have trouble with a councilman who runs with mobsters.

She said Lee had seen mob boss "Nicky" Scarfo—who is also charged in the $1 million extortion case—maybe three times in six years. I said that was three times too many.

She said their relationship has been exaggerated, particularly since a picture was taken several years ago of Scarfo leaving the Beloff home at the shore. The Beloffs were celebrating the birth of their first child.

"He was passing our street at the shore, he saw the car, he stopped in to congratulate him," Diane said.

Which means he knew where they lived, what their car looked like, and that they had a baby. This doesn't sound like strangers in the night.

"I think I've probably run into [Scarfo] more often than Lee in the last couple of years, recent years, because I go to the food store and the little shops in Longport, and Lee doesn't," Diane said.

I asked if Lee has relationships with other mobsters.

"I wouldn't say so much relationships as contact. There's a lot of different ones that have been in and out of the neighborhood office to have license work done, registration work done.

"They're the kind of guys who like to take care of everything in their neighborhood, too, so whoever has a problem ... they'll bring that problem to the office."

I asked if she meant mob soldiers, meaning little guys.

"Even up there a little bit," she said, meaning higher-ranking hoods.

"They'll come into the office and have things taken care of for them. They get serviced the same as anyone else."

What are their names?

"I'm drawing a blank."

And it's OK to service an organized-crime figure?

"Lee's a city councilman. Those people are paying taxes the same as anybody else in the city. If they want a pothole in their street fixed, they should have that pothole fixed."

I have trouble believing that a ranking mobster would visit a councilman to get a pothole filled, especially considering the mob's connections in the cement industry.

Diane said Lee entertains a lot, spends tons of money on food and drink. She doesn't deny that his company has included mobsters.

"Lee was single for a lot of years. He was used to going to bars, going to nightclubs. His lifestyle in that regard hasn't changed. You frequent those kind of Center City places, you run into people like that. That's what happens in the fast lane."

It depends on your steering.

More in a couple of days.

KEEPING FAITH IN A SHAKY STORY

February 18, 1987

It reads like a dime-store novel.

A web of politics, organized crime, wheeling and dealing, the young wife nursing the kids, the old girlfriend perched in a secret love nest.

City Councilman Lee Beloff has at least two problems in this story—he is the main character, and this is not a novel.

Beloff faces six charges of extortion—one of which suggests that the mob offered the muscle but made the mistake of counting on Beloff and his sidekick for the brains.

Yesterday, Beloff's attorney tried to dump as evidence a recorded discussion between Beloff and an old girlfriend who was living in an apartment Beloff allegedly extorted from a developer.

I am told you can bet the farm that, on the tape, Lee and the old girlfriend are not discussing the trade of Moses Malone.

I don't know how much of the tape will come as a surprise to Lee's wife, Diane. But if she gets hit out of the blue, it won't be the first time.

When the charge first surfaced, Diane and Lee had a little chat.

"For me, personally, the toughest part was reading it in the paper before discussing it," Diane said in an interview last week.

She said she had known some details, but not all, so she confronted her hubby, who caught his first glimpse of Diane when she was 15 and he was 32. I asked how it went.

"I'm still here, aren't I?" she said, sitting on her living-room couch.

"Obviously, it's something we resolved. I don't think it was ... quite as big an issue as it was portrayed to be. She was an old girlfriend of Lee's, um, and she was going through some problems in her life.

"I mean, I don't want to sit here and say, yes, he definitely had an affair with her, no, he didn't, yes, he admitted it, no, he didn't. I'm not going to comment on that.

"I think that whether or not anything took place, it was certainly blown out of proportion. ... [Lee's] the kind of guy that's remained friends with all his old girlfriends and all his old wives. And he's also a very soft touch. Whether it be girls, guys, whatever, he started carrying less money to the office because he'd get hit up all the time. You go to Lee with a hard-luck story and he's going to help you out."

Diane said they're closer now.

"Up until now there was never any major thing that we had to face together to force us to be totally honest."

In this case, patching up your marriage doesn't fix your legal problems. The woman in the apartment is walking, talking evidence in the government's case against Beloff.

But Diane said that this is all a terrible mistake, and that when Lee has a chance to explain, he'll skate.

I don't know what kind of story you tell to explain (A) a free apartment from a developer who wants legislation, (B) cashing a $9,000 check from a second developer, or (C) holding up legislation when a third developer hedges on a payoff.

Or how you explain mobsters on you like shadows.

But I'm open-minded.

Diane talked most freely about the alleged $1 million extortion of Will Rouse involving Lee, Bobby Rego, mobster Nicky Crow Caramandi, and mob chief Nicky Scarfo.

"Apparently Caramandi did go to the City Hall office a number of times," said Diane, and Caramandi also "kept pestering the Fifth Street office on some licensing things."

You can go with the feds' theory that Caramandi and Beloff were cooking up trouble. Or you can go with Diane's theory that Nicky the mobster needed help getting a license.

If it's a tossup, you might consider Crow's opinion. He says they cooked up trouble.

Diane said Nicky Crow is an "alcoholic murderer" and that she has "a little problem with credibility there." She says what really happened is this:

"It appears to me that he had a scam going on and used Lee's name to get the scam going," she said.

"It's been documented that Caramandi approached the Rouse organization. Rouse never says that he met with Lee. None of the people of his organization say they met with Lee. That's strictly Caramandi and Rouse, Caramandi trying to pull a scam. I mean, it certainly wouldn't be the first time in history that someone used someone else's supposed influence and name to pull off a scam."

So there you have it. It was mere coincidence that Beloff mysteriously held up legislation sponsoring Rouse's project. And it was coincidence that Caramandi was at Marabella's restaurant one day—the day the feds say Beloff gave a hand signal indicating the deal was on.

Wise up, Diane. Dump the bum.

GOING TO COURT WITH LEE BELOFF

March 27, 1987

It isn't easy to get inside Room 15A of the federal courthouse, where there's a line most of the day to watch City Councilman Lee Beloff and his sidekick, Bobby Rego, on trial for their unique style of constituent servicing.

For those of you unable to make it, I'm going to tell you what it's been like for the last two days.

You've got some intrigue, some mobsters, some G-men, some corruption, some sex. They already hit the bonanza on the sleaze meter.

There have been several mentions of Little Nicky Scarfo, conductor of the South Philadelphia Boys Choir. But not all the action is gripping.

Some members of the audience fell asleep yesterday when the prosecution played several hours of tape-recorded conversations between an informant, John Pastorella, and Nicky Crow Caramandi, a choir member and multiple murderer.

The problem was that the tape was barely audible, with the exception of frequent colorful language by Caramandi that I have not seen in any hymn books. At one point, Caramandi complained:

"I'm dealing with imbeciles."

I don't know if he was referring to developers, Rego and Beloff, or the entire City Council.

You hear an occasional gasp in court, like when one developer said Rego told him the long-range plan was to extort $1 million a year, and when the same developer said Beloff claimed to own 15 or 20 judges.

And then you had Pastorella saying that another developer ran the risk of incurring a headache if he didn't pay up, because Caramandi volunteered two bullets for the job.

But after careful observation, my guess is that the element of sex is generating the most anticipation from the audience. There's a lot of whispering about when the occupant of an allegedly extorted apartment love-nest will take the stand, and how Mrs. Beloff will react upon seeing the love-nestee, who allegedly rubbed beaks with Mr. Beloff.

Here's another observation: Beloff and Rego haven't put on their defense yet, but if I were Rego, I might sell my lawn furniture.

At this early stage there's already been enough testimony to reaffirm that Philadelphia is not a normal place. Let's take the subject of personal finance, since a clear pattern has been established in this case in which Rego and Beloff walk around town with enough change in their pockets to buy TWA.

Two bank officials testified that Beloff came into their bank with a $9,000 check. The check was made out by a developer to a mystery man by the name of D'Arbo, who may be alive, may be dead, may not exist.

For the sake of discussion, we'll call it a third-party check.

Well, it turns out that the bank has a special arrangement with Beloff in which he can cash checks for other people, sometimes without even endorsing them himself.

So Beloff comes in with this $9,000 check that just happens to be from a developer who claims it was part of an extortion payment. (I'm keeping an open mind about this until I hear the defense version.)

Anyhow, Beloff makes it abundantly clear to the teller that he really would rather not have his name on the check, thank you. The teller checks with the manager, who says no problem.

This sounds like one of those rare banks where the customer comes first. So I'm switching to the South Philly PNB at 10th and Oregon.

PNB, by the way, does not stand for Pals of Nicky Bank, but for PHILADELPHIA NATIONAL BANK. You may want to call today and tell them you'd like to open an NQA account (No Questions Asked).

While we're on the subject of check cashing, here's another possibility you might consider when you're in a jam. I didn't know about it until former councilman and state representative Jimmy Tayoun strolled into court.

Jimmy said he cashed checks for Rego totaling $16,000. No, he didn't ask what they were for. What's the big deal? He helps friends.

And then Jimmy left court, but it was like his shadow stayed.

One more item about personal finance. If you know the right people, you can make bets without posting the money.

Pastorella said that while he was undercover, he and Nicky Crow placed a $30,000 football bet—it was actually a pledge—with the Mastronardo gambling empire, which later attracted the interest of feds.

It's a free ride, Nicky told Pastorella. If we win, we collect. We lose, "I'll take care of it with the broker."

They lost. Nicky took care of it.

I'll keep you posted on further financial tips, or maybe even some news.

THE BANK EXPLAINS ITSELF

=========== *March 30, 1987* ===========

I promised to keep you abreast of developments in the extortion trial of Councilman Lee Beloff and chief aide Bobby Rego.

In particular, I promised to pass on personal finance pointers, since it was learned in Beloff's trial that Philadelphia National Bank has a swell program that puts customers first.

Unfortunately, because I was busy looking into that, I didn't go to court Friday, when the witness stand was filled by a couple of experts on local politics—a mobster and a mistress.

I would have been confused in court, anyway, based on what I heard about the testimony of the woman. How can you gauge the integrity of a witness who has the poor judgment to cat crackers with Lee Beloff but the keen insight to call Bobby Rego a slimeball hoodlum?

Back to the bank. Many of you followed my suggestion to call the 10th and Oregon branch of PNB and ask about their NQA (No Questions Asked) account. PNB said it had a heavy volume of calls, and the folks at the bank were none too pleased.

Here's some background:

Two bank employees testified that the bank had a special deal with Beloff in which he could cash third-party checks. One day Beloff had a $9,000 check that was made out to a man who may be dead, and who, for all we know, may be voting in the May primary. It was written by a developer who says it was part of an extortion payment. Beloff went to cash it and told the teller he didn't want his name on it. He walked out with $9,000.

After a few readers called PNB Friday, the bank located somebody who is good with words, who wrote a statement to explain that you can't do what Lee Beloff does. They read this to subsequent callers.

When I called, the bank manager said he was not at liberty to talk. I should have said I was Lee Beloff and asked him to send a truckload of money over, but I'm not a sarcastic kind of guy. (Which is why I'm not putting the phone number for the bank branch in the paper again.)

The manager told me to call PNB's public-relations office. Gary Brooten answered and said he was just a spokesman, but I think he's one of the big wheels.

"This is Steve Lopez," I said.

"How do I know that you are?" he said.

Geez. They cash a $9,000 check, no questions asked. You identify yourself and they want to conduct an investigation.

11

Brooten said they had calls from people impersonating reporters. I gave Brooten my phone number and he called me back. I was about to ask, "So how do I know you're Gary Brooten?" but I'm not a sarcastic guy.

Brooten said bank employees were shocked that some callers used abusive language. Me too. I thought all callers would use abusive language.

Brooten said bank officials told them, "There is no NQA account." They also told them PNB doesn't "discuss the accounts or transactions involving individual customers."

One bank employee had testified that Beloff was one of a few customers with special privileges. Brooten wouldn't tell me who the other VIPs are, or whether they're politicians.

He did say I was wrong to suggest that only the "rich and powerful" enjoy such privileges. He said exceptions are made for ordinary people who happen to be good customers.

I asked Brooten to get hold of some ordinary people who can cash third-party checks without signing them, and have them give me a call so I can give PNB some more publicity.

I asked the holding time on checks for people who are not special. Brooten said, "You're asking me some specific questions about policies that I can't answer off the top of my head."

Since the spokesman could not answer them off the top of his head, I suggested he answer them off the top of a bank brochure, which is where spokesmen put that stuff for handy reference.

He followed my instructions perfectly and located the information. The hold on local checks is up to three business days. I asked if PNB earns interest on that.

He said yes.

I told Brooten that if I worked in the bank and someone tried to cash a third-party check and refused to sign it, I would have called the police.

He said we know things about Beloff that the bank employees had no way of knowing back then. Yes, and we know things about PNB that we didn't know back then.

I had one last question for Brooten. Does Beloff still enjoy this special arrangement with PNB?

He said he couldn't tell me. But he wanted to make it clear that what happened in the Beloff case was not policy, but an exception to policy.

I said that was precisely the point.

SUITABLE ADVICE FOR THE MAYOR

January 10, 1986

I walked into Today's Man on Chestnut Street and a salesman approached me.

"Can I help you?" he asked.

"Yes," I said. "I'd like to buy 18 suits."

Abe Klotzman almost choked.

"What's the matter?" I asked. "Hasn't anyone ever bought 18 suits before?"

"Yeah," he said. "One time a guy came in and ordered about 20. But it was for a choral group. I never sold 18 suits to one guy."

He said he had been in the clothing business for 40 years.

"What's the most suits you ever sold to one person?" I asked.

"I would say about seven. You can only wear them one at a time."

So I asked if he had any idea why Mayor Goode would buy 18 or more.

"I think that union gets deals for him," Klotzman said.

You might say that's an understatement. The Amalgamated Clothing and Textile Workers Union furnished at least 18 suits—and maybe more—for the mayor at a price well below the rate paid by non-mayors.

This was spelled out Tuesday in an Inquirer story that in part ran next to a Boyd's ad for a 40-percent discount on suits. In my view, the story raised many important questions.

For instance, what about the mayor's socks? Does he buy 18 pairs at a time, and if so, is one of the unions getting him a deal?

Another question is—why does the mayor need so many suits? When I called his office to find out, press secretary Karen Warrington asked if I was serious. Certainly, I said. I asked how many suits she had.

"About 40," was her answer.

She said she would ask the mayor about his suits, and it took quite a while for her to call back. She finally called late yesterday with an answer:

"No comment."

I could understand 18 suits if Goode were a fashion plate and bought, say, six Miami Vice suits, six European cuts and six Western cuts. But when the mayor goes to his closet, he sees nothing but lifeless blues, browns, and grays.

Just to be fair, I called other politicians to see how many suits they own. New York Mayor Ed Koch refused to comment. Aides to Chicago Mayor Harold Washington are still researching.

Governor Thornburgh owns 12 Brooks Brothers suits.

"Six for summer and six for winter," said press secretary David Runkel. "He buys them one at a time."

The mayor of San Jose, California, the 15th-largest city in the nation, has an even more modest wardrobe.

"I have about a half-dozen suits," Tom McEnery said. "The most I've ever bought at one time was one."

Does he know why anyone would need 18 suits?

"Some people like to change clothes often," McEnery said.

That must be the case with Mayor Goode. And you know, this would have been a dinky little story if the mayor were up front about the suits and his association with the union. I mean, we're talking about just a few thousand bucks here.

You get the feeling that the mayor himself has turned it into a bigger story by apparent contradictions about when he paid for suits, and by saying things like:

"I feel fundamentally that I should not go around indicating what I buy with my personal dollars." And:

"... I expected to pay for the suits and was, in fact, billed and, in fact, paid ..." And:

"What I wanted to imply was that I did not ask anyone for any free suits; that I did not receive any free suits; and I asked to be billed and, for those I was billed for, I, in fact, paid."

Do you get the feeling that when the mayor starts saying "in fact," the facts get foggier? Well, apparently the folks at the Ethics Board have that feeling, because they are reviewing what Goode did with his personal dollars.

I think there's only one way for Goode to get himself out of this jam now. He ought to hold a news conference in his closet. He should attach receipts and canceled checks to all 18 or more suits, and tell the whole story.

I believe that if he does this, he can, in fact, avoid continued questions on the subject of what he, in fact, does with his personal dollars. And then he can turn his attention to some of his more serious problems.

By the way, Mr. Mayor, if you'd like to cut your losses before this thing gets out of hand, I'm a 40 long.

CONTRACEPTION AND
THE LEGISLATOR

March 24, 1988

Apparently we're on the verge of a medical breakthrough involving sex. Things are happening so fast in this area, I think it's important to keep up on developments, so today's column will be devoted to this subject.

Before addressing the breakthrough, which has been discovered by a Delaware County legislator, I would like to spend a moment discussing something I saw in the current issue of Newsweek magazine. In a story about sex in the '80s, there is a photo of two women wearing condoms on their ears.

You're married a few years and it's frightening, the stuff you miss. The picture tested the limits of my imagination. But the story explained everything.

It turns out the condoms are being worn as earrings. Geez, and I thought it would be something weird.

The women are smiling, which I guess is about all you can do while little Trojans are rappelling your earlobes. The condoms are in clear wrappers and come in different colors so as not to clash with your chosen ensemble. They are selling like crazy.

Next thing you know somebody will be selling jewelry for your privates.

I can't say I fully understand the point, but as close as I can figure, condom earrings are a combination fashion-social statement.

I see a practical side to this thing, as well. Let's say a woman is a little lonely, but she's having trouble getting that point across to guys. For the male who isn't quite sure where she stands, the confusion can pretty much be erased when she shows up with two nights worth of fun on her ears.

So I am in favor of condom earrings, especially since they can be important tools in the safe-sex campaign. And since many men are wearing earrings these days, I think it might not be a bad idea for guys to do the same, although they might wish to go with diaphragm earrings.

Let's move on now to the aforementioned medical breakthrough. It involves the potential discovery of a form of contraception so effective it is almost in the same mathematical area as abstention.

It was almost by accident that I stumbled onto this. I was looking at the Daily News and saw a photo of Stephen Freind, a Republican state representative. Ordinarily when I see a picture of Freind I turn the page quickly. But this time, I was grabbed by the headline, which referred to Freind's "rape-pregnancy theory."

Freind is the man behind legislation in which a victim of rape or incest

15

would not be eligible for a Medicaid abortion unless she reports the case to police. For reasons Freind doesn't understand, because they deal with humility and sensitivity, not all victims call police.

Births to poor women have gone up 25 percent since the last time abortion funding was cut in Pennsylvania. You do not find Freind leading the charge to pay for the care of these children, many of whom have lives that make abortion seem humane.

But let's get back to his theory, which he spoke of on a radio show. It goes like this: The odds of a rape victim getting pregnant are "one in millions and millions and millions." This is because the trauma of rape causes a woman to "secrete a certain secretion" that kills sperm dead.

Sounds a little far-fetched, but something tells me Freind knows more about secretions than I do.

Dr. Freind was unavailable yesterday. He may have been conducting research, because the Daily News reported that he said he'd have evidence for his theory in a week.

Meanwhile, doctors in this field have expressed a touch of skepticism. I think the doubts were best summed up by the specialist who said, "That's nonsense."

If it is true, however, can you imagine what it means? If somebody can bottle it, the Stephen Freind mystery secretion could become the most effective form of contraception ever.

I doubt if Freind intended to promote a potential multimillion dollar contraceptive industry. But pharmaceuticals have to be scrambling, this very moment, to get his secretions on the market.

I would call it Freinds No More.

Here's a feisty little sperm buster—imagine an army of miniaturized gun-toting Stephen Freinds entering the bloodstream—that gets the job done every time out, except for that rare one time in millions and millions.

So I don't know about you, but I can't wait to see Freind's evidence of the state of the art in contraception.

It'll be a dark day for medical science if he shows up at the press conference wearing condoms on his ears.

A STANDUP GUY'S
STICKING POINT

March 8, 1988

So Harold Jacobs gets out of bed at 8 Sunday morning and goes for a stroll on South Street. You remember the day. Sunny and springlike, light breeze tickling your skin and making you feel good to be alive.

Then he saw Jimmy Tayoun.

The councilman and a couple of colleagues were working from the back of a station wagon with a glue pot and some posters.

Tayoun, wearing gloves, would slop glue on a poster and then plaster it onto a utility pole. Or a store window. Or newspaper box. Or telephone stand. Or U.S. mailbox.

Jacobs moved in closer. The posters announced the 30th birthday of Tayoun's Middle East restaurant and a week of festivities at the "Garden of Eating and Belly Dancing." I guess the week's highlight would have to be the special appearance by the "World's Oldest Grapeleaf Stuffer."

Jacobs, an art professor, noticed the poster's sketches of camels and a belly dancer who has "The Middle East" painted on her stomach.

"You shouldn't be doing this," Jacobs told Tayoun. He says Tayoun responded: "Why can't Jimmy Tayoun do what everybody else does?"

Jacobs told Tayoun it's illegal to post bills and he ought to be setting a good example, not following a bad one. But Tayoun, who last week criticized Council colleagues for being too ethical, ignored him. So Jacobs went home to get his Minolta.

Jacobs says Tayoun told him to give up the camera. Jacobs refused and also refused to stop taking pictures. Jacobs says Tayoun nosed up and nudged him slightly. Unfortunately a fistfight did not break out.

So Jacobs snapped pictures from every angle. I reviewed the photos yesterday, and I particularly like the shot in which Tayoun smears a poster onto a newspaper box.

Yesterday Jacobs and I went to Fourth and South, and I could see 30 of the posters. "He's polluted the street," Jacobs observed.

I especially like the Tayoun touch on mailboxes. What better way to complement the handsome emblem of the U.S. Mail eagle than with a belly dancer and two camels?

To my surprise, when I peeled a poster off a Daily News box, red paint came off. This is powerful glue; maybe a home recipe Tayoun whipped up at the Garden of Eating.

When I called Tayoun, he first said he didn't put up the posters; his staff did. Then his memory cleared up.

"It's my 30th anniversary and I want the world to share it with me," Tayoun said, adding there's $2 off dinner tonight during the belly dancer reunion.

He said he put up about 200 posters and "there is no law on the books to my knowledge" that makes it illegal. He asked if I didn't think he was actually improving the appearance of South Street, since he put his posters over some raunchy ones in which "some guy is wearing a dress and his penis is hanging out."

For me it's too close to call.

Tayoun said he won't remove the posters after the grapeleaf-stuffing extravaganza is over because other people will just plaster over them.

Not that I question Tayoun's integrity, but he is the guy who illegally slapped up a patio at his restaurant and created a storm with a slur against a disabled public official and was at the center of a flap over his lobbying for billboard companies.

Otherwise he's a standup guy. But to be safe I made a few calls to make sure it's legal to put up posters.

Turns out Tayoun made a mistake. You need permits and permission, and as far as the Planning Department and I could tell, Tayoun violated up to three city codes.

Each one carries a possible $50 fine and up to 30 days in jail. Unfortunately, I believe the law says you can multiply those numbers by 200, the number of posters involved. My math shows 17 years and $6,000.

Geez, I almost forgot the federal laws on mailboxes. One law says you can't hang anything on mailboxes. Another law says you can't "willfully injure" a mailbox. Bound by civic duty, I reported to Postal Inspector David Fast that, to the best of my knowledge, peeling the camels and belly dancer will surely rip federal paint off the mailboxes, thereby causing injury. The penalty is three years and $1,000 per mailbox.

Fast asked, "Could Jacobs testify to the fact that he witnessed Tayoun putting these posters on mailboxes?"

And I said: "Yes, sir, to the best of my knowledge."

To cover all the bases, I notified the FBI and U.S. Attorney's Office.

Whatever happens, I hope it doesn't interfere with the "King Tut Night" Tayoun has scheduled for Friday at the Middle East.

Yo Jimmy. Turn yourself in to me and I'll ask them to go easy on you.

DANCE FEVER WITH THE MAYOR

January 8, 1988

"**S**teve Lopez, please."

Speaking.

"Please hold for the mayor."

The call came the other afternoon. It usually takes a few moments for the mayor to get on the phone, which gives you time to wonder what's bothering him now.

In his previous call he was teed off because I noted that he was standing in deep doo-doo in connection with Sen. Vince Fumo, who has pulled a fair number of tricks for the OK to obtain a piece of public property.

But I couldn't imagine anything he'd be upset about this time. Unless maybe it was my Wednesday column, which pointed out that his inaugural address was a little weak and that the kazoos and fog machines had captured the essence of his administration.

I also noted, after looking at pictures from the Inaugural Ball, that as long as he's around, I am not the worst dancer in Philadelphia. The way he moves, you figure he's a quart low.

"Steve," the mayor said.

Here we go. A lecture on his leadership ability.

"Do you seriously believe you're a better dancer than me?"

I guess I really got to him.

"You seriously believe that?" he said again.

Sure, I said. I can outdance you.

"Well then," said the mayor of Philadelphia, "I challenge you to a dance contest."

Me and Wilson on the dance floor.

I got a headache.

I must admit that I've never seen the mayor this loose. Somebody over at the Big Top must be advising him. They must have said:

"Look, Wilson, the only way to get this yo-yo off your back is to play the game his way. Call his bluff."

Unfortunately, the mayor and his advisers failed to take one very important fact into consideration.

I am a dancing machine.

"How about the Twist?" the mayor asked.

19

In my mind's eye, with the mayor doing the Twist, I see him accidentally knocking down walls. The contractor hired for the repairs gets indicted.

Sure, I said: Let's Twist.

"We'll hold the contest in City Hall," Goode said, "and sell tickets. The proceeds will benefit the homeless."

I have long supported the idea of selling tickets to events at the Big Top, but in this case it would be another Band-Aid approach to a serious problem. I suggested we use the Spectrum.

"The Spectrum?"

Sure, why not? You want the homeless off the streets or not?

I had him boxed in. Goode probably realized that a mayor and a columnist, doing the Twist in front of 17,000 people, would be a career low point and an embarrassment.

He wouldn't look so good, either.

"Let's add a couple more dances," the mayor said, trying to talk his way out of a jam.

A couple more dances?

"Yes," Goode said. "How about the Chicken and the Slop?"

I said there was no need to bring City Council into this.

The mayor had a belly laugh, which I'm sure will be taken personally by Council President Joe "King" Coleman. That's why I mention it.

When he stopped laughing, it occurred to me that I had never heard of the Chicken or the Slop. He probably figured that, and also that I'd back out.

"No problem," I said.

The mayor said we could add a dance from my era. I asked if he'd heard of Grand Funk Railroad. He probably thought I was talking about SEPTA.

He hadn't heard of the J. Geils Band, either, or Creedence Clearwater Revival. I should have known he wasn't one for the classics.

Anyhow, a lot of the details are still under negotiation. I told the mayor I insisted on a mutually verifiable agreement not to take lessons, and I did this for a very simple reason. I don't trust the man.

I'm figuring six months from now we'll find $20,000 in vouchers for lessons, at taxpayers' expense, from the Arthur Murray School of Dance.

"Let's appoint three independent judges," Goode said.

This is fine with me. Currently in Philadelphia, many judges are out of work and would be well suited to determine the winner of a contest, as they are familiar with the phrase, "The envelope, please."

Which worries me. At this point in his career, the mayor can't afford another defeat. Somebody in his camp might bribe the judges.

I'll keep you posted on developments and ticket availability, but I've got to run now. I've got a meeting with my bookie and some guy named Baryshnikov.

WHAT IT'S LIKE IN THE POKEY

August 7, 1987

We all know the numbers by now. Ex-councilman Lee Beloff got 10 years, sidekick Bobby Rego got eight, and mob poohbah Nicky Scarfo got 14.

But that doesn't close the book on this historic case in which, as the judge put it, Beloff "attempted to make City Council one branch of the local Mafia."

In fact, it just raises a whole new set of questions.

What's it really like in the federal pokey? Can you get veal medallions in wine sauce? Do they have a tanning studio? Are the conjugal visits limited to wives? How do you make the transition from ex-con to political consultant?

I happen to have all the answers, thanks to some hard research. I interviewed three local experts. Here are their names and credentials:

Former Congressman Ozzie Myers (2 years, 17 days). Former state Sen. Buddy Cianfrani (2 years, 3 months). And former Councilman Harry Jannotti (4 months).

Get out your notebooks, Lee and Bobby. The masters speak.

Probably the first concern of two guys who eat practically every meal at the most elegant restaurants in town is this: How's the food on the farm? Let's hear from our distinguished panel of experts.

Jannotti on breakfast: "Special K was my favorite. Every once in a while I'd have some eggs. If they had pancakes, I'd have pancakes."

Myers on lunch: "It changes every day. One day they'll have grilled cheese, on occasion maybe a hamburger, french fries." (Jannotti recommends the pork chops.)

Jannotti on dinner: "I liked the spaghetti." Was it the real thing? "Oh yeah. They had Italians cooking it." (Myers adds: "It ain't Le Bec-Fin, but it's ample.")

You may have heard the saying, "Sound body, sound mind." Well, that applies in prison as well as the outside world. Our experts now address this subject.

"I was on the softball team," says Myers. He looks fairly quick and shifty, so my guess was center field. "That's right! I covered a lot of ground."

This is purely speculation, but judging by the physiques, I don't see Lee or Bobby in center field, although I do see a role for them in the softball program.

I see them bribing the pitcher and making book on the game. You put Nicky Scarfo at shortstop, where he can turn the double play and also shoot the pitcher in the back of the head if he doesn't throw the game.

But there's more than one way to exercise at the federal farm.

"I played a little boccie ball at night," Jannotti says. "You'd have teams. You and another guy. I was pretty good at it."

Perhaps Lee and Bobby can join the South Philly All-Star Team, which is to the boccie program at Allenwood what the Yankees have been to major-league baseball.

There is a consensus among our panel of experts that the best way to make time fly is to keep busy.

"I always planned on doing a lot of reading, and finally I had time to catch up," says Myers. Nothing like intellectual stimulation to ease the tedium. I asked Myers what type of literature he favored. "I was always very interested in sports, so I read a lot of sport magazines."

Another way to pass time is to get a prison job.

"I drove a small tractor," Jannotti says. You mean you plowed the fields? "No, I mowed the grass."

Every farmer starts somewhere.

"I worked in the power plant as a meter reader," says Myers.

I see Lee and Bobby in the prison business office, capitalizing on their considerable check-cashing skills.

The thing to remember, Myers says, is that there are many opportunities in the federal prison system. Myers did his undergraduate work at Allenwood before working toward his masters at Loretto. He recommends the latter institution.

"I put in a request for a transfer ... and was accepted," he says. Probably scored high on the SAT. "It was the best thing because it broke up my time. I spent the last 5 1/2 months at Loretto before I got into a halfway house."

One thing about prison, it gives you time to see the error of your ways.

"I was set up!" Jannotti says.

"I wasn't contrite or sorry then and I'm not sorry today!" Myers says.

Best of all, a stiff prison sentence is a warning to other politicians.

"South Philly politics will never change," Cianfrani says. "People are going to serve their people, do what's right by their standards, even if it may not be right by the standards of other people."

So don't feel sorry for Beloff. This is a badge of honor. And he's got a great future as a political consultant.

THE ATTORNEY GENERAL
AND SINNING

========= *September 29, 1993* =========

I never thought it would come to this, but I'd like to say a word or two in defense of Pennsylvania Attorney General Ernie Preate, a good Catholic boy who may never again be allowed to take Holy Communion.

On Friday, Preate violated a church doctrine that dates to 1738. He joined the Masonic Order.

In doing so, according to one Catholic view, Preate may have condemned himself to hell. More important, however, he may have hurt his chances in the race for governor, which Republican Preate is bound to enter in the event he doesn't get indicted for anything.

In a state with three million Catholics and 170,000 Masons, Preate has raised serious questions not only about his religious loyalty, but about his ability to count.

Catholics, never a group to hold a grudge, say that one of the original goals of Freemasons in England was "the destruction of the papacy." And 255 years later, Preate's church officials have not forgotten.

Scranton Msgr. Neil J. Van Loon—who decided not to chat with me—told The Inquirer's Robert Zausner that joining the Masons is a mortal sin and that a Catholic who dies with a mortal sin on his soul is condemned to hell. Or to work for the Turnpike Commission.

Van Loon said the sin of becoming a Mason is not as bad as, say, murdering someone. He said it is more like the mortal sin of using birth control.

I spoke with Preate yesterday and informed him that if, in addition to being a Mason, he's using birth control, he can kiss his tail goodbye. He might be better off just murdering someone, although it might look bad for an attorney general.

Frankly, I respect Ernie for his response. He said his faith is a personal matter for himself and God.

"I'm trying to live a better life as a human being," said Preate, who, according to published reports, is under investigation by the FBI for matters involving campaign contributions, but has denied any wrongdoing.

I asked Preate why, as the campaign gears up, he suddenly decided to become a Mason. He said he met Masons through joint anti-drug efforts and liked what they were about, and the Masons obviously liked Ernie, because they speeded up his indoctrination.

Masons are a private, God-fearing lot who use secret handshakes and signals, much like members of the state legislature. I don't know a lot more about Masons, except that they perform many good deeds and acts of charity. And, of course, they make those jars.

Tom Jackson, grand secretary of the Pennsylvania Grand Lodge, tells me the Catholics are wrong about them. He says Masons don't have it in for Catholics or any other group. They even have Catholics as members, and encourage them to support their church.

Some Masons, as you know, become Shriners, who are known for wearing fez hats and driving miniature automobiles in parades. Which would, in my opinion, be an excellent way to campaign for governor.

Close your eyes for a minute, and work with this:

Ernie Preate, motoring about *Pennsylvania: Land of Giants*, with knees high and tassel flying.

But Preate says you have to work your way up the ladder to become a Shriner, so he won't be fitted for a fez or drive small cars anytime soon. Besides, he said, he did not join the Masons for political purposes. If anything, he said, his membership hurts him politically, what with Catholics raising eyebrows.

And that is logic you can't argue with. Until Ernie, whose political strategists encourage him to speak as little as possible, says this:

"I didn't seek publicity about it."

With all the secrecy surrounding Masons, maybe Ernie thought nobody would find out, and he'd have the Catholic votes and the Freemason votes as well. After all, there are two paths to success in politics, and one of them is rare in Pennsylvania.

Have something interesting to say.

Or join every damn club you can.

Myself, I think what really upsets the Catholics is they don't have any secret handshakes. That has to be it. They've got the funny hats.

Maybe if Ernie cuts a deal.

Bless me father, for I have joined the Masons.

For your penance, give us 10 Our Fathers, 5 Hail Marys. And 3 handshakes.

IT'S A YACHT, NOT A BOAT

September 20, 1990

At six minutes before 10 yesterday on the sixth floor of the federal building, a courtroom door swung open and in walked one of the great thieves in Philadelphia history.

In the grand tradition of local crooks, he had been caught with his pants down and then argued that there's nothing wrong with doing business in your shorts.

As such, there was no remorse and even less fear in his countenance as he walked tall in a suit the color of the cloudy sky and sat at the table where years are subtracted from the lives of great thieves.

The courtroom was appropriately jammed on sentencing day for the once and forever king of clout, the former grand poobah of the city employees union, Earl Stout.

"He maintains to this day," defense attorney Elizabeth Ainslie argued to the judge, "that he acted with no criminal intent whatsoever."

Persuasive as that argument was, it had not found its way into the hearts of a jury that in May convicted Stout on 40 counts of conspiracy, racketeering, theft, and mail fraud for bamboozling $700,000 from the union men and women he represented.

And so the job yesterday for U.S. District Judge J. William Ditter Jr. was to add up the damage in years and dollars.

On the wall behind the judge, the copper seal of the United States had rotated slightly and was crooked. As Ainslie pleaded for leniency, the seal seemed to rotate even more off center. This might have been an illusion, but probably was not.

"Mr. Stout is not an evil man," Ainslie said. "He is a good man."

The seal began to wobble.

"Perhaps," she added, "he's too good."

The seal spun around 17 times.

In a rambling, unfocused, and curiously personal plea, Ainslie called Stout "the most unforgettable person I have ever met" and a man who "acted with the best motives in the world." At one point, she sobbed:

"I hope he considers me a friend. I consider him a friend."

Ainslie also told the judge that Stout—who without rank-and-file knowledge raised his salary by $80,000, hired ghost employees, had union people work on his private property, paid $100,000 a year to a former judge for doing nothing, and enriched friends and relatives with the money of union members who were kept in the dark—was a generous man.

Judge Ditter paused only briefly before balancing the count on Earl Stout's philanthropy. "Unfortunately," Ditter said, "he was generous with other people's money."

In watching Ainslie empty her heart, it was not hard to see why Stout once held his union's unquestioning trust. He apparently has a way with people. A way that, in the beginning, did a lot of good for city employees who were making peanuts.

But in the end, and in keeping with the tradition of leadership in Philadelphia, Stout used the power of elective office to get all he could while the getting was good. And among those who made it possible was a man named Frank Rizzo.

In 1975, when the union won its biggest salary increase ever, Mayor Rizzo gave Stout full coverage on hospital care. And, as if to seal Stout's support in the next election, Rizzo gave up the city's right to audit union books.

It was a perfectly shady match of political need with personal greed.

And to this day, as the city teeters on the edge of bankruptcy, it struggles to pay the richest employee benefits package in the universe.

But even as red ink gushed from every window of City Hall, Earl Stout, leader of street sweepers and trash haulers, floated above it all on a $500,000 yacht.

"I've made it much better for the workers," Stout, now 67, once said.

"Our people got more than anybody in the whole United States. I make a nice salary. ... And my only vice is the boat. I just took all my money and put it in the boat. And I think I deserve that. I don't think that's no shame to say that I got a yacht. Don't call it a boat, please.

"It's a yacht."

Ditter, who never reached for a hanky during Ainslie's portrayal of the wonderful and generous Earl Stout, sentenced him to 3 years and 10 months in prison and ordered him to restore nearly $450,000 to the union. In the tradition of great local thieves, Stout showed no emotion.

In arguing that he couldn't afford restitution, Ainslie had said Stout's only asset was the equity on his boat.

When the king of clout resisted the urge to jump up and tell the court it was a yacht, not a boat, you knew Earl Stout was dead.

CAMDEN'S OWN YOSEMITE SAM

January 4, 1990

I met Camden County Prosecutor Sam Asbell once. He seemed like a decent guy. I don't know why they're calling him Wyatt Earp in Jersey.

Asbell goes to the office New Year's Day to read his mail. He comes out at 5 p.m. and gets into his 1987 Lincoln Town Car.

Here's where Asbell, being a safe motorist, takes that one extra little precaution. He lays a sawed-off shotgun in his lap.

Yeah. He says that's how he travels. Plus he carries a 9mm semiautomatic, just for insurance. "But as far as I'm concerned," he says, "there's nothing better than a sawed-off shotgun."

We sent the wrong people to Panama. Asbell and a hockey team would have bagged Noriega in 20 minutes.

I'm not going to second-guess a gun expert, but I recommend against a shotgun in the lap. Men were born with certain reflexive urges. They don't think. They just scratch.

Boom.

All right, Asbell says that as he drives away, two men are following in a green Toyota. A station wagon.

The men start shooting and we've got Miami Vice, no palm trees. They get up to 80, 100 miles an hour.

"My back window blew into the back of my head," Asbell says.

After a while, he stops, the Toyota pulls alongside him and Asbell cranks away with his shotgun.

"I saw his head smash into the front window," he says of the passenger. "I know I hit him. I saw his head explode."

It may be time to revoke Sam's West Coast Video card.

The Toyota speeds off. Asbell runs after it, firing the 9mm. Then he goes to the police.

There are no witnesses. No car. No body. The first thing cops and prosecutors always ask, of course, is, Did you get the license? Asbell saw the exploding head, but not the license.

Camden is awash in theories.

(A) Too much combat fatigue and he just snapped. (B) Sam's team lost the Cotton Bowl and he was fighting mad. (C) He shot up his own car to impress the new governor and get reappointed. (D) It really happened.

All four options are scary.

I'm going to assume he's telling the truth. Maybe he heightened the reality, but it's basically the truth. Asbell has thrown out three reasons for someone to kill him.

(1) Retaliation for prosecuting drug dealers. (2) An act of terrorism by the KKK. (3) A robbery attempt.

Number one is possible, but is a Toyota station wagon the car of choice among drug dealers?

Number two is possible, except for one little problem. Asbell said the guys in the car were black. I suppose it's possible that two black KKK members are driving a Japanese car, but don't bet the house.

Number three is possible, but if you want to rob somebody, do you go to a deserted county building, wait for a guy to get in his car, and then chase him through town?

I happen to own a green Toyota. I want that out in the open.

But I have witnesses who can put me in Philadelphia at 5 p.m. Monday. I was at Penn's Landing, dodging bullets from across the river.

Another thing. My Toyota is a truck, not a station wagon. But since the engine is pretty much the same, I consider myself something of an expert witness in this case.

The ride is pretty smooth. One time my dog Gretchen jumped out at 30 m.p.h. and was unhurt. (Do not try this at home.) Though my Toyota has never seen 80 miles an hour, I suppose it's possible. The doors would fall off, but it's possible.

At 100 m.p.h., Toyotas begin ejecting the occupants. So I don't know how easy it is to lean out the window and aim a gun at a car that's speeding along in the dark.

To find out more, I called Car and Driver magazine in Michigan.

Peter Charlik, a technical assistant, said that shooting out of cars "is not on our test procedure." But he said an '87 Lincoln Town Car has 150 horsepower. A Corolla station wagon has 102. The Camry wagon has 115, unless you choose the "sport" option of 156.

Charlik says that unless our drug dealer/bigot/robber chose the "sport" option on a Camry, he might have had trouble keeping up with a Town Car.

So what really happened? I don't know. Asbell's story is a little bizarre, but that would figure. Here's a cowboy who enjoys hitting the streets with the narcotics strike force. In a recent story, which had a picture of Sam holding his shotgun, Asbell said: "A couple of times a week I get down and get dirty with these guys. It's neat and macho. My wife thinks I'm insane."

Well, I don't know. But a guy who's reading his mail on New Year's Day and has a sawed-off shotgun for a lap dog maybe needs a rest.

REMINISCENCES OF A FIGHTER

October 24, 1989

She sits in the chair where her husband died.

The morning sun has found an angle through the window and divided the room into fragments of shade and textured light. It falls on Besse Weiner that way, too, leaving her half in the room, half with Max.

The death certificate will say the official place of death was the hospital, but for Besse Weiner, Max passed on here in his patched-up recliner at 3 o'-clock on Sunday afternoon.

He died at the age of 77 in his East Oak Lane den while plotting ways to beat out two guys half his age for the job of city controller. And when the little man with the funny hats left, it was a natural disaster to the conscience of the city.

"He died with his boots on," says the Rev. Paul Washington, a longtime friend who expected nothing else. Father Washington has dropped by to pay respects. His hypnotic voice is rich and resonant, soothing to the soul. Besse eases back against the burgundy chair now as if she is leaning against her husband.

Its arms reach around embracingly and take her floating off through 50 years of a marriage dedicated to doing good things for little people. Fifty years that always seemed to have begun yesterday.

"I had just given him lunch," she says, as if this whole thing were just too incomprehensible, that he could be gone just like that. "He wanted something else, I forget what, and I went into the kitchen. I was gone five seconds. When I came back he was dead. He died right here."

She says she started slapping him. Her eyes well up over the thought, and the room grows cold.

You can hear the slaps, faintly. Over the chair is a painting of Max when he was a classical mandolinist. He used to sit here and play for Besse, when he was younger. You can hear the music, faintly, off in the distance, coming from a time when both of them were young.

In painful mourning, Besse Weiner is a gray sketch of beauty, lost in her love, wisps of silver hair aglow from the morning light.

"He loved the grandchildren," she says, pointing out a 10-year-old photo of the two of them—about 7 and 5 at the time—standing behind protest signs at one of Max's eight zillion demonstrations against the great injustices of the world.

The phone keeps ringing. It doesn't seem to bother Besse. Every call affirms her husband's selfless mission.

A short, frail, bespectacled man, Max was Goliath's David as a senior citizen, Mr. Peepers with a knockout punch. To see him stroll rumpled and droopy-eyed into the Big Top arena that is City Council and take on the lions was a thing of beauty.

With his slingshot of facts, logic, and moral outrage, he was the voice of the little guy, for whom he saved literally millions of dollars on gas fees, bus fares, and telephone bills.

What many people don't know was that Max was only half of a team. All of his causes were Besse's as well, and she worked as hard, if not harder. Max was the front man.

Besse says she has a thing against public speaking that goes back to first grade. Her teacher mistakenly thought Besse was misbehaving and slapped her in class. Besse staged her first demonstration—refusing, for the rest of the school year, to speak when called upon.

When age made them slow down, they threw out going to the movies, things like that, because their work was never done. The day Max died, they had worked together on a leaflet for his campaign. They had worked together since the 1930s.

"We both went to Simon Gratz High and I knew him because he was on the debating team, drama, and he was a tumbler. He didn't know me."

She was working in Harrisburg a few years later for the Liquor Control Board, making $37.50 a month. One of her friends told her one night that some guy was organizing non-union employees and needed help mailing fliers.

Guess who.

She entered a room and found Max bobbing up and down in a chair. He would stuff an envelope, pop up, slip the envelope under him and then sit on it to squeeze the air out before sealing and moving on to the next.

They were married several months later, and Besse has been bouncing on envelopes ever since, often after getting home from the paying jobs that supported their causes.

She says living through the Depression gave them their conviction, and that Max had found things in philosophy books, as a young man, that lit in him a perpetual flame.

She says this as she sits there in the chair where Max died, her partner and her lover.

THE POLITICAL PROCESS

A CIVIC LEADER

November 20, 1990

I sat down Sunday to pay the bills and came upon a $20 parking ticket. I put my pen to a check, but something stopped me.

I got up and went into the other room to dig out the Saturday paper.

There it is. Top of Page One.

Milton Street, court aide, thumbs nose at traffic fines.

By L. Stuart Ditzen.

T. Milton Street, the assistant budget director of Philadelphia Traffic Court, owes $1,967 in fines to the court—and has no intention of paying.

"Why the f- should I pay?" demanded Street, a former state senator.

I had already addressed the envelope to the City of Philadelphia, Parking Violations Branch. For a moment, there was a temptation to enclose not the check, but the quotation in the preceding paragraph.

I ended up sending the check, but I didn't feel good about it. The thing is, I don't have Milton's connections.

"If people see that he's failing to respond to his obligation," the president judge of Traffic Court said yesterday after suspending Street, "why should they respond to theirs? I think it's terrible. It's disgusting."

Judge George Twardy also suspended Milton Street's son, Milton Jr., who had 11 unpaid tickets.

Some dads teach their kids how to fish.

Five other employees were suspended as well.

In Milton Street's case, Twardy had toyed with the idea of a penalty other than suspension.

"I'd like to go in and wring his neck," he said in Saturday's story.

I don't know what stopped him. Nor do I know why news of Street's attitude caught Twardy by surprise.

"Holy cripes!" Twardy said in the Saturday story when told of Street's unpaid fines. "I can't believe it. I'm really shocked."

As a local gentleman once asked of me—where'd this guy come out of, a tree or what?

Milton Street has almost single-handedly sustained the debt-collection industry. He has owed the state, the city, the feds, the gas company. Never has one man worked so hard to pay so little to so many.

But he's smooth behind the wheel.

"I had a choice," he said in 1981, discussing a warrant for his arrest on unpaid speeding tickets. "Either spend the money on tickets or elsewhere. I chose to spend it elsewhere."

The next year he was nailed twice for driving with a suspended license. In Saturday's story, he said his traffic fines are nothing.

"I got $62,000 I owe in taxes."

Last Wednesday, the Department of Licenses & Inspections visited Milton's vending truck at Temple University. The truck once was parked beside a no-parking sign, but Milton set it right. He had the sign moved.

Last week, an acquaintance of Milton's was operating the truck without a vending or health license.

Yum.

And so it was shut down. L&I Commissioner Don Kligerman said Milton called to explain why the acquaintance was operating the truck. Because his son Kevin was in jail (over a fatal auto accident).

This is not a family, folks. It's a roving public-relations emergency.

And while some cities might look at a résumé like Milton's and wonder why he wasn't in jail, Our Town took a look and wondered why he wasn't in Traffic Court.

Something suggests it wasn't Twardy's idea. First clue: Milton once stood outside Traffic Court and screamed for Twardy's dismissal, calling him a drunk and a hack.

Twardy denied both charges.

So we're left with some questions. Who hired Milton, and why, and aren't Milton and Traffic Court a match made in heaven?

Well, Traffic Court being a Republican patronage shack, and Billy Meehan being the party's chief hack, it's a fair guess that Meehan put Street there as a favor for God knows what.

Meehan and Twardy won't talk. But sources say Street was put there to pry more money out of the city through his brother.

Councilman John Street.

What was God thinking?

John Street, in fairness, is now considered one of the city's budget experts after living for years by the family motto. You know it. You love it. You wish it could be yours.

"Why the f- should I pay?"

Milton Street should never have been hired. And if there were a single self-respecting Republican official in this city, Milton wouldn't have been suspended yesterday. He would have been fired.

And hired by the Parking Authority.

LEGISLATION IN PHILADELPHIA

December 5, 1986

In 1983, Joe Logue and his wife bought the newsstand at 18th and Market for their son.

"It's so Jimmy could have something after we've departed," Joe says.

Jimmy, 23, has cerebral palsy and lives with his parents in Kensington.

"Twenty-three and a half," Jimmy says.

Joe and his wife, Jean, figured that once trained, Jimmy could handle the job on his own. So every weekday, from 6:30 a.m. until 6 p.m., Joe and Jimmy sell newspapers, magazines, and snacks at Jimmy's News Stand.

Business is good. Eighty-five percent of the customers are regulars, and Jimmy knows whether they want a Cosmo or a Newsweek.

But unlike many newsstands on Market, theirs has no electricity. That means no light or electric heater. Jimmy doesn't move fluidly to begin with. When it's freezing, handling change is impossible.

They used a kerosene heater last year. "Gave me terrible headaches," Jimmy says.

They have a propane heater this year. But Joe is afraid Jimmy might accidentally knock it over and start a fire. And they still need light.

When the newsstand becomes a freezer, Jimmy goes into the warm lobby at 1760 Market. And Joe tells his story to City Hall, which has given him the cold shoulder for three years.

For Logue to get electricity, Councilman John Street has to introduce legislation, because that's his district. Logue says Street has never responded to his pleas.

A lawyer who works in the 1760 Market building took up the Logues' cause. But the lawyer, Brian Rosenthal, says Street has not responded to his two letters and several calls.

For starters, something is wrong with a system in which you need legislation to plug in a heater.

When I called Street last week, he had no acceptable defense for ignoring the Logues. But his comments about street sales made sense.

"Without a doubt, some of the junkiest vending stands in all the world exist on Philadelphia streets. Vendors ought to be allowed to do business, but there's a better way."

He's right. The Logues run a neat business, but Center City is littered with miniature flea markets.

Street said the city needs a plan for vending carts and newsstands.

Some newsstands have lights, he said; some have lottery machines, some have heaters, some are dangerous, some look awful. He's right.

A year-old vending bill by Mayor Goode has gathered dust because Street and others say it doesn't go far enough. It doesn't propose design standards, for one thing. And Street says he won't introduce legislation for Jimmy's News Stand or anyone else until there's a better plan.

Which sounds quite responsible. But that's not the whole story.

Joe Logue says that while Street ignored him, the councilman introduced legislation for someone else to get electricity.

"I never did," Street told me.

Council Bill 293 was introduced October 4, 1984. It gave a businessman two blocks away from the Logues the OK for "underground wires to be connected to his newsstand."

The names on the bill are Councilmen David Cohen and John Street.

At a hearing on Bill 293, swift action was urged, for an interesting reason. The manager of the newsstand has a disability worsened by cold weather.

The bill was withdrawn on a technicality and reintroduced November 14, 1984, as Bill 364. With the signatures of Cohen and Street.

Although it never was passed, a source said the owner of the newsstand was allowed to install electricity pending the outcome of Bill 364.

When I checked that newsstand yesterday, the lights were on.

On Monday, when the Daily News was delivered to Jimmy's News Stand, it carried a story about John Street and his brother Milton, who operates a vending truck.

It said Milton Street drove his truck to Temple University and went into a tizzy when he couldn't find a parking space to his liking. Another vendor quoted Milton as saying: "If I don't vend, nobody does."

On October 9, John Street introduced a bill banning vending on that street.

"If my brother Milton can't vend there, no one can," the Daily News quoted him as saying.

The Daily News said Street backed off the bill after his brother and the other vendors worked things out.

Although Milton Street's van was closed yesterday, it was parked in the spot he coveted—between two signs that say "No Stopping Any Time."

A brisk wind cut through Jimmy's News Stand yesterday afternoon. It figures to get a lot colder.

LIBERATING THE
COUNCILMOBILE

February 7, 1988

It was windy and cold, but someone had to watch for cops. That was my job.

You wait, interminably, you wait; convinced you have plotted the perfect crime, convinced as well that something will go wrong.

At 10:20 a.m. Wednesday, the door rolled up on the city garage at Front and Hunting Park.

"Come on," I prayed.

"It'll work," an accomplice reassured.

Then, at 10:25, bingo. The blue-and-white van rolled haltingly down the hill toward me. The driver and passenger signaled thumbs up.

The Councilmobile was mine.

City Council President Joe "King" Coleman had kept it under wraps for two years, a symbol of waste and indecision. Now it was liberated.

My driver gunned the engine and clouds of smoke enveloped the van. Finally we were all inside, congratulating each other.

It was an inside job because it had to be. After Councilman Angel Ortiz wimped out, I called Councilwoman Joan Krajewski and asked if she wanted to help me turn the Councilmobile over to its rightful owners—the taxpayers of Philadelphia.

"Count me in," she said. She called Republican Councilman Brian O'Neill "for bipartisan representation."

After a strategy session outside the garage, I had sent the two Council members inside. Just tell the garage attendant you're curious, I said, and you want to take a ride. And be firm.

They followed orders perfectly.

"The seat belts don't work," said O'Neill, who was driving.

"The radio doesn't work," said Krajewski.

"And the telephone doesn't work," said Krajewski's aide, Carol Nicastro.

Too bad. The thing only has 354 miles, but I think the warranty is up.

I borrowed Nicastro's lipstick to make signs for the windows. One said "Councilmobile," the other "Deals on Wheels." We were ready to roll.

We got about 20 feet. "What did this damn thing cost?" Krajewski asked.

Thirty grand, I said.

My plan was to spin up to the Northeast for some door-to-door constituent servicing, which was the stated purpose of the Councilmobile. Then we'd circle

City Hall while I called Coleman through a megaphone. I figured we could slap the city-financed portrait of Coleman on the grille and visit neighborhoods for private screenings of Coleman's $20,000 videotape of the inaugural.

The Councilmobile stalled again.

"Thirty thousand dollars and the engine doesn't work," Krajewski said as we died next to a smashed truck and a field of trash. "What a mess. Whose district is this?"

O'Neill noticed "Jack Kelly for Council" signs on poles. It looked like we'd be stuck here a while.

"It's been in the garage so long it doesn't want to leave," O'Neill said.

We checked under the hood. Looked fine, but the Councilmobile grunted, sputtered, smoked, and stalled again.

"This is just like City Council," O'Neill said.

It took 40 minutes to go three blocks. In one violent spasm, Nicastro was thrown to the floor. We stalled again next to the Franklin Diner.

"At least we can get cocktails here," Krajewski said.

"We're going to get killed," O'Neill said, trying to merge.

He suggested we call a tow truck. Instead, we convulsed into a gas station. While a mechanic unscrewed stuff under the hood, I called Coleman's office. They said he was busy.

"Just tell him it's Lopez," I said.

"Of The Inquirer?"

"Yeah. Tell him I've stolen his Councilmobile, but we're having some mechanical difficulties. We hope to be on the road again soon."

"I'll give him the message."

I went up to a customer who had brought his car in for a lube job.

"Excuse me, sir, but this is your lucky day. Have you heard of the Councilmobile?" He said yes.

"We're on the road today to service constituents. I've got two Council members here to help you."

Robert Cromartie said he had some abandoned cars in his neighborhood. I led him to the Councilmobile. The mechanic, Jimmy Nelson, said the Councilmobile had some serious carburetor problems. I asked if we could be of any service to him.

"We got bats in our neighborhood," Nelson said.

Hey pal, this ain't the Batmobile. On our way out, I noted the van is smooth in reverse. "It's like City Council," Krajewski said.

We sputtered back to the garage. It had taken 70 minutes to go two miles, with a top speed of 12 miles an hour and four cases of whiplash.

Hey, Joe. You might want to consider a trade-in. This is not a vehicle fit for a king.

A CALL FROM CALIFORNIA

May 15, 1987

"**H**ello, Steve?"

Oh no.

"How's everything in Philadelphia?"

Fine, thanks.

"Just thought I'd check to see what's new."

Nothing is new.

"Come on. No juicy local news?"

Well, the state pitched in $5 million for the 200th anniversary of the Constitution.

"I mean big news."

Mike Schmidt hit his 500th homer.

"Don't you have an election coming up?"

Not that I know of.

"Come on."

Well, maybe.

"What are you trying to hide? I figured with all the trouble the city's had, there'd be some good reform candidates on the ballot."

That's right.

"Well, tell me about them. Let's start with the mayor. Who's going to replace that guy Wilson Goode?"

What do you mean, replace him?

"Isn't he stepping down after the city torched that neighborhood where 11 people died? We saw it on the news out here in California."

He's running for re-election.

"But I thought his own commission criticized him for what happened."

Well, they did say he was grossly negligent. And they mentioned something about a reckless disregard for life and property.

"I can't imagine a stronger denouncement."

You must have missed the grand jury presentment last week, concerning the rebuilding project.

"What did it say?"

Something about a litany of mismanagement and incompetence on the part of the mayor. I forget the exact wording.

"My God. Two weeks before the election. It must have killed him."

Don't jump to conclusions.

"How far back is he?"

He's ahead by 20 points.

"I don't understand."

Don't try to.

"Except for MOVE, has he been a great success?"

I said don't try to understand.

"This ought to be a walk for the Republicans. I'll bet ever since the bomb was dropped, they've been grooming some young turk to lead the city out of the dark past."

Ever hear of Frank Rizzo?

"Isn't he the guy who ... "

Yeah.

"Now don't tell me he's ahead in the polls, too."

Bingo.

"Do you mean it may be Goode against Rizzo in the general election? They could be the worst and second-worst mayors in United States history."

It's debatable.

"What is?"

Who's first and who's second.

"I hope some decent people are running for City Council."

Sure. Take Happy Fernandez. Bright young Democrat.

"The mayor must have put her on his slate to help his own image."

No, he went with Fran Rafferty.

"What's he known for?"

A fist fight at a Council meeting, taking his shirt off on TV and announcing he was going to get bombed, and introducing a resolution to honor the Roofers Union, which had 13 people accused of racketeering.

"Is there anything good you can say about Mayor Goode?"

He didn't endorse Harry Jannotti for Council.

"What are his credentials?"

Only one conviction. Remember Abscam?

"He was convicted in Abscam and he's running for Council again?"

Get to know us.

"You can't possibly have a worse candidate on the ballot."

Ever hear of Lee Beloff?

"Who's he?"

A councilman with some friends who happen to be gangsters. One of them was just convicted of extortion and the feds say Beloff was in on it. Beloff has a trial coming up—six counts of extortion.

"He'll be glad when that's over."

Not particularly.

"Why not?"

He'll go on trial for vote fraud.

"I'll bet nobody is supporting him."

Three names stand out. Former state Sen. Buddy Cianfrani, former U.S. Rep. Raymond Lederer, and former state Rep. Matthew Cianciulli.

"Why do they stand out?"

All convicted of corruption.

"I guess your only hope is that Philadelphia's young people will set higher standards in the future."

The Young Democrats of Philadelphia just endorsed Beloff.

"It's quite a city."

Why don't you visit this summer?

"What for?"

To celebrate the Constitution.

A SUPERINTENDENT GETS THE PICTURE

March 17, 1993

Rumors have been flying again about the possibility of School Superintendent Constance E. Clayton leaving Philadelphia, and I thought maybe I should say something about this before it's too late.

It might be best if I direct my comments to people in New York and Washington. If the rumors are true, those are two of the places where she might land.

First of all, I can't recommend Clayton highly enough.

Just the other day, I was looking through Report Card, a newsletter produced by Clayton's vast and talented public-relations staff and mailed by the thousands to parents and employees. And I was reminded, on Page 3, of the superintendent's "oft-repeated statement."

The Children Come First.

This appeared just above a photograph of Clayton. It was one of seven photos of Clayton in the six-page newsletter, and appeared on the page just before the partial listing of outstanding achievements by students. (A note explained: Space does not permit a full listing ...)

My guess is that if more students were listed, one of the seven photographs of Clayton might have gotten bumped. (She photographs far better from the right, it seems to me.) Or, even worse, they might have had to kill the "time-lapse photo" of the PE building message that read:

Phila Salutes Dr. Clayton 10 Years.

If ever there was any doubt that we're getting our money's worth from Clayton's PR staff—last time I checked they had 14 employees and a budget of just under $1 million—let me be the first to give an A-plus to Report Card's tribute to Clayton for her 10 years as superintendent.

As a school district parent, I can't tell you how reassuring it is to be reminded by Clayton and her staff that she is doing a tremendous job.

Of course, there are critics. Some say administrators, principals, and teachers are intimidated into paralysis by Clayton's tyrannical style.

Some have a problem with Clayton's refusal to let anyone see data that would let the public know whether the schools are improving. And while everyone in the field agrees that huge schools must be broken down into schools within schools that govern themselves, some say that Clayton herself, despite her claims to the contrary, is the biggest obstacle, because she can't bear to give up any power.

For the sake of argument, let's say it's all true. If you ask me, that only makes Clayton all the more shrewd.

If schools are failing and students lagging, is there a better strategy than to hide the evidence and have your PR machine make you out to be God's gift to education? I think not.

The next question is this: If Clayton leaves Philadelphia, where can she best benefit America? And the answer, obviously, is in Washington.

Rumor has it that she lost out on the job of deputy secretary of education. But if President Clinton is half as committed to children as he claims, there has to be a place in D.C. for Dr. Constance E. Clayton.

And as hard as it is to admit, I wouldn't be surprised if Washington raids more than just our schools. Clinton might also come after our joint City Council committee on education and public safety.

I can think of no better word to describe the committee's report on school violence than astounding. It begins with a poem by Councilwoman Jannie Blackwell. A poem written in a way that makes it accessible, you might say, even to second-graders: "Just endless joy and boundless hope, for we are caretakers of the rope, that binds us all and keeps us free and let's [sic] us know what we can be."

(Space does not permit a full listing of the beautiful stanzas.)

But there is room for this:

"This shooting was widely publicized and will cause this 17-year-old's name, Calvin Saunders, to go down in history as synonymous with the issue of violence in our schools. ... It is sad when a student is shot in a school lunchroom with a sawed-off shotgun."

Sad, indeed.

But here's a happy conclusion:

"We have an excellent School Board and School Administration who are trying as hard as possible to alleviate the problem of violence in pubic [sic] schools."

If we lose Clayton, maybe we can get Clarence Thomas to run our pubic schools.

In any event, from Clayton to Council, Philadelphia is rich in education leadership. And in these tough times, we have a moral obligation to share the wealth.

Help yourself, Mr. President.

We ask not what our country can do for us.

HUSH MONEY,
CAMPAIGN-STYLE

November 10, 1993

Should we be surprised?

I don't think so.

It's getting so that nothing in politics, and nothing in New Jersey, surprises. But this sets a new standard.

Now we learn that the Christie Whitman campaign spent a half-million dollars encouraging black voters to stay home on Election Day.

And not only were they largely successful, they are bragging about it. Republican kingmaker Ed Rollins, in a Washington Post story, says Whitman's camp paid black ministers and Democratic workers to discourage any kind of enthusiasm for Governor Florio, who lost by a hair.

"We played the game the way the game is played in New Jersey," Rollins told reporters. "To a certain extent, we suppressed their [the Democratic] vote."

Ordinarily in sleazy politics, election-day money is used to encourage people to vote. In New Jersey, election-day money was used to turn back the clock about 30 years.

Usually, it's called Walking Around Money or street money. Party bosses keep wads in their pockets, and when they see the right conditions, they drop it like seeds.

The recipients, unless their brains have been removed, know exactly what they're supposed to do.

In New Jersey, which sits at the cutting edge of politics these days, innovative Republicans used a simple twist. Instead of Walking Around Money, they passed out Sitting Around Money.

Here's how Rollins, who is paid huge sums of money for his talents, explained it to the Post:

"We went into the black churches and basically said to ministers who had endorsed Florio: 'Do you have a special project [that needs financial support]? We see you have already endorsed Florio. That's fine. But don't get up in the Sunday pulpit and preach. ... Don't get up there and say it's your moral obligation to vote on Tuesday, to vote for Jim Florio.'"

The story came across the wires last night, and it was not immediately clear exactly what kind of response the Republicans got in the black community when they waltzed in with this proposition.

Nor is it clear why there were no reported sightings, just before the election, of white people with bad haircuts flying out of black churches and landing on their butts.

To tell you the truth, I'm not sure exactly which part of this is worse: that offers were made, or that they were accepted.

Asked how the payments would be made, Rollins said, "We made contributions to their favorite charity."

Rollins said Whitman campaign workers also approached black mayors they knew were unhappy with Florio, and told them:

"How much have they paid you to do your normal duty? We'll match it. Go home, sit and watch television. And I think to a certain extent we suppressed their vote."

Congratulations, Ed.

A truly insulting thing, it seems to me, would have been to ask blacks to vote for Whitman. Asking them not to vote for Florio was definitely the high road.

As for Whitman, a spokesman named Carl Golden claims he doesn't know anything about the black thing, and neither does Whitman.

Which creates two possibilities.

They're lying, which is bad enough.

Or this is a governor-elect who doesn't know what the hell her top adviser is doing, which is worse.

What we do know is that Whitman knew damn well what she was doing earlier in the campaign when she hired the guy who came up with the Willie Horton ad for George Bush. The one that, as I have pointed out, carried this lovely message:

Scared of Negroes? Vote Republican.

After realizing it didn't look too good, Whitman fired the guy.

In this case, it's not clear if Whitman will fire anybody, since she is, as she says, ignorant of the matter.

But whether she knows about it or not, she ought to say something.

I mean, it could well be that paying blacks to stay home and watch television is her idea of an anti-crime bill. If so, she ought to provide a little more detail than she did when she promised to cut income taxes 30 percent without explaining how.

Actually, I think I can see it falling into place. Maybe she's going to cover the income tax loss by bringing back the poll tax.

'THE GRAVEYARD OF
REAL IDEAS'

===== *November 14, 1993* =====

I know I took some shots at him the other day, but on second thought, I think we should all thank Ed Rollins.

With just a few stunning comments, he has crystallized for America what is wrong with the way we elect people to office.

Rollins, as you know, is the Rambo of Republican hired guns. When things looked bad for Christie Whitman in her run for governor of New Jersey, she called in Rollins, who narrowly pulled it out for her.

But Rollins wasn't satisfied with that. He wanted to explain to everyone just how wonderful he was. Unfortunately for Ed, he got so comfortable with the spotlight he didn't know he was on fire.

Rollins bragged to the national press that the Whitman campaign cruised through black communities tossing cash out the window to ministers and pols. All the Republicans asked in return, Rollins explained, was that black people, rather than vote, stay home and watch television.

Nice work, Ed. Maybe on the next election day, free bus fare to Trump Castle for Puerto Ricans.

Whitman has, of course, denied that it happened. So have many black ministers. No surprises there.

If it happened, who'd admit it?

Ed himself disappeared after people noted the staggering ignorance of his remarks. But before crawling into a hole, he said his comments were exaggerated and inaccurate, whatever that means.

The irony is beautiful.

Ed Rollins, champion image maker, sadly in need of a spin doctor.

Actually, his opponent tried to help. Jim Carville, Governor Florio's guy, while admitting to no training as a psychologist, suggested valor as a motive for Rollins. "He did a somewhat courageous thing by admitting to this," Carville said.

Maybe a medal. Maybe a human rights award. Maybe Ed and Jim can go on tour, each one explaining what the other is saying.

Guess what, folks.

We don't have elections; we have fund-raising events. We don't have candidates; we have cartoons. And they are drawn by megalomaniacs the likes of Ed Rollins.

Let's say he was lying. Is that any more comforting?

In the last 15 years, Rollins has had more to do with shaping political strategy in America than anyone else, and yet he is so far removed from reality that he had no clue his comments were degrading to blacks and insulting to everyone else.

Does he know that people gave their lives for the right to vote?

This is what it's come to. Elections that are just as much a contest between superstar spin doctors as between political candidates.

Rollins and Carville don't give a damn about New Jersey. They were hired for their ability to reduce problem-solving to simple slogans, and to reduce candidates to their most marketable form. But their greatest gift, by far, is understanding how shallow the voting public is.

When Whitman futzes with the impossible trick of balancing the budget while fulfilling her pandering promise to cut income taxes 30 percent, Rollins won't be around.

He'll be in the next state—if anybody will have him—spending millions of dollars on new ways to conceal the windup crank in the backs of his clients.

Whitman and Florio spent $5.9 million each. In Pennsylvania, a losing candidate collected $1.3 million from lawyers, party bosses, and other wildlife in a run for Supreme Court.

This is what was meant by: I can't define obscenity, but I know it when I see it.

As for street money, which is scattered like confetti on election day to get out the vote, or, in New Jersey, to keep it home, I have a few thoughts.

I don't care if it's legal. I don't care if it's been going on forever. I don't care if it seldom makes a difference.

It should be banned.

Street money is to politics what prostitution is to sex.

Wear a condom at all times.

Last week, while Ed Rollins was busy securing New Jersey's place at the cutting edge of bad politics, a quiet development caught my eye in Pennsylvania. Teresa Heinz, wife of the late Sen. John Heinz, explained why, after months of consideration, she decided not to run for Congress.

"Today," she said, "political campaigns are the graveyard of real ideas, and the birthplace of empty promises."

MAYOR RENDELL AND THE ELECTION SCAM

December 8, 1993

I dropped by City Hall Tuesday around noon, carrying some flashcards, and went up to see the mayor.

I'm not as concerned about the Second Senate District election —won magically and narrowly by a Democratic Party hack bankrolled by the mayor and other pals—as I am about the city budget.

As you know, Democrat Bill Stinson pulled 80 percent of the 1,757 absentee ballots, beating Republican Bruce Marks by 461 votes and giving the Democrats a one-vote majority in the Senate.

It was, without question, the sleaziest local election during Ed Rendell's term as reform mayor. As of last Wednesday, 220 people had told Inquirer reporters they were misled or hoodwinked into voting for Stinson.

Also on Wednesday, Rendell said:

"It occurred on both sides. Five paid people on [Marks'] campaign staff voted by absentee ballot for convenience even though they were in the district on Election Day."

I brought two flashcards with me to the mayor's office.

One is less than two

Five is less than 220

Frankly, I don't know how you can compare five Marks people voting for their boss to dozens of people having no idea who the hell they voted for. But I do know that in addition to being less than 220, five also is less than 280, the current number of people who say they were misled into voting for Stinson. And if we've got a mayor who finds five and 280 comparable, do we want him in charge of a $2 billion city budget?

Before I could work it all out in my head, the mayor called.

No, he said, he didn't mean to compare five to 220, or 280. He was just suggesting that if five of Marks' paid staffers cheated, it's possible that further investigation will turn up widespread dirty tricks for Marks.

It's wrong no matter where it happened, he agreed, and responsible parties ought to be prosecuted. Rendell said he's been saying as much from the start, but maybe became too partisan "when Marks turned it into a political football." But don't overturn the election, he says, before the investigation is done.

A few points here.

First, I haven't suggested overturning the election. But plenty of flim-flam has been established, and I wouldn't be surprised if, before this newspaper stops knocking on doors, the number of people who say they were misled will cover Stinson's margin of victory.

It may or may not turn out that Marks' people cheated. But The Inquirer has not pursued Stinson exclusively. Reporters have knocked on doors of people who had absentee ballots signed in their names. So far, not a single one of the 280 say they were misled by the Marks people.

And while Rendell has supported an investigation, he has also given us the "it occurred on both sides" stroke, as well as blowoffs like: "What's happening here, to some degree, is the forces of Marks were taken by surprise and outworked."

Did I mention that Ed used to be district attorney? But that was long ago. Way before he was able to raise huge sums of money and help out the best and brightest political candidates. Take, for instance, the $50,000 in loans to Bill Stinson.

Then there's $21,000 more that Rendell's campaign committee gave to two people. Ruth Birchett, from the Mayor's Office of Community Services, who took a leave to work on Stinson's campaign, and Joe Martz, deputy commissioner of public property, who left to become Stinson's campaign chief.

So the mayor's in fairly deep, and Stinson lands in Harrisburg a lame duck. Even Rendell said yesterday he doesn't see how Stinson can run for a second term after this fiasco.

But even before this, Bill Stinson was no John Adams. He wasn't even Grizzly Adams. If Rendell hadn't been so busy working on a national image, he might have found a candidate who (A) had a pulse, and (B) didn't need a magic show to get elected.

Too late to do anything about that. But not too late for Mr. All-American Mayor to do what he should have been doing for four weeks.

Quit treating this thing like an annoyance.

Go after the scammers.

Slap people around, chop heads, and explain why Democratic Party boss Bobby Brady has kept a lower profile than a ghost employee.

And promise to be the guy who writes the election reforms.

MAKING FORGERY WORK FOR YOU

Ordinarily, I don't like to get personally involved in politics. But I think I can be of some assistance to current and future candidates, so here goes.

It has to do with signatures on nominating petitions, absentee ballots, and whatnot. As you may have noticed, there has been some trouble in this area here in the birthplace of Democracy.

First we had problems in the Second Senate District, and now it's the Second Congressional District—which apparently slept through four full months of news—where Chaka Fattah alleges that U.S. Rep. Lucien The Solution Blackwell's troops collected dozens of phony signatures.

Having seen some of the Blackwell signatures, I can see where Fattah might have gotten suspicious. I'd say the tipoff might have been the one sheet with 50 signatures in absolutely and irrefutably identical handwriting. (In fairness, it was excellent penmanship, at least.)

Then again, it might have been the complete sets of identical names, first in one handwriting style and then in another. I don't know.

But in any event, it seems that some general guidelines might be useful to Lucien The Solution Blackwell supporters and, for that matter, to anyone who remains uncertain on how to craft a proper forgery.

First of all, just to clear something up, a simple caution. Despite tradition and history, it is NOT LEGAL to forge signatures. That's why it's important to make at least a half-hearted effort to conceal your fraud.

As a case in point, a close examination of the Declaration of Independence is quite revealing. Clearly, John Hancock signed for Benjamin Franklin, who was in his cups that day at the City Tavern.

The loops are almost identical, and the Ks are obviously the work of the same man. But John Hancock, seasoned statesman that he was, had the good sense to throw off the King of England by abbreviating Franklin's name, which appears Benj. Franklin.

Both men, by the way, lived in the Second Senate District. This explains why, with the aid of a magnifying glass, a third Adams appears among the signers. There's John, of course, and Samuel. But place the glass over a cleverly illegible signature, and you'll see Grizzly.

To summarize:

(A) Forgery dates back to our forefathers and used to be of a much higher quality, and (B) Lucien Blackwell has no respect for history.

We move on.

When forging signatures, it's always best to have righthanded and lei_
handed staffers. They should be given frequent reminders to change pens every
10 to 15 names, and follow this sequence: Sign with both eyes open, close the
left eye, close the right eye, close both eyes.

From Lucien Blackwell's forces, we learn another useful tip. Take the number of legitimate signatures required by law, and multiply by eight. Blackwell,
who needed 1,000 honest signatures, actually collected 8,000.

And that's the kind of vision and careful planning Lucien The Solution's
crack team brings to Washington. Only through years of experience does a staff
come to know that as much as 87.5 percent of their boss's support could be bad.

I spoke with Chaka Fattah yesterday and he told me that in reviewing
Blackwell's petitions, he was particularly impressed by the number of "men
who are housewives and people like Hennri and Sharlet who can't spell their
first names and people who keep addressing themselves as living next door to
where they live or two doors down."

Picky, picky, picky.

Blackwell did not return my call. But then, I left eight numbers, only one of
which was accurate.

Let's say, for the sake of illustration, that he did call me back. As a seasoned politician, he had already taken steps to mitigate the significance of any
bad petitions.

He married Jannie Blackwell.

As Jannie's husband, Lucien could have told me: "Look, you wretch. I'm
married to a City Council person who's fighting tooth and nail to keep a convicted drug dealer and former organized-crime member on the city payroll as
her aide, and you're bothering me about a few lousy signatures?"

From John Hancock to Lucien Blackwell, quality endures. Vote early and
often, and keep the dream alive.

STORY OF A BRIGHT GUY

October 28, 1987

A word that gets thrown around too much in this town is "bright," as in, "He's a bright guy."

This has been happening for years with a man named John F. Street. What I'd like to do here today, as a public service, is set the record straight on this matter.

If we get time, maybe we can also look into how it is possible for Councilman Street, a gas commissioner, to receive gas service despite stiffing the company for $5,600. But first things first.

I think I understand how Philadelphians get confused about who's bright and who isn't. Let's use an analogy.

In sports, when announcers find an athlete whose grunts sound polysyllabic, they call him articulate. He is not genuinely articulate, but when compared to other athletes, he is a genius.

Nine times out of 10, when you call somebody smart, it's based on a comparison.

John Street serves on City Council. Do I need to draw pictures?

You put a bag of groceries in the seat next to Fran Rafferty, the groceries could get into Harvard.

Another reason people might have started calling Councilman Street bright was because they couldn't find anything else to like about him. He is rude, arrogant, and loud.

As far as I can tell, these are his better qualities. On the down side, he cuts deals for friends and loved ones, bullies and browbeats people he doesn't like, and does not pay his bills.

By this last comment, I don't mean he's an occasional nickel short at the checkout stand.

This is the councilman who stuck the city for $9,200 in sewer and water fees. This is the gas commissioner who owes the gas company $5,600. This is the ex-student who ignored $8,900 in student loans. This is the model citizen who is $9,600 in the hole with the IRS.

As you may know, these details are currently floating around in bankruptcy court. This is not the first time Street has gone for a swim.

In 1982, when Street defaulted on an agreement to repay back taxes and water charges, the Revenue Department threatened to garnishee his wages. Street declared bankruptcy, which prevents creditors from grabbing a piece of his take-home.

On Monday, the city controller announced plans to attach the wages of 86 city employees who owe city taxes. Street was not on the list. He's bankrupt again, so they can't cut into his paycheck. There's a pattern here.

What I'm wondering is how such a bright guy, with a $60,000 family income, living in one of the more affordable areas of the city, ends up $54,000 in hock. You know he isn't running up a tab at charm school.

I put in a call to Street.

Mr. Taxpayer said news of his debt has been greatly exaggerated. He said the gas company actually owes him credit for gas, although he does owe PGW for space heaters. He said he is "exercising my right" not to pay his student loan.

And he left the impression that he doesn't care about any of this.

"You'll write a story or two and that'll be the end of it," he said.

Financial bankruptcy is the least of his problems. He is also morally bankrupt. Which comes as no surprise.

For years he ignored pleas from a man whose disabled son, a vendor, needed Street's OK to put a heater in his newsstand. But when Street's brother Milton, a vendor, tried to do business illegally at Temple University, and other vendors complained, John Street immediately introduced a bill to outlaw vending on that street. He said that if his brother couldn't do business, nobody would.

When a friend of Milton's needed some cash, John Street helped engineer payment of $100,000. Street said he saw nothing wrong with bestowing tax dollars at will.

This is the kind of leadership that defines the man. And his constituents must be happy. The only guy running against Street in next week's election hasn't even come out of his house.

So my guess is that we will continue to have a gas commissioner who doesn't pay his gas bills. Nobody at PGW has the guts to complain; they didn't even have the guts to cut off Street's service. And you won't hear a peep out of our heroes on City Council, who have the authority to detour Street.

And, of course, we will continue to have a councilman—head of the Appropriations Committee, no less—who doesn't pay city fees, and doesn't really care, and seems to be thoroughly enjoying the game he plays.

I can live with that. I just wish people would recognize the difference between a bright guy and a wise guy.

NO INDICTMENTS, NO COURAGE

May 5, 1988

And so it comes down to a 279-page grand jury report. The bomb, the firestorm, the kids in body bags, the smoldering homes.

It takes me back three years, to when Mayor Goode stood at City Hall even as the smoke curled up from Osage Avenue, and said the city's MOVE plan was a good one.

The report differs, and is graphic and sometimes hard. But it is missing the only page that could have meant anything. Indictments.

One reason for that is politics. Maybe District Attorney Ron Castille feared losing the case—and what it could mean to his career—more than he feared taking heat for having no courage.

It took two years for the grand jury to tell us that the Goode administration's handiwork on May 13, 1985—a bomb, roughly 10,000 bullets, 11 bodies, and 61 fire-gutted houses—was unacceptable and morally reprehensible. But not willfully criminal or with reckless disregard.

You cannot demonstrate greater reckless disregard than by sending Police Commissioner Gregore Sambor into the street with enough fireworks to blow up Ohio. Other than by having him report to Managing Director Leo Brooks, who liked to be called general.

So what we have from Castille's office is a report that does not advance what we knew three years ago, that lets police officers off the hook for lying about the bomb, and that clouds the issue of whether MOVE members were killed as they tried to escape the burning house.

The story of the report appeared in the paper on the same day as a story about Marty Graham being sentenced to life in prison for murdering seven women, a fate I have no problem with. I just point it out because Marty happens to be crackers, and you could make a case that, as such, he was less in control of his actions than Wilson Goode was on May 13, 1985.

But we could spend all night debating the relative strengths and weaknesses of Marty Graham and Wilson Goode and not make much headway.

Another story in yesterday's paper said that 15 Rutgers University students were indicted for participating in a booze bash that led to a young man drinking himself to death.

I have no problem with those charges, either. I am just wondering how alcohol poses a greater threat to a person's well-being, thereby justifying crimi-

54

nal prosecution, than dropping a bomb on a house and then standing around like Boy Scouts at a campfire.

While we're on the subject, you'll recall that Goode said he knew nothing about the planned use of a helicopter to drop the bomb.

Interesting, because Leo Brooks says he told the mayor about it. And the mayor's bodyguard told the grand jury that as Goode and his staff watched television just before the explosion, "Goode said, 'Watch this,' and, moreover, registered no surprise."

Goode has the luxury of looking ahead now, because nobody cares to make him look back.

"Upon leaving office," the mayor said of his future, "it is not my desire to enter appointive or elective office, but to teach, and write, and reflect for a while, and to become involved actively in making Philadelphia stronger."

I guess you can pull whatever sweet things you want to out of that comment and have yourself a picnic. The first thought that comes to my mind is that the mayor has made a connection between his leaving office and the city becoming stronger.

Then, of course, we have the mayor teaching. Think about it.

Mayor Goode is lucky to be in a city where accountability is not a prerequisite for success, where presiding over epic disasters is not a political liability, and where you can fit the public's sense of moral outrage into a gnat's navel.

This city re-elected him after MOVE. Talk about reckless disregard.

You can argue points of law all day. The bottom line is that monumental incompetence led to death and destruction, and nobody has been forced to pay, other than taxpayers. The bungling began long before May 13 and continued long after.

We might have gotten some satisfaction in watching city officials sit in a witness stand and squirm under the weight of criminal charges. Instead their fate was decided in secret, with politics guarding the door.

For the deaths of five children, the MOVE adults are responsible first, the Goode administration second, one gang as dumb as the other.

Criminal indictments would have been the voices of those children saying, "Watch this."

THE LIFE OF A CONVENTION DELEGATE

July 21, 1988

ATLANTA—They put me in the same hotel here as the Pennsylvania delegation, and I guess there are some advantages to that.

But none of them comes to mind when you open your door after a rough night, groggy and maybe a little dizzy, and the first assignment for your eyes is to focus on Philadelphia City Council President Joe Coleman.

Different local companies sponsor the meals every morning and I think Coleman was on his way downstairs for the People's Natural Gas Breakfast.

The hotel is 14 stories tall, 521 rooms, and they put King Coleman three doors away from me.

You walk around the lobby of the Stouffer Waverly Hotel and everywhere you turn, around every pillar, in every corner, there's Mayor Goode, or Bobby Brady, or Sam Evans.

And you can't escape. You're actually living with these people for a solid week. Then you realize they came here to offer their input at the Democratic National Convention, and it's like you didn't wake up, you're just having a bad dream.

The advantage of being so close to them, of course, is nobody can get away with too much here because they know they're being watched.

But that hasn't kept people from running up some pretty good tabs at the hotel bar, which looks like a City Council meeting every night except nobody has yelled or thrown punches yet.

So the other night I'm in the lounge and up at the bar you've got Councilwoman Joan Krajewski, City Commissioner Marge Tartaglione, union boss Jim Sutton, and civic leader Sam Evans.

It's kind of a strange crew, because if memory serves me, Krajewski once sued Evans, Tartaglione once had a fistfight with Krajewski, and who knows what else?

But I figure they're setting a good example, and maybe we should all try to get along down here, so I tell the waitress to serve up another round for the four of them.

Next thing I know, Tartaglione comes over to chat, and later on, Krajewski joins us. What I like about them is they don't sip fruity drinks with umbrellas in them. They drink beer.

Krajewski says it's a little boring down here because they don't have any casinos, but she's determined to find a slot machine somewhere.

Krajewski and Councilwoman Ann Land, in case you forgot, went to Las Vegas last year for a National League of Cities convention. Unfortunately for the Boom-Boom Sisters, a reporter, in disguise, followed them and found out they didn't do much besides play slot machines.

"This is a shame," Krajewski said. "You've got the Boom-Boom Sisters in town and no slot machines."

"You know," Tartaglione said after a swig of brew, "we ought to wear disguises and follow you reporters around Atlanta. Maybe follow you into one of them strip joints or something, what's it called, Glitters? See how you like that."

While we were on the subject of who does what, I told Tartaglione there was a question I'd been meaning to ask.

"What does a city commissioner do?"

Tartaglione took another swig, looked me in the eye and said:

"I'm not tellin'."

OK, let's try another. Tartaglione is a Dukakis delegate, and the platform is pretty much established, so what does a delegate do down here?

"I'm not tellin'."

I love this woman.

We closed the place about 3 a.m., and the next night, when I got back to the hotel following Jesse Jackson's speech, Tartaglione and Krajewski were at the same bar, same seats. So I asked if they were in the Omni arena for Jackson's speech.

"We were there, but we went out to get a drink," Krajewski said, "and when we tried to get back in we were locked out."

So I invited them to go shopping. We decided to do it yesterday, after the morning caucus and other meetings for Pennsylvania delegates.

Unfortunately the girls got up a little too late and missed those things. Hey, it takes a while for all of them to get ready. Krajewski, Tartaglione, and their friend Bernice are all sharing a room to save money.

While we were waiting for Krajewski to come downstairs, I noticed Mayor Goode in the lobby. So I told Tartaglione I was going to invite him shopping with us.

"You do and I'm not going," Tartaglione said.

The mayor introduced me to his wife, Velma, and all three of his children.

"This is some guy who writes stuff in The Inquirer," the mayor said.

We all exchanged pleasantries, and then I said:

"I'm going shopping with Marge Tartaglione and Joan Krajewski. You guys want to come along?"

Nobody in the mayor's family answered. They just stared for a second, and then laughed. Even the mayor.

Anyhow, Krajewski came down and I hired a driver named Cecil with a Lincoln Town Car. Councilwoman Land was on her way for a swim, but we invited her along, so she went up and changed.

Cecil didn't say much. He had to use the side-view mirror because, I think, he couldn't have seen through Tartaglione's hair if he had used the rear-view mirror. Plus you had some earrings in the back seat the size of shopping bags, so he had to concentrate.

The girls wanted to pick up some souvenirs for sons and daughters, grandchildren, that sort of thing. So the first store we go into is Nieman-Marcus, where Tartaglione runs her hands over a $480 sweater.

"Anybody into leather pants?" Land called out from the next aisle. "These are only $415."

That's a bit high, so I suggested to Land that she get a Class 500 grant from City Council to cover their shopping spree.

"Hey," she said, "that's something I'd vote for."

The girls also stopped in Louis Vuitton, Malletier of Paris, but couldn't find any souvenirs. Finally, at a Hallmark shop, Krajewski found a Zoobilee Zoo character for her grandchild and Bernice found some canisters with holiday motifs, and for the next hour, the cash registers of the Lenox Mall rang out like Christmas bells.

Krajewski bought a new outfit, Tartaglione and Bernice bought some boxes of peanut brittle, and they sampled all the free food.

And then we walked up to a place called The Tinder Box. Actually I think the Boom-Boom Sisters were drawn to it by a magnetic force. Krajewski was the first one to spot the Big Ticket item in the window, but she kept her composure.

"A SLOT MACHINE!"

The entire mall grew silent as people turned.

"Ann, IT'S A SLOT MACHINE."

The Boom-Boom Sisters went inside and inspected two types of slot machines. Krajewski pulled the arm a few times and her eyes lit up.

"You know, they're really fun," she said.

"I'll take the big one."

That took a $60 nick out of Krajewski's credit card. The girls also bought some Michael Dukakis-for-President Cigarettes and some trick golf balls.

Unfortunately we did not have a forklift, so we had to carry the bags out to the Lincoln Town Car and Cecil helped us put them into the trunk.

The girls said they were going to set up the slot machine in the hotel lobby and pay for their trip to Atlanta with the money they make.

They may not be as serious or influential as some of the other delegates in town this week, but this country is stronger because of people like them.

HOME OR AWAY,
THE TRADITION LIVES

════════ *July 22, 1988* ════════

ATLANTA—With delegations from all 50 states attending the Democratic National Convention, it's hard for any one group to distinguish itself.

But you had to figure it was only a matter of time. And yesterday, as the convention drew to a close, a single state became the talk of the city.

It was the state that needs a special prosecutor for every occasion. Of course, we're talking about the proud state of Pennsylvania.

It seems the commonwealth's best and brightest cranked up the presses and ran off several dozen phony credentials so non-delegates could get into the convention.

Actually it was ingenious for its simplicity, and my only disappointment is that nobody made any money off the deal. There were only isolated reports of credentials for sale.

The word is that the counterfeiters simply Xeroxed credentials. And it was done for the first and foremost of all Pennsylvania political causes.

As a favor to friends and relatives.

A secondary reason was to stack the room, increasing the chance that someone might actually clap or open his eyes during Governor Casey's speech.

And so on Wednesday night, while America braced itself to hear the ideals of Democracy on the night a presidential nominee was selected, and while Governor Casey held the spotlight at the podium, about 15 Pennsylvanians were hauled off the convention floor by security bouncers and tossed out of the building.

"Some of our people were on the run," said a delegate who was afraid to give me his name. He was describing the scene when the *federales* swept through the entire Pennsylvania delegation.

Where'd they go?

"One guy hid in Mississippi."

You're kidding.

"Another guy retreated into the high Sierras of Colorado."

You mean Rockies.

"Yeah."

Another undetermined number never even made it into the building.

Harold Rosenthal of Philadelphia, who said he got his credential from a guy in a bar, was taken to an FBI agent and videotaped before getting booted.

All over the place, inside and out, if you were from Pennsylvania, you were a suspect. Just like back home.

"We've got another one," the cops would say. Or, "He's from Pennsylvania, make sure you check him."

Some people may not have known their credentials were bogus. But after enough phonies turned up, even people with legitimate credentials were corralled.

At one point, there was almost a quorum of Philadelphia City Council members in detention. George Burrell, Gussie Clark, and Angel Ortiz were held under a canopy outside the Omni Arena along with Eileen Vignola, wife of Joe Vignola.

Eileen, pleading with the *federales,* made the mistake of using the following argument in her defense:

"My husband is running for U.S. Senate from Pennsylvania."

She had to leave the building.

I've spent the last 24 hours trying to get to the bottom of it. And although some of the details are sketchy, there is never a shortage of Pennsylvania politicos willing to rat on each other.

"I don't know about the credentials," a Philadelphia Council member told me, "but I know Councilman Angel Ortiz drove his city car down here, and he's not even a delegate."

So let's have it, Angel.

"Hey, I needed a car. I'm working down here. If that's the biggest sin you've got on me, I can take it."

Actually, in what is probably the biggest political surprise of the convention, Philadelphia delegates appear to have had little or no role in the bogus ticket scam. That's probably why we haven't seen any federal indictments yet.

This looks like a Bucks County deal, and it's nice to see some new people getting to meet FBI agents.

Although there weren't many outright confessions from the Bucks County brigade, there were even fewer denials. In fact, there was a lot of boasting.

Ray Regan, a supervisor from Warminster Township, said this scam continues a long tradition that is a source of pride in Bucks County.

He spoke from his heart about the convention in which credential I.D. numbers were carved into a potato, which was used as a stamp to get non-delegates past a security check.

Asked how many people managed to stay in the Omni Wednesday night with phony papers, a grinning Regan said:

"Pennsylvania beat the DNC [Democratic National Convention] by a considerable margin."

Regan also said he could easily get five people into the building on one legitimate credential. You go into the building with your own credential, borrow someone else's, and go back out with the two credentials. Then you bring in a friend and repeat five times. "That's the legitimate-credential method," he said.

"Hey Ray," I said. "Can you get Eagles tickets?"

He didn't answer.

State Sen. Craig Lewis, who was on several top-10 lists of suspected ringleaders, admitted he referred people to places where he had heard they could get serviced. But he said he didn't run the scam.

One delegate came up with a pretty simple explanation, and it says something very basic about Pennsylvania politics.

"Delegates, spouses, you've got people who expect something to be worked out. It got worked out."

And what a smooth job. As far as I know, it's the first time an entire delegation was raided during a convention, and delegates had to flee across state lines.

But you have to give them credit for ingenuity. The whole delegation can probably get back to Pennsylvania on three airline tickets.

THE PARKING JACKPOT

July 27, 1989

O ver the last two years, a West Philadelphia man named Robert Hamilton has had 28 parking tickets left on his windshield.

Records suggest he has paid several. The rest have been dismissed.

Not to get too personal, but I suppose we should note that Hamilton is a high-ranking public official. And since we've gone that far, we might as well say where he works.

The Parking Authority.

I think this is called irony.

Hamilton makes $45,000 a year as assistant to the executive director of the Parking Authority, a funhouse for Democrats with political connections. He is the husband of Shirley Hamilton, who rakes in $80,100 a year as Mayor Goode's chief of staff.

For all that money, Mr. Hamilton seems chronically short of quarters. While hard at work for the agency that enforces Philadelphia's parking laws, he has picked up tickets all over the city, at all hours.

But he gets some kind of discount.

Nearly $1,000 worth of tickets and penalties have been dismissed in the two-year period, records show. The tickets were on Hamilton's personal car, which he uses for work.

When confronted with the rather lengthy list of his violations, Hamilton had an explanation. He said he is authorized to park anywhere in the city while on city business.

He said the authorization came in letters. I asked to see them.

He said he misplaced them.

Hamilton suggested I call Clayton Carter, City Council chief of staff, to confirm that Carter granted such authorization.

Carter told me he had never authorized anyone unconditional parking privileges. If anything, Carter said, he might have authorized Hamilton to park in the 1500 block of JFK Boulevard back when Carter was in the managing director's office, but he doesn't recall doing so.

Carter said no city official had authority to grant someone full exemption from parking ordinances.

News of Hamilton's privileges also surprised Webster Fitzgerald.

He is Hamilton's boss.

"I would suggest ... that Mr. Hamilton needs to pay parking tickets ... like every other citizen. That's the bottom line," said Fitzgerald, executive director of the authority.

Fitzgerald said Parking Authority employees should serve as models.

"If [Hamilton] is scoffing, he should be towed and he should be booted," Fitzgerald said.

Fitzgerald later said he would not be opposed to tickets being dismissed if Hamilton is on city business and time expires on a meter.

Unfortunately for Hamilton, only seven of his 28 tickets were for expired meters. The rest were for parking in loading zones and prohibited areas. Such as near a fire hydrant.

Some citations were given at night. Let's take January 26. Hamilton was cited at 9:26 p.m. for parking illegally at 55th and Haverford.

Hamilton said his job often required him to attend night meetings. He said he did a lot of work associated with the mayor's minority set-aside requirements for firms bidding on Parking Authority contracts.

He said he saved money for the city by using his own car, even though he was offered a city car, and because he pays for the gas. Besides, he said, he's up to date on his tickets.

Hamilton said he appeared before a hearing officer last Friday at the Parking Authority office at Broad and Callowhill. Hamilton said he was told he had 12 outstanding tickets for an accumulated debt of $473.

He said he told the officer about his special authorization. It was like pulling the arm on a slot machine.

When the bells stopped ringing, nine tickets disappeared. Hamilton, who earlier had paid $50 on the debt to avoid having his car booted, paid just $40 more and was clean.

This happened even though Hamilton did not produce his authorization letters, which, we have noted, cannot be found. When asked the name of the hearing officer, Hamilton said he didn't know.

I'd have sent a gift. A card at least.

Dominic Cermele, a former Traffic Court judge now in charge of hearings at the Parking Authority, said Hamilton did appear before a hearing officer Friday. Cermele said he can't comment on specific cases, but city employees can have tickets dismissed only if they were involved in emergencies.

Cermele said he had talked to the hearing officer about some mistakes that were made last week so they didn't happen again.

Hamilton also had a pretty good day in court on May 31, 1988. He was looking at 13 tickets and $518 in fees and penalties. He paid $60 and hit the highway an unburdened man.

Arrogance has its privileges. Or is it the other way around?

TURBULENCE AT AIR FUMO

===== *September 19, 1993* =====

W ell, here it is Friday evening at Northeast Philadelphia Airport, and I'm getting tired of waiting.

Hold on. Here comes a guy now. Hey, he looks like a pilot.

"Excuse me. Sir? Did David Cohen send you to pick me up? You know, Mayor Rendell's chief of staff?"

He's shaking his head like I'm nuts or something.

I don't know what happened. I called Cohen's office Thursday morning and left a message. I'm sure it was clear, because I remember the receptionist reading it back to me.

"You're at Northeast Philadelphia Airport, and you want Mr. Cohen to send a plane for you."

This would be correct.

"So you can visit a friend in Pittsburgh?"

That's it. A depressed Pirates fan who needs my help.

So where's my damn plane?

Hey, I read Wednesday's story by Inquirer reporters Emilie Lounsberry and Gary Cohn. The story that said Cohen made arrangements for a plane to pick up State Sen. Vince Fumo in Atlantic City last year, and he flew to Erie to see a friend over Fourth of July weekend.

All right. We know that David Cohen, Ed Rendell, and Vince Fumo are so cozy they occasionally discover they're wearing each other's socks.

Hell, we might as well just call this the Vindell Administration.

But the airplane. That's a little incestuous. Unless, of course, this is a new kind of service available to all taxpayers. Which, until further notice, I'm going to believe.

Because, frankly, Cohen isn't talking. We don't even know whether he offered the plane out of the blue, or if Vince just snapped his fingers.

But we do know that the pal Fumo visited in Erie was state Supreme Court Justice Stephen Zappala. And just five days after they had their lakeside chat, the Rendell administration asked the court to hear a case involving labor contracts.

Zappala drafted the order by which the Supreme Court agreed to hear the case. Two months later, the court ruled in favor of the Rendell administration. Or, should I say, the Vindell Administration.

In any event, these details are being looked at by the folks involved in the grand-jury investigation of the state Supreme Court. They also might want to take a look at the fact that Zappala presided at Fumo's second wedding and later didn't disqualify himself from a decision not to review a child-support ruling against Fumo's first wife.

As you may recall, Justice Rolf Larsen has reportedly testified that Zappala told him he met with Fumo and talked about the city's labor case.

But in fairness, we don't know that Fumo and Zappala talked about the labor case in Erie.

According to the Inquirer story, Zappala and Fumo have said they talked about the legislature's budget cuts for state courts. As Fumo reportedly explained it to investigators, he flew to Erie to assuage Zappala's concerns about those cuts.

Allow me to recap.

Fourth of July holiday weekend. Vincent is at his place down the Shore. David Cohen calls a campaign contributor who has access to a plane. Fumo flies to Erie and back, because Justice Zappala is depressed about court budgets.

Hey, I know these are all New Age guys, but is this a little too sensitive?

If I were Vince, I'd have called Zappala and told him to get a grip. Maybe light a few firecrackers. Have a beer and enjoy the holiday.

But I've learned something. When friends are in need, you drop everything and borrow a plane.

That may be why Vince recently got his own pilot's license. Now he can fly across the state and meet with whatever judge might be depressed. As you know, Vince takes a keen interest in the judiciary, and has helped clear a path for Russell Nigro to the high court.

I don't know why Vince doesn't step up to the bench himself. Think of it. Vince and the Supremes.

But here's what worries me, aside from the fact that you can't become a justice in this state without wading through the political cesspool. What if Nigro gets elected, and then he and Zappala get depressed on the same day?

Who does Fumo rank higher?

And can David Cohen get two planes?

By the way, it's cold out here.

David. David? Where's my plane?

SENATOR, LEFTOVERS, FOOD FOR THOUGHT

November 1, 1992

It wasn't too long ago that U.S. Sen. Arlen Specter's son called my bosses to discuss my work and asked whether they had any kind of internal compass that might keep me from batting his father around.

Well, at the risk of finding myself on both sides of an issue, like a certain senator I know, the answer is yes and no. And with the election just two days away, I'd like to explain.

The policy of this newspaper, wrongheaded though it might be, is for me not to endorse any candidate as the election draws near.

So in the race between Specter, who supports the desperate President Bush, and Lynn Yeakel, who supports Bill Clinton, my options were to:

(A) Start writing about Arlen's good side, (B) Take some shots at Yeakel, (C) Say nice things about both of them, (D) Rip both of them, or, (E) Do one of those wifty personal columns about something noncontroversial, such as what's in my refrigerator.

To stay on good terms with both the management and the reading public, I have chosen (E).

All right. So I opened my refrigerator. I looked inside.

And I saw a can of Coke.

Hey, that's what I saw. A can of Coke. And of course my first thought was of Supreme Court Justice Clarence Thomas and Long Dong Silver.

So I quickly looked away from the Coke, because this isn't supposed to be about the fact that a Senate panel, led by you-know-who, spent roughly 10 minutes looking at whether a rookie judge was qualified to be on the high court, and a week discussing penises, breasts, and pubic hair.

But next to the Coke was a container of leftover pea soup. Unfortunately, this reminded me of *The Exorcist* and Sen. Orrin Hatch.

So I looked away again, and this time I saw some Ocean Spray cranberry-apricot juice. Which, believe it or not, was the same color as Sen. Strom Thurmond's hair.

No matter where I looked in my refrigerator it was hard to shake the image of that famous nose-picking panel of ethical giants, who included a plagiarist, a savings & loan scoundrel, a guy who was completely unintelligible, and a guy who drove a woman into a creek.

In other words, as the Senate goes—a Senate made up of 98 white men and two women—they were the best and the brightest.

But this is about my refrigerator.

On a rack above the Ocean Spray was a piece of apple pie, which made me think of Specter's primary opponent Stephen Freind. And the amazing coincidence that by handing Thomas a seat on the bench, Specter siphoned some of the conservative crackpot vote away from Freind.

Next to the pie was a jar of popcorn, which made me think of the movie *JFK*. Which reminded me that outside the theater, my sons said they didn't understand the magic bullet theory everybody was laughing at. So I got a running start and dived through the back of a car, emerged out a side window, hovered, entered another car, and landed in the driver's seat unscathed.

But I digress.

Much of what was in my refrigerator was unidentifiable. Some of it looked mushy, mysterious, and half-baked.

Which brought to mind the campaign of Lynn Yeakel. A campaign that has been a textbook study on how to blow momentum.

First you sit around and do nothing. Then you defend yourself against charges that you're a tax cheat and a bigot. And then to catch up, you surround yourself with celebrities instead of real people.

So do what you have to do, folks. Whichever lever you pull, you're taking a risk.

Specter's a decent senator who does OK except for those occasions when his spine drips into his shoes. I mean, if the White House had asked Arlen to pave the way, Pat Boone would be on the Supreme Court.

Yeakel's a decent person with good intentions but no political savvy. Some people kind of like that. Some people think she doesn't have what it takes to last 10 minutes in the shark tank.

If you're on the fence, you might consider the words of Larry Yatch, the Specter fan who characterized the pitch of women candidates as, "Here, I've got breasts. Vote for me."

Or you might consider the reaction of Claire Sargent, a U.S. Senate candidate from Arizona, who said:

"Well, I think it's about time we voted for senators with breasts. After all, we've been voting for boobs long enough."

'THIS DEPARTMENT IS UNIQUE'

September 14, 1994

Having once rented a limo to take Marge Tartaglione and the Boom-Boom Sisters to a shopping mall instead of attending dry meetings at the 1988 Democratic National Convention, I can fairly say Marge knows how to have a good time.

But she doesn't quite have the gift of gab, as I was reminded yesterday while listening to the tape of a long interview she did with The Inquirer.

Reporter Mark Fazlollah questioned the city commissioner for his Sunday story about the fact that Philadelphia—surprise, surprise—spends far more for parts and maintenance of its voting machines than any city in the galaxy.

Wheels, cotter pins, nuts, and bolts—you name it, we're paying top dollar and then some. And then there's the $875 jackpot for each of 80 Election Day mechanics for a day's work, while other cities pay $125.

I'm not sure if, in the two-hour interview, Marge answered a single question. But she took stabs at everything from automobiles to indoor rainstorms, and from "breakfastses" to "how the department is ran."

And so without further ado, folks, welcome to Marge's World. And keep in mind that she's a public official entrusted with the sanctity and integrity of the voting process.

Marge on technology:

"It's like my husband, he used to have a gas station, all right, when they were, a car came, a new car, they'd lift up the hood, everything was metric tools, now it cost them a fortune to go out to buy the metric tools, somebody says, Oh, come on you could use these, he says, Yeah, and strip the bearings or strip whatever it is ... now these [voting] machines are antiquated, they're antiquated, now as, how old is this machine, all right, 45, if you were a mechanic 45 years ago, the younger generation, everything is changed, you take the new machines, you take the computers, and it's gettin' harder and harder, like it's gettin' harder and harder to get parts ..."

Or to complete a sentence.

Marge on public administration:

"All right, I am the supervisor of [unintelligible], get Bobby Lee over at Spring Garden Street, you, you sign in to Bobby Lee, you're with Bobby Lee on this company and says that Fazio went here, this Fazio's timesheet, Bobby Lee signs that Fazio's timesheet is indeed correct ... over the warehouse, whatever the supervisor signs in, signs that this is the true document, because you know that I can't be over Wissahickon Avenue, Spring Garden Street, that's why they're the supervisor ..."

That's what I figured.

Marge on workplace hazards:

"I get blamed for many things, you know, you live in the fishbowl, you live in uh, uh, the fishbowl, between the FBI coming in and saying I rigged the election to ... now Ed Rendell is D.A., I got arrested, my husband's birthday, took me from the polling place in handcuffs ..."

Blow out the candles, hon.

Marge on election systems that might be better than ours:

"Now we went, the three commissioners, Marian Tasco, John Kane, and myself, went to Chicago to observe their election looking at new machines ... and the commissioner, head of everything, said 250,000 votes were stolen, so I said you can't, these machines are out ... and in Florida ... they put little punch cards, so the humidity and the rain swept up, oh, they got wet, they put them in microwaves, tried to dry them and they lost the whole election ..."

Either way, we're better off.

Marge on freak weather:

"You saw how deplorable the warehouse, was not, let's be fair, the roof leaked, the machines get wet, the curtains were horrible, replace the curtains, when I say deplorable that every time it rained it rained harder inside than it rained outside."

Marge on the new motor voter laws:

"My husband bought me a Chevy, it's two weeks old, I'm drivin' to Harrisburg and I'm in Lebanon and all smoke was comin' out—two weeks—I go out of the car, it's me, my daughter, pick up the hood, I don't know, I pick up the hood and saw smoke, yeah, smoke, I don't know nothin' about a car, gentleman stopped in a pickup truck and he said, Oh hon, he said, you got trouble ... and I'll take it to the gas station, you get a tow truck ... I'm responsible if the election don't go off, I'm no mechanic, Mark, if you go into a gas station and he says, If you don't get this done your car's not gonna drive, what are you gonna do?"

Shoot myself in the head?

Marge on understatement:

"Let me tell you something. This department is unique."

'WHO THE HELL ARE THESE PEOPLE?'

May 9, 1993

So I thought we'd play a little game.

I'll stick a bunch of names in the next paragraph, and you tell me what they have in common.

Greg Reed. Matthew M. Sarsfield. James M. Munley. Joseph Sabino Mistick. Robert P. Horgos.

Anybody got it?

I'll give you more names.

Michael A. Della Vecchia. Jon Pushinsky. Thomas G. Saylor. Amy Putnam. Gerald M. Bigley.

Still stumped? Try these.

Dante Bertani. Peter J. O'Brien. Ralph D. Pratt. William J. Atkinson. Sandra Newman.

Admit it. You don't have a clue.

What those people have in common—all 15 of them—is that in nine days, when you walk into that little booth and flip the lever that closes the curtain behind you, those names are going to stare back at you.

They're candidates for state judgeships. Your job is to determine who among them—and seven others, for a total of 22—are best qualified for the state Supreme Court, Superior Court, and Commonwealth Court.

And then, depending on what county you live in, you'll have maybe another dozen or so people you know nothing about who are running for Municipal and Common Pleas Court.

Of course, you've faced this problem before. You remember walking into that booth, looking at dozens of names and thinking:

Who the hell are these people?

But don't feel stupid. It's virtually impossible for anybody to be adequately informed. If you're one of the few people who do their homework, you can read about all the candidates in this newspaper. But even if you do, you're not equipped to figure out which person might make a better judge than another.

So I'd like to make a few suggestions, and you can feel free to clip this handy voters' guide and take it into the booth with you.

1. If you don't recognize any of the names as being from your region, pick a name that has a nice ring to it. For Supreme Court, for instance, Dante Bertani is more pleasant to the ear than John L. Musmanno.

2. Go with your own ethnicity. If you're Irish, for example, and you don't

70

know any of the candidates from Adam, you should go with Peter J. O'Brien for Superior Court. And you know you will.

However, be careful. One year in Philadelphia, William Marutani got a lot of votes in Italian communities of South Philadelphia. Another year, so did Henry DeBernardo. And you can just imagine how those voters felt upon discovering that Marutani was Asian and DeBernardo was black.

3. Go with any name you've heard of, or you think you might have heard of. You can even go with a name you haven't heard of if it sounds at all similar to the name of a friend, or possibly somebody you sat next to in eighth-grade civics class.

4. Look at the names on the cards you were handed upon entering the polling place. Only trustworthy, reliable people, with nothing but the public interest in mind, stand outside polling places shilling for candidates they might never have met except to hear them promise to be fair in some ward leader's basement.

5. Close your eyes and just go for it.

Some of you may be wondering what these tips have to do with the qualifications of the candidates. The answer is nothing.

But don't be concerned.

For the most part, the candidates are sponsored, bankrolled, and, in some cases, built from scratch like Frankenstein, by party bosses and politicians for whom legal scholarship doesn't even figure into it. So you'll be right in tune with democracy as practiced here in *Pennsylvania: Land of Giants*.

In March, in fact, the state's most respected politicians staged what amounted to a gelding exhibition and horse-trading auction to determine which candidates to saddle up for Supreme Court.

It's been this way forever in Pennsylvania, one of only eight states that has no merit selection of judges at any level. And proposals for change never get out of committee because politicians like the way things are.

Quite a surprise, then, that our Supreme Court is a national laughingstock, that you could cover the Spectrum with the robes of judges who've been tainted, and that many Pennsylvania judges think Night Court was a training film.

Because of these problems, in fact, you'll find a constitutional amendment on the ballot, floating somewhere in that alphabet soup of names you never heard of. It would end the private wrist-slapping of unethical or crooked judges and make it easier to suspend or dump them.

That's May 18, and don't forget.

Vote early and often.

THE NIGHT THAT FREIND FLIPPED

April 1, 1992

At this point in the Pennsylvania campaign for U.S. Senate you have to begin wondering if, perhaps in his youth, Stephen Freind missed a tetanus shot.

Frankly, I have no medical training, and I'm not even certain that missing a shot can make steam come out of your head. So my observation is that of a mere lay person.

But if you saw Freind's debate Monday night with Sen. Arlen Specter—a wobbly pup in his own right—or if you saw photographs of Freind during one of those moments when the Lord Jesus entered his body and then tried to jump out of his suit, well, you have to wonder about the guy.

I should make it clear, right here, that I'm not complaining about the direction of the campaign—I kind of like it—nor am I surprised.

I think I've noted previously that in a region where a doctor sold mail-order heads, a Wall Street investor presided over a basement colony, and a financial adviser might have purchased nine million pairs of used underpants, it's only natural that politicians are going to be a few sandwiches shy of a picnic.

Maybe it's something in the water. Maybe it's the scrapple. Frankly, I think it all starts with the Mummers.

If you're going to make such a big deal about grownups strutting around in ostrich feathers, you've got to figure there's a risk of eventually becoming the laundry-sniffing capital of the free world.

Like me, you might have been dismayed Monday when, after the debate, fisticuffs broke out between aides to Freind and Specter.

But don't fret. There's plenty of time left for the candidates themselves to box each other's heads in.

Here, I'd put money on Specter, because something tells you he'd throw punches from implausible, unbelievable, inconceivable angles.

It's also possible that with a single punch, Specter could hit Freind six times.

On the other hand, we all know God is in Stephen Freind's corner.

"I'll never apologize for accepting Jesus Christ as my Lord and savior," he said in the televised debate.

If I were Specter, I'd have interrupted at that point and done a Woody Allen routine.

"Not to be facetious or didactic, Mr. Freind, but could I interject, at this juncture, that Jesus was a Jew?"

Freind's eyes would have rolled back in his head. Actually they were already there. And you know his supporters would have begun ranting, perhaps debating whether the Holocaust actually occurred, or possibly whether rape victims release microscopic nuns into the bloodstream to attack sperm with rulers.

Instead, Freind was allowed to continue.

"And I'll never apologize for saying that my first priority ... [is] to spend eternity with God."

I'd have been happy with a balanced budget. Maybe a national health policy. And Freind's first priority is pitching a tent in heaven.

What's this guy running for, U.S. Senate, or God's press secretary?

It's not like Specter hasn't offered Steve Freind a big enough piece of his chin. There was JFK, and Specter's half-baked explanation.

And last week, Specter, in a move even sleazier than his televised whipping of Anita Hill, tried to put some political spin on it. Now that election day is closing in, Specter suddenly sees the error of his ways. Although he says the devil made him do it, speaking through the body of Sen. Strom Thurmond.

Meanwhile Freind, with all that stuff to work with, is drowning in the foaming saliva of his own righteousness. I don't want to pass judgment on him. But if he makes it to heaven, you know what God's going to say the minute he walks in.

"Steve, good job making babies and all. But this thing about you can't get pregnant if you're raped. What the hell were you thinking?"

Frankly I don't know if Freind is going to make it upstairs. After the debate, and just before the fistfight, he was seen pounding like a lunatic on the door of the room where Specter was being interviewed.

And then he denied it to the TV station manager who saw him.

I quote now from the Daily News:

TV Guy: "Did you pound on the door?"

Freind: "I did not pound on the door."

TV Guy: "That, sir, is a bald-faced lie."

And it certainly is not appropriate behavior for a man who, moments earlier, had made witness to a live television audience, accepting Jesus as his Lord and savior.

At least the underpants man wasn't a hypocrite.

FORM FOLLOWS DYSFUNCTION

I called home the other day to talk to my parents about my upbringing.

My father answered the phone, and I said that State Sen. Vince Fumo, in a Philadelphia Gay News story, had called me "a jealous, demented child of a dysfunctional family."

"What does he know about us?" my father asked. Then he put down his slingshot and called to my mother.

"Grace, some senator in Philadelphia is calling us a bunch of misfits."

My mother, who was forging signatures on a ballot petition, got on. "How'd he find out?" she asked. "How'd he even know about John?"

My brother John is a comic. He shaves his head, appears on MTV, and makes fun of U.S. Sen. Arlen Specter out West, so that we have bicoastal coverage.

So, in other words, yes. I am demented; we are dysfunctional.

This is why Vince and I connect.

Not to be presumptuous, but when Vince blew a synapse last week in Harrisburg, making fun of Attorney General Ernie Preate and calling a federal judge a brain-dead Republican senile hack during a long, rambling breakdown, who did he sound like?

It's bad enough that the Democrats stole a bunch of votes in the Second Senate District election. Do I need Vince Fumo stealing my material?

I'm not sure what's gotten into him. But I suppose it could be that a man who owns a Jet Ski, hunts quail with semiautomatic weapons, and snaps his fingers when he needs something from Mayor Rendell—an airplane, for instance—is insecure.

Through my many years of dysfunctional family therapy, I know that an insecure, controlling person often develops conspiracy theories to rationalize not getting his way.

And Fumo, after his Senate candidate was indicted and his power went from Jet Ski to blow-dryer, said he believes that The Inquirer and the Republicans have "conspired to manipulate and manufacture whatever news they could."

Here, we have transference. The words "manipulate" and "manufacture" describe perfectly the Democrats' vote-gathering tactics.

And, as the Republican senile hack judge put it, "At least $4,000 was specially allocated to implement this scheme from a political action committee associated with Democrat State Sen. Vincent Fumo."

This could be what's eating Vince. Or it could be he knows I've been trying to contact his pal Tom Myers, who flew with him from Atlantic City to Erie—in the plane provided by the mayor's office—to meet with Supreme Court Justice Stephen Zappala.

There's one thing I never understood in the grand jury's report on its investigation of the Supreme Court. Zappala told the grand jury that he and Fumo talked only about court funding, not about a case involving labor negotiations between the Rendell administration and city unions. Fumo said the same thing.

But Myers told a different story. He said the conversation was purely social—not about court funding.

My feeling is that it would have been better if the three of them had conspired to manipulate and manufacture a story. Any story. Just as long as it was the same story.

Lack of communication is not uncommon, however, in dysfunctional families. To their credit, the Democrats have been much better about this in the Second District fiasco. Rather than denounce the fraud, they have consistently blamed The Inquirer for reporting it.

And the thing about Fumo is that he's so smart, he can help us better understand politics even when foaming at the mouth. I quote now from his Harrisburg screed:

"You know, there is an old saying ... Democrats steal the tickets; Republicans steal the whole train. ... Steal the tickets, yeah, I know about stealing a $5 ticket, I can associate with that."

I'm disappointed. I'd have figured Vince for boosting the train.

Moments later, after criticizing The Inquirer for coming up with only 300 dirty votes, and Ernie Preate for indicting Democrat Bill Stinson "even though it is OK for Ernie the attorney to launder cash," Fumo, whose party hoodwinked and bamboozled poor black and Latino voters, said:

"Goodbye civil rights, goodbye democracy."

I feel that I can help you, Vince. Come by the house, I'll introduce you to the family, we'll pull wings off of birds or something.

It's going to be OK.

CONGRESS MUGS THE CRIME BILL

August 17, 1994

At times there is the appearance, faint though it is, that they are talking about crime control in Washington.

At other times you might get the impression they're taking a look at health care reform.

Both of which would make sense.

The daily American death toll from crime rivals the daily death toll in the Bosnian war. A two-night stay in a hospital costs roughly the same as a new Oldsmobile and involves 10 times as much paperwork.

But don't be fooled by what might look like good intentions.

Washington is where good intentions go to die, and there is a slaughter in that town this summer.

Despite the fact that they throw out different topics of discussion from one day to the next, there is really only one subject of any interest to those in Congress.

The war between Democrats and Republicans.

Everything they do is connected to it. Every topic, every vote, every sound-bite. Every campaign contribution they raise from every lobbyist, no matter how corrupting the process.

Not that it's a new game. Not that there are even any new moves.

But I don't know of a time when more issues were framed by this one.

A clear attempt has been under way most of the summer to destroy President Clinton by destroying two bills essential to his survival.

Crime and health care.

There is nothing wrong with going after a President. Politics is not meant to be, and never has been, very pretty. And Clinton has certainly left a few doors open since he took up residence in the White House.

But there is something wrong with sabotaging compromise and with trampling public interest.

Take the crime bill.

From the beginning, it was all wrong.

Yes, we need more prisons. Yes, we could use more police officers.

But neither of those things—and not the death penalty, either —will make a dent in the problem.

Given the political realities, though, the crime bill had to be loaded with those things. And even then, they couldn't move it.

It had opposition from some black Democrats and it had opposition from the NRA, which vowed that anyone who voted to ban assault weapons was dead meat.

But the latest problem was the charge, by Republican Newt Gingrich and other giants, that the crime bill is filled with pork.

There is no way for me to explain to you, in so small a space, the obscenity of that position.

The "pork" is the only part of the crime bill that would make a difference.

It's the prevention end of it and it includes things like youth counseling.

Things like keeping inner-city schools open at night so kids can have a safe haven and use the library or gymnasium.

Things like a late-night basketball program that clears the streets and has cut crime in cities where it's been tried.

We actually have a situation in which elected representatives, entrusted with public policy, are in favor of military style assault weapons and against education, recreation, and counseling.

Finally, late last night, some progress. The story out of Washington was that President Clinton had met with Gingrich and 12 other Republicans.

"I think the President accepts that he will have to accept less money," Gingrich said on his way out of the White House.

The AP reported:

Among changes being considered by Democratic leaders are the reduction in some crime-prevention measures—seen as pork by some Republicans—and an increase in law-enforcement provisions such as prison construction and police department aid.

With this kind of compromise, they may get it through. And they will pat themselves on the back and give the appearance that they did something about crime.

President Clinton and the Democrats will declare victory. The Republicans will say they brought the Democrats to their knees.

Nothing but the partisan war will be advanced.

And then they'll move on to health care.

A FEEL-GOOD CRIME BILL

August 24, 1994

Two weeks ago a photographer and I went to a drug-infected corner in North Philadelphia, just above Lehigh, and although it wasn't clear who was more of a threat to whose happiness and well-being, the dealers won a war of nerves with the visiting journalists.

They wanted to know what we thought we were doing on their turf, and made it clear that we were disrupting a brisk enterprise, although our presence hadn't exactly put them out of business.

After a while it got intimidating enough that we decided to find another corner, nearby, for the photographer to capture the essence of the neighborhood. But it took three or four stops to find a clean corner.

Yesterday morning I went back up to the first corner with a different photographer. We parked, got out, and a teenage emissary greeted us.

He looked at the name printed on the car. The Philadelphia Inquirer. And then he asked:

"What are you doing? Inquiring minds want to know."

Again, business slowed, but didn't stop. The kid, 16 or so, suggested we use a mural as a backdrop for a quick photo. He pointed to one he said was for a friend who was shot dead "right there," and he motioned toward a spot 20 feet away.

When I tell people these stories, they often ask the same question.

If I know where these corners are, then police must know. So how can drug dealers operate around the clock without getting hauled in? Especially if, as we know, drugs play so big a role in American crime.

The answer is simple. Maybe not simple enough for Congress to understand, but not quite rocket science, either.

There are more dealers than cops.

And guess what.

There always will be. Even if you spread 100,000 more officers around the country.

There also, unfortunately, are more drug dealers than jail cells.

And guess what.

There always will be, even if you build a brand new jail in every city.

And there is a reason for that. A reason having more to do with economics than with crime. Simply put, it's supply and demand.

When you stand on those drug corners in the American wasteland, you see endless streams of customers. Through broken-down streets and past shutdown factories they come. On foot, by car, by cab.

They aren't scared away by the threat of violence, or arrest, or even by the horrifying sight of annoying journalists standing around with notebooks and cameras.

And the more you watch it, the more ridiculous the crime bill looks, at least as it concerns cities. Or, as Robert Kahle of Wayne State University in Detroit put it:

"Hiring more cops to solve the crime problem is like hiring more ambulance drivers to cure cancer."

Actually, I don't go as far. I'm not going to tell you the police couldn't use some help, or that drug dealers shouldn't be dragged off the streets and locked up.

But you don't need to spend more than 10 minutes out there to see that the only chance—as many police will tell you—is trying to cut the demand for drugs at least as much as we flail away at the supply.

And you don't need to be a genius to see that in a place where all the legal jobs have dried up and half the kids don't see a reason to even bother with school, no amount of death-penalty clauses or jail cells is going to take junior off the corner and put him on the college track.

The problems are deeper, the solutions more complicated. The way to start isn't to flex our muscles but to admit to the disease, which runs through every American street.

Cigarette companies lie about addiction. Beer companies sell sex and glamour. Hollywood glorifies violence. Crumbling smokestacks have crushed neighborhoods and broken families. With so much anger and fear out there, violence will rage until crime and addiction are no longer such natural responses.

We need a jobs bill, not a crime bill. Unfortunately, there are few people in Congress honest enough to tell you that what now sits in the lap of the Senate is simply a political bill.

It's filled with things you want to hear, and might briefly give you a warm feeling. But you'll remember it, sooner or later, as the same sensation you often had when you were in training pants.

SPENDING THE TAX SAVING

March 9, 1994

The specials last night at La Campagne in Cherry Hill were rack of lamb, Dover sole, and magret of duck.

Myself, not knowing what a magret is, I probably would have gone with the sole or the lamb.

But that was before I asked the executive chef, Olivier de St. Martin, about the prices. La Campagne is no greasy spoon. Dinner costs $35 per person, and that's a la carte.

If you want, say, the salmon noriel as an appetizer, and maybe the cappuccino cheesecake for dessert, you're up to $50 per person, and that doesn't include wine.

I explained to Olivier that I was looking for ways New Jerseyans might celebrate Governor Christie Whitman's first income tax cut—5 percent—but I don't think the tax cut buys dinner for two at La Campagne.

And I must say, it was a big letdown for me. If you saw the pictures of Whitman putting her signature on the tax cut, it looked as if quite a picnic was underway. The governor was flanked by legislative leaders who smiled and applauded—at first I thought it was an awards banquet for the Hair Club—as if Whitman were signing the Magna Carta.

But it turns out that for the couple who earn $50,000 a year, this tax cut amounts to about $57. And in fact, 70 percent of the state's taxpayers earn less than $50,000. Their savings will average $37.

This leaves several options. For the $50,000 couple, maybe they can flip a coin, and one of them can go to La Campagne this year, and the other can go next year. But that's only if Whitman sticks to her campaign promise to cut income taxes every year, for a total of 30 percent.

Another option is a cheaper restaurant. And so I called Ponzio's on Route 70 in Cherry Hill.

The special at Ponzio's last night was baked Swiss steak, at $9.90. It came with a tossed salad, rosemary potatoes, garden peas, and rolls.

Now let's say you have a couple of belts apiece before dinner, then coffee and pie à la mode afterward.

I know it's hard to believe, but guess what: You're under $40!

Unfortunately, 70 percent of all New Jerseyans will have to do without the pie à la mode. But the $50,000 couple will have plenty of good eatin', a pleasant dining atmosphere, and enough change to buy milk on the way home.

So I guess this must be what Governor Whitman is talking about when she says the tax cut will stir economic growth in New Jersey. It means 30 percent of all New Jerseyans can go nuts one extra night at a diner.

Provided, of course, they have no children. If they have children, Ponzio's may be out of the question. Personally, I would suggest Pizza Hut. Or hey, forget dinner altogether, and maybe celebrate the tax cut by going to a ballgame.

But again, the under-$50,000 family of four doesn't make the cut. I called the New Jersey Nets, and the cheapest seat in the house is $10. So the $37 break is just shy of a ballgame.

You know what, though? It might be advisable to hold on to your tax savings for a while. At least until you know what programs Whitman axes to pay for her tax cut. Because to provide that whopping $1 a week average in extra spending and investment money, Whitman has to come up with $285 million.

Thus far, she hasn't fully explained the magic of this, and some people are leery. They say this sort of trickle-down thinking is the stuff George Bush called voodoo economics, and it helped produce both the gazillion-dollar national debt and the bazillion-dollar deficit.

Others say Whitman may have to can state employees. And still others say that if income taxes go down, you can bet dinner at La Campagne that property taxes will go up.

Whitman says she'll reveal specific cuts March 15. I don't know about you, but I wait with bated breath.

Until then, in fairness to Whitman—whose family income was $3.7 million in 1992—I should point out that for some people, the 5 percent tax cut will be more than enough to buy dinner at La Campagne.

Whitman says her own personal $11,829 tax savings will go to charity rather than French restaurants. As for the rest of the New Jersey residents who earn more than $100,000, they'll average a $470 cut.

And so to that elite 7 percent, I say bon appetit.

Chef Olivier, by the way, recommends the chocolate mint truffle.

MR. LOPEZ, AT YOUR SERVICE

May 2, 1993

You will remember, of course, the Philadelphia city employee who said he slipped on ketchup at the Sansom Street Oyster House and won a disability claim.

And maybe you'll recall the police officer who injured two fingers, won a lifetime disability, and then became a physician, a campaign bankroller, and one of the two doctors whose nursing-home contract was just renewed despite allegations of neglected patients and overbilling.

Hall of fame performances in an all-star town. And, you'd think, impossible to top.

But now we have Michael R. McAleer, who found out he was losing his $51,600-a-year job at the Parking Authority, so he went upstairs to the Pension Board to check on his retirement benefits.

And McAleer, a ward leader, of course, tripped out of the elevator, naturally, and filed a claim that could add a workers' compensation check to his pension.

Pain in the lower back. Numbness in the shoulder, arm, and hand.

Last year, when warned that he could lose his job as director of labor relations because of his performance, he filed a claim saying he was suffering from job-related stress.

And in 1987, while on disability because of a car accident, he ran a write-in campaign for City Council.

He's got everything he needs.

He's an artist.

He's a patronage pro.

You might also have read, in Vernon Loeb's Friday dispatch, that McAleer contends that two people helped him up off the floor.

One being a "Mr. Lopez."

Let me say, right off the bat, that while I have helped a few people up off the floor in my time, and have in fact even been helped off the floor myself a time or two, I'm not sure I can recall helping Mr. McAleer up.

So on Friday I reported to the scene—the 20th floor of Two Penn Center—to see if it refreshed my memory.

And I have to say it didn't, although I'd like the authorities to know I'm willing to be a witness on the off chance it comes back to me.

Anyhow, with nothing else to do, I decided to make sure nobody else got hurt coming off elevators. Because with Mayor Rendell erasing 130 jobs at the Parking Authority—including four ward leaders, two of whom have been indicted in their lives—I frankly expected piles of hacks to come tumbling out each time the elevator doors whooshed open.

But over the course of my hour on the case, 50 people got off safely. Some of them wondering, as I offered assistance, who the hell I was.

"Mr. Lopez," I said.

Who?

"Mr. Lopez. I'm the elevator monitor."

"The what?"

"I help people who've fallen and can't get up."

Some of them seemed cautious toward me in the same way they might be cautious toward someone with underpants on his head.

I also rode the elevator and made several unsuccessful attempts to fall while disembarking, much like my unsuccessful attempts to slip on ketchup at the Oyster House.

Some people just don't have it.

Then I called McAleer to see how he was feeling, but he didn't call back. And so I called his attorney, Marge Koral, and explained that I was Mr. Lopez, but not *the* Mr. Lopez, as far as I could recall. Although I had spent the morning waiting for someone to fall out of an elevator.

"You did what?"

Koral said she didn't think McAleer had been to a doctor, but she was sure he was seriously hurt "by the way he was holding his body" when he told her his story. Besides, she said, he had two witnesses.

Not that he knows who they were or how to find them, but they saw him fall. Koral was sure of it.

Koral, for fans of political history, was a protégé of Herb Fineman, the Philadelphia state representative who went to jail. And she was a ward leader herself, which was how she met McAleer.

She said she has handled dozens of these kinds of cases, and she's sure that checking on your pension qualifies as a job-related function.

McAleer's claim will now be investigated, not by the Parking Authority, but by Riley & Fleming Adjusters, a longtime contributor to political campaigns in this town. And if it's denied, Koral tells me, she's going straight to Harrisburg to file for workers' compensation.

And, this being *Pennsylvania: Land of Giants*, anything can happen.

We'll keep you posted with future postcards from the Hack Hotline. And until then, remember:

It's a city of bottom feeders.

With no bottom.

So watch your step.

WHERE NO GOOD DEED
GOES UNPUNISHED

===== *January 15, 1995* =====

Here now the story of a man with a noble cause and a clear conscience, who made the mistake of testing them both in Philadelphia.

By an odd set of circumstances 14 months ago, Eric Schnurer, chief of staff for Lt. Gov. Mark Singel, found himself filling a slot on the board of the Delaware River Port Authority.

This is like waking up one day and finding yourself in a spider web, and all the bigger spiders are wearing party hats, driving Cadillacs, writing checks to consultants, and eating the smaller bugs.

Schnurer, 36, an expert on constitutional and civil-rights law, didn't particularly want a thankless unpaid job at the port. He took it because he was asked by his boss and because he believes in public service.

Last month, he wrote a column for The Inquirer because he thought the public should know that millions of dollars are handled like play money by the politicians who run the agency known for patronage, secrecy, and sloth.

He might as well have climbed the Benjamin Franklin Bridge, put on a pair of cement boots, and jumped.

Not 10 minutes have gone by without Schnurer hearing, either through the grapevine or directly, about the misery that awaits him.

He'll be tossed off the board. He'll never get a job in Philadelphia. He'll never get a job in Pennsylvania.

Friends were stunned. My God, he'd taken on the mighty DRPA, which is run, for all intents and purposes, like the private estate of State Sen. Vince Fumo.

The latest threat to Schnurer's professional well-being came last week, when Mayor Rendell, second in command in the Vindell administration, called Schnurer's outgoing boss, Singel, asking him to dump Schnurer.

Singel didn't call me back, and Fumo's office hung up on me five times in one minute, a personal record. Schnurer thinks that by law, he's on the board until 1998. But one theory is that as a replacement in 1993, he had only until that term ended last year and can be forced out now.

One problem with Schnurer, says Rendell spokesman Kevin Feeley, is that he misses too many meetings. (Schnurer says he's attended more than half. He missed some because of work obligations in Harrisburg, and because he picked up a viral infection on a visit to Africa.)

When Schnurer does show up, Feeley says, there's a "question of whether he votes Philadelphia's economic development interests, and the mayor's view is he does not."

Edwardo, Edwardo, Edwardo.

Nice as it would be to have the usual yes-man in there, drooling on himself and rubber-stamping every project you cook up, the DRPA is not a piggy bank for city development.

Schnurer, appointed by the governor's office, doesn't represent the Vindell administration. He represents Joe Blow. And he's not out to block economic development. He's out to make sure DRPA doesn't hose away so much on pet projects rammed through by politicians that it comes up short in its primary purpose —operating bridges and ports.

Executive Director Paul Drayton, one year on the job, has some of the same concerns. The problem is that politics gets in the way of reform.

Drayton and I recently looked at some sloppy, vague resolutions on the dishing out of millions of dollars. It was no wonder there was confusion on the board over a small concern—did members just sign over $6 million to $8 million as a grant, or as a loan?

Go to lunch with these people. You can't lose. One staff member —they're afraid to be named for fear of losing their jobs—told me Schnurer didn't have all his facts straight in his column, but he raised the right issues.

"Eric is really trying to be a voice for the interests of the public and wants to make sure DRPA's business is done in a professional and forthright manner. And he's on the right track in pointing out some of the problems and pursuing reforms."

Schnurer, still in shock over the fact that big-shot politicians would come after a little guy like him, says he won't go quietly.

"Everybody who knows me well knows my father was the biggest influence in my life, and he brought us all up to believe what we should try to do is make a difference."

Fine. But Eric's father, who lives in Arizona, didn't know Eric would end up in Philadelphia, where no good deed goes unpunished.

LIFE AROUND PHILADELPHIA

THELMA'S LUNCHEONETTE

April 6, 1987

Somebody's voice came tumbling out of the Hi-Fidelity Deluxe Radio, next to the sign that says a fried bologna sandwich goes for $1.35, and I don't know if it was Vic Damone or Perry Como, but he was singing "You Gotta Have Heart" while the 64-year-old waitress tried to pick up a 30 year-old customer.

"I'm lookin' for a man," said Rose the waitress, who noted that fish cakes would replace meatballs on the menu today. "I don't want no old guy, can't even walk straight."

Thelma's luncheonette is a cross between a diner and your kitchen. It was my first time in the place.

"I like your beard," said Rose. "You wanna go to Atlantic City?"

I've found a home.

My dad raised me to stay away from any restaurant that's part of a chain, because somebody a thousand miles away is making a profit and has no idea whether the scrambled eggs are runny.

I sensed that Thelma's was not part of a chain. Having no sign out front was a clue.

"It blew down in Hurricane Agnes and we haven't put it back up yet," said John Serbin, who owns the place with his wife, Thelma.

I asked when Agnes came by.

"I think it was 1972."

Thelma's is almost hidden on the ground floor of a clump of three-story rowhouses on Main Street in Manayunk. John says he doesn't need a sign because business is fine.

A friend had told me how to find it. He said it's three doors down from the barber shop with the sign that says, Girls' legs shaved. $2.50 each.

This really threw me. I didn't know if it was $2.50 for each leg or each girl.

"The barber's retired," Rose said of her brother-in-law, "but if you bring your girl around he'll shave her legs."

I decided to think it over with coffee and a doughnut. Rose held up a freshly scrubbed pot and noted for diners, "You won't find no scum on these." She even scrubs the salt and pepper shakers.

"This place hasn't changed," said Officer Jim Clarke, a regular for 25 years. "Great food, fresh every day. You heard of a mom-and-pop store? This is a mom-and-pop restaurant."

Thelma's has 10 lollipop chairs, a Formica countertop, and knotty pine walls. Dispensers for Stanco aspirin hang on a wall, waiting for the company's second life. One wall has pictures of Thelma and Rose as young knockout babes, and John cruising Main Street in his 1931 Ford.

Thelma's sells gloves, $1.25, for mill workers. Plastic garbage bags are on sale because John got a deal. The empty egg cartons are free, in case you need a place to store golf balls.

I asked John where he was from.

"Manayunk."

What street? "This street."

Far from here? "I was born in the barber shop."

The barber shop is at 4111 Main St. John and eight brothers and sisters, including Rose, were raised there.

John later bought 4109 Main St. Then 4107. Then, 35 years ago, he bought 4105 and opened Thelma's. He and Thelma raised three children above the luncheonette and now have eight grandchildren, one great-grandchild.

A door in the luncheonette opens into John's and Thelma's living room. On Tuesday and Thursday, their daughter Sissy takes over for Rose, and Sissy's baby granddaughter sits in a crib in the living room and watches the action.

"Everybody in the place talks to her," John says. "What an education that kid's gettin'."

The future of Thelma's is threatened only by the demise of Vaculator, which made vacuum-type brewers like the one at Thelma's. Nobody wants the coffee any other way.

"I called the company in Chicago 10 years ago and told them to send me all the parts they had," John said.

They sent 72 coffee pots.

"I got 60 pots left. But I only got enough filters for eight more years."

I asked John how he stayed open all these years with mills closing, other restaurants disappearing, everything changing.

He said the key was not changing at all, making the place feel like home, the customers like family. He said he learned a lesson during the Depression, when Tony the Butcher fed John's family on credit.

"Today you got mills layin' off, guys without much money, you help them out. They get back on their feet, they don't forget you. When we got flooded out by Hurricane Agnes, the guys from the Littlewood mill come in here, helped us rebuild. I don't forget that."

Thelma grilled onions, the radio played "In the Mood," Rose flirted. John looked around and said something about improvements.

I told him not to touch a thing.

LUCY'S BLUE LIGHT

March 12, 1989

Not long ago, Lucy Perez's 14-year-old son gave her a three-speed bicycle. He told her he had worked hard, selling flowers and shining shoes, and he wanted his mother to exercise and lose some weight.

The bike was put to good use. After Victor Corcino ran away from home the last time, Lucy would pedal around North Philadelphia, looking for her son. She would pedal east of Broad Street and west of Broad Street, through neighborhoods that used to be owned by people but are now owned by drugs.

She prayed as she pedaled, hoping it was not too late.

A month ago, her brother had a premonition and told Lucy to prepare for bad news about Victor. A week ago, she had her own vision. She says she saw a flash of blue light, and for her it symbolized death.

Last Tuesday, an awful feeling came over her. She went to Victor's room and touched his books, his clothes, his paintings. Things that were black, like his shoes, seemed to be alive. She saw some flowers and imagined a funeral.

About 2:15 p.m. Wednesday, Victor was shot near Ninth and Clearfield. The bullet entered his chest and came out his back.

Lucy, racing the ghosts, rushed to St. Christopher's Hospital. An hour later, the blue light was gone, and Victor with it. He had said he wanted to own a store when he grew up.

She is in the car now, riding to the Medical Examiner's on a gorgeous day that is melting the late snow. She is wearing black, and in a few moments she will have to identify the body of her second of four sons.

Police don't know for sure that it was drugs, but that is where they're looking. Victor was arrested recently for selling marijuana, and it was the lure of money that put him on the corner where he was shot.

Lucy's brother had helped her look for Victor. Night after night.

"He told me he didn't want to be poor. He wanted to buy things," the brother says. "Jewelry. Clothes."

The search led Lucy's brother to Ninth and Clearfield, where the dealers are brokers of little boys' lives.

"I told them I'm Victor's uncle and I want to take him home. They said he's a runaway. He's ours now."

Another relative was chased away by men with bats and knives. The law of the streets said Victor was theirs. There is no court of appeals, here. There is no childhood.

"Ever since his father abandoned him, I think it hurt him in his heart," Lucy

91

is saying in the car. "He ran away, the first time, right after his father left. He was like 9 years old."

And she was left to raise four kids in a neighborhood that waits to pluck them away. Lucy's back yard abuts the yard of the Mazzccua family. In December, 17-year-old Keith Mazzccua was gunned down in a shootout on the street and his 11-year-old sister took a bullet in the leg. It was drug-related.

"I have students who can't read or write," says Sylvia Rider, principal of Kenderton School, which Mazzccua and Corcino children attend. "But talk about drugs, they're all fluent, they all have personal stories."

Victor graduated from Kenderton at 13. The Corcino kids are known for bright personalities and artistic talent—soldiers in the army of kids with Main Line potential and North Philly limitations.

The day after Victor was killed, the school nurse led students in a discussion about losing loved ones to tragedy. It's one subject that requires no remedial work.

On the way to the morgue, Lucy is looking at passing cars and people on the streets. Victor is everywhere. He is walking to school, he is selling flowers, he is opening the door of his store. The absurdity of the routine movement of life is pulling soft tears out of her as the car pulses through traffic.

"I did the best I could do as a mother, God knows. I still serve the Lord, because I know that if I do, I'll get a second chance to be with Victor. That's what I live for now."

Lucy walks strong, with her brother, into the room where Victor lies. She comes out wearing his death, crying for all the mothers and fathers of lost children, and for all the babies growing up in neighborhoods their parents used to own.

He was only a boy, and he died violently in a place where the murder of children is becoming small news, to the dishonor of us all.

The day Lucy went to the morgue, Ninth and Clearfield was crawling with dealers. A half-dozen worked the corner where Victor was shot, another half-dozen nearby.

They wore the stain of Victor's blood, as do all pushers and users, and they stood under the glare of Lucy's blue light.

THE FACES BEHIND CASEY'S NUMBERS

=== *February 13, 1994* ===

When Pennsylvania Gov. Casey says he is cutting welfare for people he calls "able-bodied," there is a clear suggestion in it. With a good kick, maybe they'll get off their duffs and go get a job.

And so on Thursday, as he drives his wife to the El in Northeast Philadelphia, 53-year-old Vincent is not as angry as he is surprised. Maybe you could even say he is shocked. He can't believe this is happening.

He always had a job. Twelve years with a steel company until that went under, and then 20 years as a mechanical inspector for a company that makes airplane parts. That company went bankrupt last March.

Now, every day is a search. Vincent and his wife, Jeannette, have answered ads, knocked on doors. Nothing. When unemployment benefits ran out in December, he did something he never imagined.

He and his wife applied for welfare. Payments started last month. It isn't much—$316 a month plus $200 in food stamps—but it's all they've got.

And now, under Gov. Casey's plan, it'll be gone, too. They figure they'll go from $316 a month to $316 a year.

Five years away from owning their house outright, they stand to lose it. They're already three months behind on the $191 mortgage, and foreclosure is being threatened.

Vincent is taking Jeannette to the El for a ride to Center City. She heard the Philadelphia Unemployment Project can help keep you from being thrown out of your house.

Statewide, about 160,000 people will take a hit in Casey's plan. We need welfare reform, he said, and this will save $88 million. In the next stroke of his pen, he cut business taxes.

Jonathan Stein of Community Legal Services calls the cuts not just cruel, but short-sighted. They may just create greater costs.

"The business cut will amount to about $400 per company," he says. "That's about the price of one health-club membership, and doesn't mean much to a company. But the welfare cuts will mean that someone can't put food on the table, or pay the rent, or pay for a prescription that might prevent a more expensive hospital stay."

The day Jeannette goes to the Philadelphia Unemployment Project, business is brisk. With 48,700 people unemployed in Philadelphia, says outreach

93

worker Evonne Tisdale, all kinds walk in. Black people, white people, the homeless, the chronically poor, and the newly poor.

I'm on the phone with Tisdale when Jeannette walks in. Tisdale puts her on.

They have one son, 25, Jeannette tells me. She's worked before, but she spent most of her adult life as a homemaker. She did have a hobby. She went around her block helping elderly neighbors who were falling behind. She'd run errands and make calls trying to prevent utility shutoffs. Now she makes those calls in her own behalf.

That night, I head over to Jeannette's home. She and her husband live in a neat stone rowhouse on a nice little street near Roosevelt Boulevard. Jeannette takes me inside to meet Vincent. There's a problem, Jeannette says. Vincent is uncomfortable. He doesn't want to be in the paper. No last name. No street name.

I turn to Vincent. He is slender, handsome, soft in manner and voice. He doesn't want to say what he's about to say.

"I'm embarrassed."

His despair quiets the room. Jeannette sighs.

"I've always provided," Vincent continues. "It's a humiliating situation."

He describes what it feels like to stand in a supermarket checkout line with food stamps.

There is no point in telling him there is no shame in it, but I tell him anyway. I begin to add that with his taxes over the years, he paid for the safety net. But it's an absurd thought. The governor has just cut the net out from under him.

"He sure picked a tough time," Vincent says.

There's fear alongside his embarrassment. What happened to the factories where people used to make things? Is he already too old for anyone to hire him? All he and his wife can do, Vincent says, is keep looking. Maybe they'll catch a break.

I leave their house reminded how close we all are to the edge. And wondering whether Casey, who is good with numbers, ever sees faces.

WATCHING A BOY'S WORLD
FALL APART

June 20, 1993

Officer Robert Hayes' three sons decided some time after 1:30 in the morning that they were hungry and wanted something from McDonald's, but not just anything. They wanted the special Jurassic Park meals

And so the search began for a McDonald's open that late, and somebody found one and brought food back to the boys at the hospital. If nothing else, it was another piece of proof for Bobby, a 10-year-old and oldest of the three boys, that this guy must really be Mayor Rendell.

"When his mom introduced us," Rendell recalled, "Bobby looked up and said, 'You're not the mayor.' I had to show him my driver's license."

Three hours earlier, Bobby Hayes' father and his partner were shot during a traffic stop in West Oak Lane. A 19-year-old man believed to be a drug dealer was arrested. And now doctors at Einstein Medical Center were trying to save Robert S. Hayes and John Marynowitz.

The wives were there. The boys. Other family. The wives talked about the irony of the timing, what with Father's Day coming up. Marynowitz and his wife have a boy almost 2.

And Mayor Rendell, who always knows what to say, didn't this time. He'd never done anything like this.

The night dragged and the air went out of the room and the city became these little boys with their brush haircuts, just like Dad, summer at their window, taken from their sleep to wait for their world to be decided.

"The two younger boys sort of half did and half didn't understand what was happening. The 10-year-old knew right away," Rendell said. "He was terrified from the moment he got to the hospital.

"There's not much you can say. I told them it's going to be a long night and your dad needs you guys to be brave. We talked about food and sports, who plays what sports."

First it looked as if one cop might make it and the other wouldn't, and it flopped through the night. The mayor, keeping vigil with Police Commissioner Richard Neal, felt more helpless as he watched the families brace at each turn.

He's the mayor, this is his city. He's supposed to have solutions for every problem, maybe even a miracle now and then. This night, he had neither.

"I was struck with total despair at how we've evolved to a point where we're such a violent society, that we resort to guns and to deadly force almost without an afterthought.

"A more clear sense of punishment could help, but it's not the sole answer by any means. Where does it end? How do we stop people? Yes, I felt frustration and helplessness. And if you told me I could do anything I want to make it stop, I'm not sure I'd know what to do."

Bobby Hayes' brothers went home in the middle of the night. Bobby stayed and fell asleep on a chair.

"As the night wore on," the mayor said, "literally every officer in the squad came to see the wives, and it didn't matter if they were white, black, Hispanic. It was all the same, and they hugged. Like family."

A little before six, the doctor came out and said Officer Hayes had gone into cardiac arrest.

Rendell says he knew then.

He thought about being at school when he was 14 and getting that call from his uncle telling him his father was sick real bad. He didn't want to go home, because he knew.

He looked at Bobby again, struck, as a parent always is, by the innocence, sad and beautiful, of a child asleep. And he imagined his son lying there.

And when the doctor came out about 6:40, having just told Mrs. Hayes the news in another room, Rendell wanted to run up and say no, don't tell Bobby. Let him dream. Let him sleep a while longer.

"I didn't want to watch because I knew it would be horrible, and yet something forced me to watch. The doctor woke Bobby up and put his hands on the sides of his head, trying to comfort him. It was the worst thing I've ever seen in my life."

Gone, all day Thursday, was Rendell's usual unflappable manner. He kept breaking up as he recalled the vigil. In the evening, as planned, he took his son and some pals to a Phillies game to celebrate his son's birthday. Never, he said, did it feel better to be with his boy.

For Father's Day, Rendell planned to be with his family at the Shore. "Not a minute will go by," he said, when he doesn't think about Bobby and the rest of the family of Officer Robert S. Hayes, who died at 45.

DROPPING IN ON A VICTORY PARTY

May 12, 1988

Y ou could convict me for a lot of things, but never for failing to look at both sides of a story.

Last year I asked attorney Bobby Simone for an interview with reputed mob boss Nicky Scarfo. Among other things, I wanted to see if Nicky had any idea why a bunch of guys he knew were shot in the head.

Simone didn't produce. And so, with only my imagination and what seemed like 40,000 indictments to go on, maybe my columns about Nicky's trials and tribulations were a shade to one side, I don't know. Some people seemed to think so.

So on Tuesday, after Nicky and eight associates were found not guilty of the Salvie Testa hit, I dropped by the victory party.

The defendants themselves had to celebrate privately, as they are still locked up for other business ventures. But a gang of sympathizers swept out of court and over to the Four Seasons Hotel to pay tribute to the jury system in America.

It probably was the first party at the hotel in which a man in a bathrobe threatened to swim buck naked in the fountain and $100-a-cork hootch was sprinkled on the appointments.

Hotel staff, perhaps concerned that a party celebrating acquittal in a gangland slaying might scare the pants off hotel guests, ran the revelers into the Washington Room, next to the Audio Visual Script Design convention room.

And that's where I found myself by late afternoon, peeking through the door, two thoughts in mind. Either I shouldn't have called this the most inept branch of the American mob. Or I shouldn't be here.

I looked back at the fountain, and in my imagination it became a larger body of water. A river maybe, possibly an ocean. No lifeguards on duty.

But sometimes you have to just swim. And so I took a deep breath, threw open the doors, and waded in.

It felt good. But I knew I couldn't hide forever in the Audio Visual Script Design room.

So I eased into the Washington Room, where I saw a happy crowd of men, women, and children. I went up to Oscar Goodman, who represented Crazy Phil Leonetti. As an ice-breaker, I asked Goodman if he was still planning to get naked.

He said no, and asked me to sit. I did so, hoping to be put at ease by the man known for brilliant defense of heavies. In a kind voice, he said:

"You remind me of a journalist in Las Vegas who did similar work. He passed away."

I saw the river, the ocean.

"These guys don't like you."

I guess I can understand that.

"They dislike you very much."

Come on, Nicky doesn't read this stuff. Does he?

"They read it. Of course they read it. They hate you. Lee Beloff hates you. Diane Beloff hates you."

But I love all of them.

"I respect you, but if you're going to write negative stories, you should write the other side as well."

That's why I'm here.

"This is a great day. The message is that you can't build a prosecution on the paid-for testimony of two sleazeballs like [ex-mobsters] Tommy DelGiorno and Nicky Caramandi."

A woman named Joy sat at the table. She was at the hotel on business and got swept up in the party.

"They're friendly people," said Joy, who was deep enough into a bottle of champagne to make Sasquatch look friendly. "The world is made up of so many wonderful cultures, and that's what this is. This is a culture."

As she spoke, one of the cultured made a discovery.

"Lopez?" he said.

Yes sir.

"Steve Lopez?"

Pleasure to meet you.

"Get the [hockey puck] out."

A few others joined in.

"I want to talk to you," said one.

Politics? The budget deficit?

"You're a mother—."

Yet another said:

"You killed Frank Rizzo."

Hey, I love the Bambino.

"You killed Rizzo for mayor. Get the [hockey puck] out. Get out!"

One man held the doors open while a posse rode shotgun. As I left, Joy was saying, "It's a culture, that's what it is."

Attorney David Chesnoff apologized. The important thing, he said, is that it was a great day for Americans because the verdict upheld the rights of all citizens against contrived and sleazy prosecution.

And that, folks, is the other side of the story. I say Salvie Testa committed suicide. The second shot in the head was his idea of insurance.

As I left the hotel, I noticed the lifelike sculpture of two men. I'd seen it before, but it never struck me that the men appear to be in concrete body casts. When nobody was looking, I walked up and said:

One of you guys from Vegas?

GOOD MEATBALLS, LOTS OF FREE PARKING

August 3, 1994

Over the course of time here, I've written about abortion and bigotry, education and crime, transportation and insurance, housing and jobs.

I have written about presidents and governors, mayors and Council members; about heroes and hacks, good guys and bums.

I have written from Moscow and Colombia, Bosnia and Iraq.

None of which ever had as many people asking for more details as did my story about parking my car in the middle of South Broad Street.

It's nice to know where you stand.

If you missed it, I first drove my car up North Broad, parked between the double yellow lines across from Vendetta's Creativity Salon, and got a ticket in seven minutes flat.

I then drove to South Broad, parked between the double yellow lines like hundreds of other good citizens, and got a meatball sandwich at Emil's Restaurant.

By the time the story ran, the car had been parked—unmoved, unbooted, and unticketed—for four days. Then the questions began.

Did you really do it?

Is it still there?

Do you have a ticket yet?

I got complaints along the lines of: How dare you mess with a tradition that has existed for decades.

But there were far more calls and letters from people asking me to investigate other traditions in South Philadelphia, such as double parking and finagling disabled parking privileges for disabilities that are not apparent to the naked eye.

While all of this was going on, I left my car in the same spot, driving down each day in another car to check on it. A week came and went. No ticket. Then 10 days.

"What are you going to do?" my son Andrew asked.

"I'm thinking of starting a business," I said. "We could sell hoagies out of the trunk."

Andrew liked the idea and has asked several times if I was serious. And frankly, I don't know.

But there are two things I do know.

(1) The car still had no ticket yesterday, which means that today marks two weeks of free parking.

(2) I love this city.

I called Linda Miller at the Parking Authority. She is the one who told me about the history of clout in South Philadelphia, and she said yesterday that she knows of no plans to challenge the status quo.

This means that responsible citizens who park at meters, and run a minute late, will continue to get tickets, whereas people like me, who abandon their cars in the middle of the street, clogging the emergency lane and obstructing the view of pedestrians and motorists alike, will get a free ride.

Except, perhaps, on parts of North Broad. Where, for no reason other than a neighborhood history of considerably less clout, you may get a ticket before the engine cools.

(I promised Vendetta I'd run an item for her again. She is still looking for a stylist at the Creativity Salon.)

As for South Broad, I called Emil's Restaurant yesterday to see if it might be possible to open a middle-of-the-street franchise out of my trunk. Nickie Francesco, the owner's daughter, answered the phone.

"We want to thank you," she said, for mentioning the meatball sandwich platter in the column ($5.95, fries and coleslaw included).

"We did a good meatball business after the article," she said.

"You're kidding."

"No. People came in asking about it. We had a run on meatballs."

It's nice to have an impact on the important matters of the day. But I must tell you I was not prepared for what Nickie said next.

"We ran the meatball sandwich all week and called it the Steve Lopez Special."

Indulge, if you will, a momentary immodesty.

I have arrived in this town.

I'm even thinking of retiring, there being no higher award in all of journalism.

Nickie and I have begun discussing a joint business venture, which will consist of meatball sandwiches being sold out of my car.

I could be the next Milton Street.

Call me a dreamer, but I envision a day when people are parked in the middle of the street, all up and down South Broad, eating the special.

(Clip this column for 50 percent discount. Double coupons for Parking Authority employees and their relatives. Plenty of free parking.)

A BOY AND HIS BROTHER

July 26, 1988

The white hearse moved along a line of trees at Mount Lawn Cemetery in Sharon Hill and then crossed the highway, catching the sun as it turned to come down the hill with the body of 5-year-old Marcus Yates.

On the day the city got tough and began shutting 500 crack houses in Philadelphia, a decision too late for Marcus Yates, the hearse stopped in front of Garden D, where a work crew had prepared the grave under a red tent.

The place they had carved out of the earth for Marcus Yates was against the highway, and his family and friends moved toward it, supporting each other so that together they could shoulder their burden.

First came the flowers from the hearse, the work crew placing wreaths around the grave site.

"Our Grandson," said one.

"Our Baby," said another, a heart-shaped one with red carnations, and it reminded you how short a time Marcus Yates was here before a bullet snuffed him out, a bullet fired during a gun battle that followed a staring contest between two alleged Jamaican drug dealers.

Marcus Yates was playing a video game in the mom-and-pop store where it happened. One brother and a cousin were wounded. And the carnage that is a part of life in the Philadelphia area—where 60 people have died this year in drug-related slaughters—had finally awakened the right people.

As the pallbearers reached for the little white casket, you wondered why, if the locations of 500 crack houses were known, nobody shut them down before Marcus Yates took a bullet in the head. And you wondered if doing it now would disrupt the drug trade for more than 24 hours, coming so late in a losing game, another desperate, "Well, I guess we better do something."

You wondered, but nothing made sense yesterday at 10:37 a.m. as the coffin came out of the back of the car and one of the pallbearers put his tiny hands under the box that held his brother.

Tony Yates was an 11-year-old man yesterday, his face a sketch of the courage that grows from anger. He took short steps, his fingers cradling the back of the casket that held the brother who had idolized him.

They had played together, fought together, watched out for each other on the street. In the safety of their room, Tony and Marcus would stretch the bedspread down from the top bunk bed, tight to the floor, and send their little matchbox cars screaming down the hill.

Anthony and Rochelle held each other, and after Tony helped place the casket over the grave, he moved between his parents and looked up into their wet eyes, as if to pass his own strength on to them.

A mourner shrieked as carnations were placed on the casket, and at 10:50, two cemetery workers named Nate and Willie began lowering Marcus Yates into the ground.

When that was done, Willie walked away from the crowd and in the shelter of his own privacy, Willie the cemetery worker wept. The job is never easy, he said a moment later, but no 5-year-old boy should die this way. Willie said he has eight children and nine grandchildren, and then he explained why this particular job was so difficult for him.

"I lost a boy the same way," he said. "It was gang-related. He was the youngest one I had, 17 years old, got shot. It was about four years ago."

When the procession drove away, Willie walked up to the grave and looked to its depth for a moment, maybe seeing his own son, maybe seeing all of our despair at the loss of innocent life. And then Willie began removing the tent and fixing up the grave site, because the ground next to Marcus Yates was waiting for the little boy's new neighbor.

Friends and family were on their way to a reception at Holy Temple Church of God in Christ, where the sign outside says, "Jesus Never Fails." Inside the church annex, Rochelle Yates spoke of the mayor's plan to shut crack houses.

"It's about time. I think if my son hadn't died, the city would still be at a standstill, like it always is."

Anthony Yates said that although he welcomed the mayor's crackdown, the fight was against weakness, against a system that allows drugs into the country, and money to be laundered, and people to live in fear of their own neighborhoods.

"This cannot be accepted as a part of life," Rochelle Yates said.

Tony Yates, the little man, talked about his brother. He had made the decision on his own—he emphasized that—to carry Marcus' casket.

He said it was his way of giving something back to the little brother who used to make him laugh.

LOCKED SCHOOLS ARE
SQUANDERED

March 6, 1994

I live one block from a library and a gymnasium, both of which I pay taxes for, but neither of which my kids can use.

Across Philadelphia and other cities, millions of people can say the same thing. Almost every public school has a library and gym. But the schools are locked in the afternoon, on weekends, and all summer.

I can't count the times I've been in a neighborhood where somebody told me there wasn't enough for the kids to do, and that's one reason they end up in trouble. Each time, a public school was no more than a few blocks away. A public school that was probably the safest, most positive place in the neighborhood.

Several years ago, before the Philadelphia City Council bought the Councilmobile to serve as a sort of traveling Big Top, there was a discussion of alternatives.

We need field offices, some Council members argued. Well, one suggested, how about using the school buildings? There's a school in every neighborhood, so why rent additional space at taxpayer expense?

It's not possible, another Council member responded. Too much hassle. Among other things, you'd have to find out who had the key to the school, and arrange for this person to open and close the building.

Yes, too much hassle. It might require one division of government to work with another. Rocket science. Bring on the Councilmobile.

Now there is a proposal, in Washington, to do just that—use the schools. It comes from New Jersey Sen. Bill Bradley, who sees locked schools as one of the nation's most ridiculously wasted resources.

Here we are, trying to reduce crime, improve education, bolster families, and restore a sense of community, and the one place in every neighborhood that could be the center of it all is locked up at 3 in the afternoon.

Open the schools, Bradley says. Open them in the evenings, on weekends, in the summer. Especially with libraries and rec centers so strapped, and with scaled-back hours.

Let kids come in and play ball and paint and get help with their homework. Bring in parents and religious groups and community leaders to help teach and supervise them.

Bradley introduced the idea last year, keeping it small.

"In this budgetary climate, we . . . introduced a modest bill—$15 million.

And then toward the end of last year, along came the giant crime bill and suddenly the Senate leadership found $20 billion to fight crime."

You've already heard about the big stuff in the bill. More prisons, more police, three strikes and you're out. The crowd-pleasing things. The things that won't make a dent.

"We looked at each other and said, 'Wait a minute,' " Bradley says. "Sure we need to fight crime, but we also need to prevent crime. And the best way is to get to kids before they become criminals."

Bradley rounded up support, and "we basically blocked progress of the crime bill" until the schools initiative was included. "Now it's in there, at $400 million—$100 million for each of the next four years."

He thinks the prospects for this piece of the bill are good. "This is one of the few things in it that could be viewed as preventive. I'd say the bill is about 80 percent punitive."

As a practical matter, that's upside down. But working in Congress isn't an act of thinking so much as an act of posing. What makes Bradley a rarity is that he's not interested in looking at the pictures.

And so while his colleagues trip over each other to propose prisons on top of prisons, here he is, quietly asking if we might also unlock the schools at a fraction of the cost.

Bradley tells the story of a man in Washington who for years has offered his house as a haven for neighborhood kids. One of them became an attorney, and is one of Bradley's best friends.

Every community has people like that, he says. "High-spirited people of goodwill." Why not give them a bigger, centrally located place to do what they do best?

"The problems in America are really three interrelated problems," he says. "Joblessness, family disintegration, and violence. Until we deal with all three, we're not going to really deal with urban problems."

Opening the schools could help with all three. The remarkable thing is that so simple an idea comes off as so revolutionary.

MOMENTARY INNOCENCE

April 11, 1993

The adults tried their best, but it was impossible to find every last one of them. So there were still some crack vials amongst the hidden treasures Friday afternoon when the children of Tusculum Street lined up for their Easter egg hunt.

The kids, most of them 6 and under, waited in front of their homes for the OK to begin. Because of the dangers in the area, which include occasional gunfire, most of them had never even been allowed to cross the street, which lies above Lehigh in Kensington. So this was a big deal.

The kids peered across Tusculum and into the lot along the railroad tracks, scanning the field for the tops of eggs. The lot had been raked clean a few days earlier by Marge, Charlotte, and Emma, three longtime residents of Tusculum. They found countless crack vials, a couple of hypodermics, used condoms, and lots of trash. Charlotte found a dead rat.

At the corner now, a teenage lookout with a big-billed cap stood atop the A Street Bridge, protecting a drug operation. At the other end of the block, a young man in a blue warm-up jacket smoked crack behind a yellow shed.

Across the railroad tracks and under the bridge, people floated in and out of a homemade fort that serves as headquarters for a colony of drug addicts and drifters.

But the kids, concentrating on the eggs, were oblivious to all of this.

Christina, 4, and her sister Nicole, 3, wore pretty purple handbands and eyeballed the field of eggs. Joey, 2, didn't seem to understand this plastic-egg concept, but he knew all he needed to know. Inside the eggs were candy, quarters, dimes, and nickels.

"We already know where the eggs are," said Christie Lynn, 6, who sat on the front steps with her cousin Christina, plotting a course. "We saw the lady hiding them."

The lady hiding them was Emily, whose 1-year-old nephew, Billy, was standing by for the hunt. Emily said she had knocked on the doors of drug dealers and suggested they send their kids out, too, "so they get to experience something positive." But none of them had shown up.

When it was about to begin, Ed and Emma came out to watch the show. They go back 43 years on this street. Back to the good old days. The days before they bought the house next door, and kept it vacant, just to make sure drug dealers didn't move in.

"You know what I do?" Ed said. "I live inside, not out."

Some residents are trapped here because the value of their homes has sunk to almost nothing with all the danger and decay. It's especially tough for Ed to see what's happened. He was a police officer for 25 years.

"You have to restrain yourself from getting involved," he says. If a neighbor happens to be a dealer, he limits conversation to this: "Good morning. Hello. Goodnight."

As Emma scrubbed their marble steps, Ed remembered a time he came outside and hit the deck.

"They were using 9mm guns, shooting at each other. You're ducking behind the rims of the wheels and when they're done you go around and you've got bullet holes in the side of your car."

The kids were ready to go now. And when Emily's nephew Billy was led to the field, that signaled the start of the Tusculum Street Easter egg hunt. Six kids in all.

Christie Lynn and Christina, working as a team, were cleaning up.

Joey, eggless, was crying. But then he spotted a green egg and lit up.

Some of the kids were eating the candy out of the eggs now and counting their money. Meanwhile, the lookout spotted someone nearby, maybe a cop, and shouted a warning to the dealers in his crew.

The kids remained oblivious.

Ironically, the crack vials in the field had pastel caps that were almost the same color as the eggs. But the cleaning crew hadn't missed all that many. And if the kids saw the vials, they knew not to touch them.

Several more kids came to join the hunt now, and as they did, Emily's family hid more eggs just north of the others, closer to the drug corner and to the bridge with the colony of drifters under it.

Ed went for his camera and got the kids to pose in the lot with their eggs in front of them. In the background were a burned-out house, a gutted house, graffiti, a few satellite dishes, maybe a drug dealer or two, and a shut-down factory that once employed hundreds.

The Tusculum Street kids smiled for the portrait. Innocence frozen.

They smiled because they had their eggs and they were happy, and because they had no idea it isn't supposed to be like this.

WINDS OF CHANGE

September 2, 1990

It was late one night in spring, the feel of change in the air, when the visitor from California sat on the porch with his son and watched his grandchildren play in the street with their friends.

The kids, there must have been eight or 10 of them, were playing kick the can.

"I didn't know anyone still played that," my father said, watching the kids and talking about when he had played the game half a century ago.

The wooden rocker creaked on the porch and a cool breeze swished through the trees. Every few minutes, the can would go clanging along on the asphalt, the sound echoing past quiet rowhouses.

The night held that indescribable yet unmistakable feel of change. It was as if each molecule of air rode the edge of a new season. The kids seemed charged by its promise. Of course the end of the school year, which was drawing near, might have had something to do with it.

"You've got a nice neighborhood here," my father said. "Really nice."

He was back home in California when the cool breezes moved out and warm, heavy air moved in. Summer had come to a quiet street in Mount Airy, and it would be a summer to remember.

Many times I would sit in the rocking chair my father had sat in and watch the kids. My father's words had given me a comfort and security as warm as the summer nights, and his voice lingered on the porch long after he was gone.

I wished he could have watched with me as the nightly gathering grew to new numbers each week, kids coming from the next street, from around the corner. Whether the game was kick the can, or kickball, or jailbreak, or hide and seek, there was no problem finding enough kids to play.

It got to where 16 or 17 kids would be out every night, a regular neighborhood gang. But it was a different kind of gang than I had seen in years past, no matter what neighborhood I had lived in, no matter what city.

There were about as many girls as boys. Some kids were as young as 5, some as old as 16.

Some were black, some white, some Asian.

Nobody seemed to notice.

Nor did it seem to be a problem that while some were barely out of diapers, others were discovering hormones that change the feel of a breeze, the glow of the moon.

Among themselves, they established an order to their games that allowed every kid to feel like an indispensable part of the gang.

In a game of kickball, you might see a gangly kid nearly six feet tall on first base, a five-footer on second, a four-footer on third, and all of them rooting for some little munchkin at the plate to clear the bases.

Some nights, during kick the can, the youngest and smallest of the gang would scamper toward my house. In a spot that really didn't look much like a hiding place, she was able to practically disappear.

She would just wedge herself in behind a fence and duck barely under the top of a short stone wall. On a dark night, other kids could walk within two feet and not see her.

As the summer wore on, the nightly show became more of an escape from the rest of the world. The city was racing toward financial doom, there was more violence and more racial hatred, the country seemed buried under S&L gloom, the world tiptoed closer to the edge of war.

But in at least one neighborhood in Philadelphia, where a little girl had the most secure hiding place in the world and differences among kids went unnoticed, the nights were long and the world was fine and summer was timeless.

I think what my father saw that night was his own childhood, his own neighborhood. I think he liked knowing there was still a place where people aren't compelled to purchase distance between each other, a place where kids aren't always glued to TV sets and computer games.

It may be, as summer fades, that it felt so good and seemed so special because we wanted it to. Certainly the neighborhood isn't perfect, the kids didn't always get along. But I prefer to believe it was a special time and will be one of those summers to remember.

The other night one of the kids came in from the street to change his shorts for a pair of long pants. A wind blew outside, a different kind of wind that carried the feel of change.

A sudden gust caught the empty rocker and sent it swaying gently. It creaked on the porch where my father had sat, where his voice had lingered long after he said he liked the neighborhood.

'AND THEY WHO DWELL THEREIN'

November 25, 1987

It had slipped away to nothing but the cold and the darkness for Georgianna, the line between life and death fading in the night.

She pulled the blankets up over her and prepared to pass, quietly, invisibly, in an abandoned house on Christian Street in a South Philadelphia winter.

She did not want to die, but she had long ago accepted death. Her feet were frozen numb, and maybe that's what it would be like. A spreading of the numbness until there was no feeling at all.

Georgianna had committed much of the Bible to memory, and her favorite passage would accompany her now: "The earth is the Lord's and the fullness thereof, the world and they who dwell therein."

Morning came, and it seemed almost unfair that Georgianna would see the light, spared for the sake of suffering, only to face death again. She looked down and realized her toes were gone, lost to frostbite. It bothered her none; she still had her soul.

Won't be doin' no runnin', Georgianna thought in the squalor of the abandoned house on Christian Street. Won't be doin' no dancin'. But she thanked God for letting her live, and then dragged herself out to look at a world that would rather not know she existed.

It was Mary Scullion who found her, two years ago now. Mary Scullion, who would venture out on the coldest nights to take people home with her. She has found people wandering the streets with broken bones, blindness, cancer, heart problems, diabetes.

"I'd like to help," Scullion told Georgianna.

"No," Georgianna insisted. When all you have left is who you are, you cover yourself with every remaining thread of dignity.

Mary Scullion came back again, as she always does. In warmer weather, Georgianna had taken to sleeping on the sidewalk near 17th and Rodman, and Scullion would look for her there. The third time, Georgianna went with her.

Scullion is Sister Mary Scullion and she runs Women of Hope, a shelter administered by Mercy Hospice.

Georgianna is one of 24 women living in Scullion's shelter. All of them have lived on the streets, all of them have been in mental institutions, all of them have held hands with death.

And yet there is more life in the former school at 1210 Lombard St., a stronger sense of human spirit and resourcefulness, than you will find anywhere else.

"Got me a job," Georgianna says. "Answerin' phones."

It's a volunteer job, but for what it means to her, chief executive officer would be no better. Georgianna has gone most of her life being told she is of no use, a helpless mental case. Now she has purpose.

"They gave me a birthday party right after I got here," she says. "I think I only had three parties my whole life."

Fourteen of the 24 women have volunteer jobs. It's almost as if there's pressure for those of sound enough mind to get off the dime and make something of their lives, or at least contribute to the care of the shelter.

Even the staff members have stories. Turhan, the maintenance man, was on the street for a year. Jerome, who is doing some fix-it work in the basement, goes home at night to a cardboard box under a fire escape on Seventh Street. He's saving up to get a place.

Amanda, who does some housekeeping for the shelter and has lived for four months at Mercy Hospice, will move into her own place today with her 14-month-old son "and have a Thanksgiving turkey —in our own house—on Thursday."

"I believe," Scullion says, "that the homeless are a prophetic presence, telling us that something is radically wrong."

She can preach—in that tireless way of hers—about all the bright minds and money devoted to weapons development while human development goes begging. But her words can't be as compelling as what she and her staff have built at 1210 Lombard St., and what it says about the force of compassion.

They will gather tomorrow afternoon in the cafeteria, Mary Scullion's extended family. Two dozen castaways—a rag-tag army of lost souls who have found themselves in each other—will share Thanksgiving dinner. And then Scullion will probably go out and search the streets again.

"I will give thanks for life," Georgianna says. "Thanks that I'm here today. Thanks to have something to eat. Thanks to have a roof over my head. Thanks to Sister Mary for coming back for me the third time.

"She didn't have to, you know."

Memories for a
Family's Pain

November 27, 1994

Eddie Polec's mother is folded like a fallen angel on the sofa, under the Happy Thanksgiving banner, trying to find the words to describe the son who was taken by a crime the city cannot forget.

Her husband watches her thoughts slide through her, and her daughter and son do, too, knowing all too well the crushing weight of memories good and bad.

"You spend a lifetime loving them, and in a moment, they're gone," Kathy Polec says. "It breaks your heart."

Kristie, 19, holds her mother's hand. Bill, 14, looks to see if he can help, too.

John Polec, a computer programmer whose son was beaten to death with baseball bats by a swarming mob November 11 while 911 calls went unheeded, squats in a corner of the room.

A picture of Eddie, 16, a senior at Cardinal Dougherty, looks out at them all.

It is, in a way, a double tragedy. First the senseless murder and five arrests so far, and then the news that if 911 had worked the way it should have, his son might be alive. Polec says he and his family are dealing with other difficulties now, and aren't yet ready to comment publicly on 911.

Eddie was a little guy—about 130 pounds. He liked to wrestle; he liked the Cleveland Indians; and he loved the family vacations in Ocean City, N.J., because he loved the water. He wanted to be in the Coast Guard.

Eddie knew he'd done well this last reporting period, but he never saw the report card. It came after he died.

"First honors," his mother says. "He worked hard, and it was the first time."

She allows a smile.

"Eddie was special," she goes on, rising on the memories now instead of sinking under them. "All parents say that about their kids, but it's true. Do you have kids? Well, then, you know that each of them brings something different to the family."

She is apologizing now to her other children for calling Eddie special.

It isn't necessary, says Kristie, a college sophomore.

Eddie, he was the one who always had a joke. Eddie's mother would hear all about it when she worked as a crossing guard over at St. Cecilia's.

You're Eddie's mother?

112

Eddie made me laugh. Eddie did this. Eddie did that.

"He had a gift," Kathy Polec says.

Eddie worked at Boston Chicken from the time he was 14. He bought sneakers with the money, and clothes.

"He just blew it all," his little brother says. "He spent money on every-thing."

"He bought me lunch when I came home from college," Kristie says.

Eddie went with her to the store one day and insisted on paying for her shampoo and conditioner, then he ran off to work.

"I went by Boston Chicken to leave the change for him, and he was in the window," Kristie says. "That was the last time I saw him."

Kathy Polec wants to share a letter she got the other day from one of Ed-die's teachers:

I wanted to write this letter just to let you know how your son has affected me and so many others. . . . Ed was the light and his friends were drawn to his warmth, his friendly smile and his kindness. . . . He would go out of his way to greet me, always with a Good morning, Mr. Esposito. And then he would pro-ceed to tell me everything he did on the weekend that passed. . . . I loved to joke with him in the classroom and watch him laugh, even when my jokes weren't al-ways so funny. . . . I'm just grateful for having had the honor and privilege of getting to know your son. . . .

Eddie's father says we can copy the letter at the library where Eddie used to study, and so we drive through the neighborhood that will never look or feel the same for him again.

That night, carloads of empty-headed kids with nothing to do but defend false honor through senseless violence—a snapshot of America—were coming in from Abington to settle the score on a rape that never occurred. A rumble, with the group Eddie hung out with at the neighborhood recreation center, had been rumored.

Neighbors looked out their windows to see baseball bats and a riot in the making, but their calls for help—increasingly desperate—produced no police. The calls went to different dispatchers, and the system is so inept that no con-nection was made.

Some dispatchers were rude. Some wasted time with ignorant questions.

"Who's got a bat, sir?"

"Is he white or black or Hispanic?"

Nearly 45 minutes passed between the first call and the arrival of police.

Eddie Polec's father is driving now at twilight, two weeks after the fact, through the middle-class neighborhood where all civility ended.

There is nothing out here to explain how human beings can be so savage as to crush another in the head with bats, or how others can be so corrupt as to stand by like ghouls.

There is nothing to explain why a 911 system has to be like rocket science in the city of Philadelphia.

There is only a kid named Eddie Polec in the last moments of life, and Eddie's father, who is out here because he has to be, honoring his son.

"This is St. Cecilia's, the church where they beat him," he says.

Wasn't Eddie an altar boy here?

"Four years. Fifth grade through eighth. I'll just go up here so you get a sense of what it was that night."

He stops at the Fox Chase Library for a copy of the letter from the teacher. "Ed will always be in my thoughts, my heart, and in my prayers." Then he stops at the Fox Chase Playground.

"Can you see that on the wall there, or is it too far?"

It says, "In Memory of Ed."

"They put that up there the night he died," he says. "And then they ran this way."

He drives toward Rhawn, and you can almost see Eddie and the Fox Chase kids running for their lives.

There had been no rape—apparently only a typical spat; some ridiculous teenage thing. But the rumor was loose, and there was honor to defend. And Eddie, who tripped and fell, became the sacrifice.

"People were out of their houses here screaming," John Polec says, and then he points across Rhawn to a side entrance of the church.

"You see those doors? That's where he died."

He drives into the church lot now and past the spot where flowers had been placed to cover the blood of his middle child, and then he heads home to take care of Eddie's mother and Eddie's brother and sister.

"I have a great family," Eddie's father says to explain his strength. "That's how I'm getting through this."

THE POLEC CASE RINGS ANOTHER ALARM

December 4, 1994

The idea itself scares me. The thought of taking a bat, holding it in my hands, and clubbing someone in the head or the face.

I don't think I could do it.

If my life depended on it, or if the life of someone I love depended on it, I could take a whack at someone's legs or shoulders. Disable them.

But beat the life out of them? The thought makes me cringe. And that's the part that troubles me more than any other in the Eddie Polec story.

How can a teenager—or anyone—take a baseball bat and beat another human being in the head?

And then, when the victim is limp and dazed, or maybe unconscious, how does someone prop him up to make a better target for other kids?

The story of Polec, the 16-year-old Fox Chase kid, has been horrifying in several ways. There was the failure of the 911 system, which everyone had agreed needed to be fixed, but which nobody fixed.

There was Mayor Rendell in one of his weakest hours, underreacting at first, and then, still without accepting a scintilla of responsibility, conveniently firing three 911 operators.

Then there were those who ran with the ridiculous and ugly notion that the operators were disciplined because they were black, and that the murder has created a stir because the victim was white.

A fine young man is dead and his family will never be the same. And I will not devote another sentence here to those who are small enough and shameless enough to politicize the Polec family's loss.

So let me get back to the mirror this case holds up to us, and to the most disturbing aspect of all: the unbelievable capacity human beings have to inflict pain on one another.

You know the story. The rumor of a rape that never occurred. Carloads of Abington kids, some with bats, driving into Fox Chase to avenge it.

"I don't think," says John Apeldorn, captain of the homicide unit in Philadelphia, "that anyone thought they'd be going home after a murder."

Then what did they think?

Did they think at all?

With 50 kids assembled, the fight started. Some kids ran. Eddie Polec was tripped when someone threw a bat, and now the attackers were part of a mob, no longer human.

115

They beat him outside the church where he had been an altar boy.

Six Abington-area teenagers have been charged with murder. Friday, a seventh, suspected of handing out bats, surrendered.

Norman Schmid, the principal of Abington High, has two points. First, that the vast majority of kids in any community aren't violent.

"We're discussing it every day, and most of our students are horrified."

Second, don't look for simple explanations with those who are violent.

Maybe it's parenting, or the nightly news, or peer pressure.

Maybe it's violence on TV and in movies, which is pervasive and almost cartoonlike, often without pain and sometimes without consequence.

Maybe it's all those things.

We live in a culture whose main activities are turning on the TV, worshiping athletes and pop idols, and hanging out at malls. And we live territorially— black against white, urban against suburban, Republican against Democrat, us against them.

As little thought and interaction as possible. As little respect.

Combine that, Captain Apeldorn says, with all the guns and other weapons on the street, and it's explosive. And so, too, is the breakdown in communication between parents and their children.

The Fox Chase altercation was rumored for a week, Apeldorn says. If just one of the 50 kids had said something to a parent, and the parent had acted, it might not have happened.

"I think it gets back to family," says Apeldorn, who talks about "everything, always," with his daughter.

"I think this society in general has forgotten what's important. The TV's always on, and if the kid has a problem, you tell him to wait till a commercial. What happened to, before going to bed at night, you hug me, you tell me you love me, maybe you have a conversation?"

Eddie Polec's father—who talked, and listened, to his son every night— told me the hardest part is that he died for nothing.

It's small consolation, I know, but if we examine what Eddie's savage death says about the way we live, and if we can feel any of his family's love for him, it wasn't for nothing.

A SONG ABOUT AN
OLD ROOFER

December 22, 1986

Did you ever get a melody in your head and, even though it's not your favorite song, you can't get rid of it?

It happened to me after I went through the newspaper and read the conversations recorded by the FBI.

The ones where Roofers Union honcho Steve Traitz chats with local judges, cronies, and other wildlife. It was even more colorful than the stuff the feds released in October.

I'm going to write the lyrics to the song, which, ironically, is about a guy who works on roofs. I've added a few personal touches.

One, two. One-two-three-four.

You better watch out.

My guys is a-punch-in-the-nose guys.—Traitz to Judge-elect Mario Driggs

You better not cry.

Let me go. Please!—A contractor, amid slapping sounds at the union hall

You better not pout, I'm telling you why.

Backhand him.—Traitz to one of his elves

Santa Claus is coming to town.

. . . That's 300 to help you with your campaign. . . . Merry Christmas.—Traitz to Judge-elect Mary Rose Fante Cunningham

He's making a list.

Judge Wallace, 300. Judge White, three. Tommy Dempsey, three. —Traitz

He's checking it twice.

Judy, two. Eddie, two. Jimmy, two. Bobby, one. . . . Mayor Marberger, two. Chief Bambi, two. . . . Judge Cavanaugh, three. —Traitz

He's going to find out who's naughty.

My guy failed me today. His [testicles] ain't what they should be.—Traitz on Judge Wilhelm Knauer

And nice.

Oh. Steve, thank you. Thank you so much.—Cunningham after getting $300 from Traitz

Santa Claus is coming to town.

OK. Tommy Miller's roof, . . . that's the head of the State Building Trades. Judge Chiovero's roof, and, and, ah, Bobby Heenan's roof in Atlantic City.—Traitz to one of his elves

He sees you when you're sleeping.

You'll never hear me. . . .—Traitz to Judge-elect Esther Sylvester
He knows when you're awake.

Now, ya know who else I wanna give 500? I wanna give Bill Simon five. He's strong.—Traitz on the Camden County sheriff
He knows if you've been bad.

If he opens his mouth, give him a . . . backhand.—Traitz discussing a colleague
Or good.

Oh, here's another judge that's strong. Judge DeMeo down Traffic Court, give him five.—Traitz
So be good for goodness sake.

And, if you can help, good. And if you can't, I understand that. I would never put you under no heat. What the hell kind of a friend would I be?—Traitz to Sylvester
Oh, you better watch out.

You got a kid goin' in front of you at 11 o'clock. Eric Burns. He's one of . . . my guys' nephews. . . . The kid's goin' in the Army, Judge, and he just needs a clean bill to get into the Army.—Traitz to Judge Mitchell Lipschutz
You better not cry, you better not pout.

Based upon the character testimony . . . the Court under the new trial finds the defendant not guilty.—Lipschutz on Eric Burns
I'm telling you why.

I was up country for, for three weeks. I bought a farm up there. Yeah. Well, you'll be up there with me. I'll bring you up there some weekend.—Traitz to Lipschutz
Santa Claus is coming to town.

Jeez, Tommy, don't let me forget nobody. . . . I ain't gonna mark 'em, Tom. I wonder how the blank I'm gonna do that?—Traitz to an enterprising elf, who suggests—I would put ah, on all the judges, put an "X" at the top of the envelope. . . . And put an "O" on the, the D.A.'s.
He's making a list.

OK. Judge King, three. Julian Harris, three. Bernie Snyder, three. Jimmy Shiomos, three.—Traitz
He's checking it twice.

One's only gutter and spout. Some gutter and spout. The other one, whatever the judge needs.—Traitz
He's going to find out who's naughty and nice.

Sometimes . . . you get somebody in front of you that's a losing case. You gotta say guilty . . . The break comes at sentencing. —Judge Driggs to Traitz
Santa Claus is coming to town.

All's I want is a break.—Traitz to Driggs
Merry Christmas to all. And to all, good night.

118

ANOTHER DAY, ANOTHER DOLLAR

December 4, 1991

Emanuel Johnson, a $40,000-a-year supervisor at the Philadelphia Water Department, gets to work at 7 every morning.

After punching the clock in his fourth-floor office in the ARA building on Market Street, he reads the morning paper.

At about 8, he goes down to the Gallery and buys a cup of coffee. Johnson, a Sludge Program Plant Operations supervisor, generally reads another newspaper when he gets back to his cubicle.

When he's done, he goes downstairs for one of six daily cigarette breaks. He smokes Kools.

Before lunch, he pops an electronic chess game onto his desk and plays against the computer. Johnson, 47, brings the game from home to help kill time.

Speaking of time, while Johnson went through his daily routine, the sludge crew ran up a $211,951 overtime bill the first two weeks of November. That averaged out to more than $1,000 for each of the 200 employees, who are now closing in on $1 million in OT for the year.

But I digress.

Johnson usually goes to the Reading Terminal for lunch.

"After lunch, I just relax," he says.

He may buy Sports Illustrated so he has something to read back at the office, where his calendar shows not a single appointment the entire month of December.

Then he'll take his cigarette breaks before cracking open a book to kill the rest of the day. Right now, he's reading *Othello*.

"It's really good," he says.

At 3:30, Johnson punches out and heads home to Olney.

Another day, another dollar.

"I have a ball," says Johnson, who wore gray slacks and a sharp tie to the office yesterday, and couldn't remember the last time he did any work. After some thought, he said:

"I guess it'll be almost two years in March."

I hadn't checked on him in a year, and was reminded of that by a Sunday story about federal Labor Department employees who sit on their hands all day. Johnson saw the story and felt a bond.

"That's me," he said.

So nothing has changed in 12 months?

"Not a thing," he said.

Except that on a wall of his cubicle, Johnson hung up a memo from Commissioner John Plonski to all supervisors. It says:

"Please review your unit's operation more carefully to determine whether certain employees are taking too many work breaks during the course of the day for smoking, coffee, phone calls, shopping, etc."

Last year, while the Water Department was pushing a $43 million rate hike, I got hold of memos suggesting things were out of hand at the sludge plant where Johnson worked.

He was accused of blowing hundreds of thousands of dollars by giving unnecessary overtime to buddies, and allowing private contractors to bill the department for work they didn't do.

He denies it all.

As for overtime, Johnson wonders how the sludge plant just ran up a $211,000 tab in two weeks without his help. Plonski, who doesn't know if he's got a job when the new mayor takes over, said he hopes to control overtime by next July.

The department decided last year to demote Johnson, but didn't follow through. The inside story was that Plonski's hot-shot executives hadn't exactly done a bang-up job minding the store, and it seemed they should get the same punishment as Johnson.

But nobody had the guts to spank them, so Johnson was stripped of his duties and quietly nudged to the cubicle where he still sits, while his attorneys haggle with the department.

Johnson wants his old duties back, not a transfer, and not a demotion.

Although Johnson's daily routine is common knowledge, Plonski claimed yesterday that he thought Johnson was hard at work all these months. When informed that Johnson was being paid to smoke cigarettes, sip coffee, play chess, and peruse periodicals, Plonski said:

"I think we better investigate that right away."

Sure thing, Sherlock.

Feel free to send Mr. Plonski a magnifying glass and decoder ring.

Plonski and Robert Sugarman, Johnson's attorney, now say they think they can work it out. But they won't say how or when.

Not that Johnson's complaining about his deal. But he says having nothing to do day after day, in a city that's going broke, can be stressful.

"I feel stagnant in my career," Johnson said over coffee. "I'm seeing a doctor for hypertension."

THANKSGIVING AND LASAGNA

November 23, 1994

At some point today, or possibly tomorrow, South Philadelphia's Joe Scavola, who is 58 and sleeps in the bedroom he was born in, finds out if he gets lasagna with his turkey.

He thinks yes. His wife says no.

I don't like being in the middle of it, but here's the story.

Every year about now, I get homesick. I think about my mother in California, and about her holiday meals. And I end up going to South Philadelphia, where food was invented, to walk the streets.

So I'm at the Italian Market, hundreds of people pushing carts up and down Ninth, filling them with macaroni and vegetables and turkey and whatnot. I go into Esposito meats, where I see a round man with a red apron, red beret, and big cigar.

Joe Scavola is yacking at customers whether they're listening or not, tossing out recipes off the top of his head, wrapping turkey and veal and sausage as if this is the only job in the world anybody could ever want.

Joey is 58, half Italian, half Irish. His brother Richie, working another counter, is 51.

"Twenty-five years I been here," says Joey. "I used to be down the corner at Giordano's."

How many years were you there?

"Twenty-four."

Wait a minute.

"I quit Giordano's when I was 30."

You retired at 30 after 24 years?

"I started when I was 6, picking papers off the floor that the fruit came in. They gave you $2 a day, with a big basket of fruit to take home every Saturday night."

You live right around here?

"A block away, on Kimball."

South Philadelphia.

Joey once worked a night janitor job at City Hall. Even then, he kept the day job on Ninth Street. His whole world is two blocks, and he's happier than anyone should be.

The Joey Scavola routine:

Up at 5:30, have toast and coffee with the 6 o'clock news, say goodbye to the wife and Aunt Veronica, dip a finger in the holy water near the marriage certificate from Pope John Paul II, make the sign of the cross, step outside, and walk the walk.

One end of the world to the other.

"I'm in my glory," Joey says. "I'm supposed to be to work at 7:30, but I usually get here at 6:45. Financially, I don't have to be here, and I'm suffering greatly with an ulcer in my leg, but this is where I want to be.

"I like people, and everybody who comes in that door is family, I don't care where they come from. I wanna die behind the counter the way I came in, with the hat, the red apron, the whole thing."

I ask Joey about Thanksgiving. He says he's a good cook, but his wife is a great cook, and she'll make turkey along with lasagna, a specialty.

It's exquisite, he says.

"She's my second wife," Joey says, opening his wallet. "She's a beauty. Looks 20 years younger than myself."

In Joey's wallet, Josephine lives next door to the Knights of Columbus. Joey is Third Degree.

"I can't make Fourth Degree, where they give you the sword and all, because it's only done Memorial Day weekend, and I always work."

Back to his beautiful wife.

"It was arranged. My first wife passed away, but her cousin's wife knew this girl in Italy, and we corresponded. I invited her to the United States, and guess what. We were married 14 days after she got here."

Joey says Josephine doesn't speak much English, but I can go knock on the door and say hello if I like.

Josephine is a set-up wife to die for. Beauty-ful, as they say.

I explain to her and Aunt Veronica who I am and what I'm doing. A story about family, holidays, good food.

"They're a lovely couple," Aunt Veronica says.

The lasagna for Thanksgiving sounds good, I say.

Josephine's eyes go cold.

"No lasagna," she says, holding her hand to make a gut. She doesn't have one, though. She must mean Joey.

"Eat pasta, eat turkey, fat stomach. No lasagna."

She is not leaving much room for discussion. But I try. Joey's counting on it, I say. After hearing about it, I was counting on it.

Josephine's voice gets an edge.

"Mozzarella," she says, making a layer with her hand. "Ground meat. Gravy. Spinach. Too much."

He talked a good game, Joey Scavola. The job, the wife, the neighborhood. But in the end, he's just another guy one plate of lasagna short of a perfect world.

A PHILADELPHIA FIASCO

January 5, 1989

I don't remember the exact hour. All I remember is waking up for the first time in 1989 and making a mistake, right out of the box.

I turned on Channel 3.

A very tinny sound was coming out of the TV, trying to be music. There was a figure on the screen. I would have said it was a man, but I could have been talked out of it.

The figure wore makeup and a sequined pantsuit. Concentric rings of white ostrich feathers rippled out from his body.

Whatever it was, the figure was doing a little jig on Broad Street. I would have said it was snowing, but I could have been talked out of it.

I thought of calling Mayor Goode, who saw snow on his TV at a critical moment in his career and has been confused ever since. Maybe I was looking at a fire hose extinguishing a burning chicken farm.

No. It was the Mummers Parade. And it was snowing.

This may be sacrilegious, but for my taste the costumes have gotten a little too fruity. There must be better ways to bring in the new year than to watch a cross-dressing birdman turn into a wet mop on live television.

Because of weather and other problems, the Mummers Parade was a fiasco this year. It was tainted by infighting, lack of leadership, cowardice, politics, and money-grubbing. All it needs is a few desks and it could become an official city department.

As a public service, I would like to review where it all went wrong.

Let's start with Saturday night's weather forecast: "The outlook for the Mummers Parade is becoming more pessimistic."

Later, the forecast got worse, predicting a strong chance of precipitation all day. By early Sunday, it was snowing in parts of the city.

Mummers officials, in keeping with local political traditions, are divided by special interests and petty concerns. So they were split 4-4 on whether to march.

This left it up to Recreation Commissioner Delores Andy. She voted to march, saying that the National Weather Service predicted light flurries followed by clearing and that Monday's forecasts called for strong wind, another no-no for Mummers.

Well, nobody at the weather service knows where Delores Andy got her dandy forecast. Whatever. The subject of light flurries brings us, of course, to Mayor Goode.

The mayor once sat in his house watching TV footage of the bombing and burning of a Philadelphia neighborhood. When asked why he didn't order

123

someone to put out the fire, Goode said he thought he saw water on his TV, but it must have been static. He called it snow.

Remind me not to go skiing with this guy.

"The mayor directly told us if the parade didn't go on New Year's, we couldn't parade again," Jack Hee, a string band member, told the Daily News, describing a dramatic curbside meeting in South Philadelphia on parade day.

At Channel 3, meanwhile, they say Goode called to ask whether the parade would be televised if delayed until Monday. The answer was no.

A couple of thoughts here.

TV should never be a consideration, because experiencing a parade on TV is like taking a vacation by watching Fantasy Island. Either you're there, or it isn't worth it.

Regarding the weather, I would like to point out that Philadelphia is in the Mid-Atlantic region. Winter promises rain, sleet, snow, wind, and bitter cold. If you schedule a parade for January 1, you ought to be prepared.

In fact, the possibility of mean weather is part of the charm of a parade in a tough, we-can-take-anything city. You want bathing beauties, sunshine, and rose-covered floats, go to California.

Broad Street, as always, was lined with die-hard, spirited spectators huddled in the chill to see a proud tradition. What they witnessed was a low point in this city's history.

Busloads of wimpy Mummers flocked past them to the judging area, where cash prizes are determined. They wanted to keep their feathers fluffy, so they skipped part of the parade route.

They were roundly booed, and while this city may be tough, it never booed anybody who didn't deserve it. When it rains in Kenya, they do not put ostriches on buses.

I give credit to those who marched in the snow, like that guy I saw when I turned on the TV. Some Mummers, by the way, have demanded city compensation for feather damage.

It's worth considering. Maybe City Council can set up a catastrophic-loss fund for Mummers. Yeah.

Get on a bus and get out of here.

YOUR TAX DOLLAR AT WORK

January 30, 1987

$\mathbf{M}$any of you constantly carp, moan, and whine about the waste of your tax dollars.

The streets aren't plowed. SEPTA should change its name to INEPTA. City Council gives $600,000 to Sam Evans without asking what he wanted it for.

I, however, prefer to dwell on good news whenever possible. So today's column—which I dedicate to those who say local government never does anything right—is about a plan to invigorate Philadelphia's economy. It is called: PROPOSAL FOR ECONOMIC DEVELOPMENT NOW.

Let's find out more about this exciting plan NOW.

The 20-page proposal, by Bob Brady, was given to Council in October.

Council President Joe "King" Coleman was so impressed that he dipped into the Funny Money Fund (FMF) and hired Brady—for $40,000 a year—as a consultant to Council's Economic Development Committee (EDC), which is so efficient it hasn't needed a meeting for three years.

Oh, I almost forgot. Brady is chairman of the local Democratic Party.

Some people say his consulting arrangement is a phantom job that will allow him to run Democratic pow-wows as King Coleman, Mayor Goode, and other Democrats seek re-election.

Nonsense.

Complaints have come from Councilman Thacher Longstreth and Republican mayoral candidate John Egan.

Maybe they haven't read PROPOSAL FOR ECONOMIC DEVELOPMENT NOW, which I like to think of as a commentary on local Democratic vision and leadership.

Let's check some excerpts NOW.

Today the creation of a process is as important as the formation of a specific plan.

Did you slap your palm against your forehead, like I did?

An aggressive and harmonious relationship with the ramifications of the labor movement is vital.

The whole Democratic think tank may have worked on this proposal.

This region represents the most remarkable potential for development of urbanization in the country.

And you thought Philadelphia would always be a country town of 1.6 million.

Philadelphia's position in the world community makes it imperative that we follow this course.

Or Western Europe could collapse.

GOAL: 1. To provide some direction to a potentially trackless maze.

He's going to straighten out SEPTA.

What makes America tick? This question can be answered in many ways and by many different people and each will believe their answer is the correct answer.

He's been to Council meetings.

A better question is what makes Philadelphia tick? What makes Philadelphia unique?

The Roofers Union.

A study of public opinion will tell you that the Council of the City of Philadelphia is made up of the most varied group of individuals than any other legislative or representative body in any city of America.

If you don't count zoos.

Council members do not possess the luxury of having their work done for them by pollsters, political consultants, and sociologists.

But they can try like hell.

This being the case the men and women serving in City Council realize the sacrifices they are expected to make by their constituents when they become elected to this fine body.

Patronage jobs for everyone.

A high quality of visual information must be made available to Council's Economic Committee at all times.

Please donate your Brownie camera to the cause.

Monitoring is the activity which enables the consultant to keep track of what is happening on a day-by-day basis.

Operation Brownie.

Finally a successful outcome of City Council's resolution is predicated upon that Council body to select an individual whose character and expertise enables that person to discharge the text and meaning of such a resolution in the spirit which was intended by that body in adoption of such a Resolution.

That was on the tip of my tongue.

This should satisfy the critics. If not, Brady submitted a résumé.

It says, among other things, that he graduated from Martin Technical School, where he studied surveying, carpentry, engineering, and blueprint reading.

I called Brady and King Coleman Wednesday and Thursday to find out about all the work Brady has done as a consultant. They didn't call back.

They may have been collecting a high quality of visual information. Let's hope they didn't get lost on the potentially trackless maze.

DO MIRACLES GROW
ON TREES?

July 17, 1988

Back in grade school, the nuns used to tell us that God is in all places at all times. So it came as little surprise to me in recent years when people reported seeing Jesus, or at least His image, on a soybean oil tank and a tortilla, among other places.

Then I heard that, in the Mayfair section of Northeast Philadelphia, people were assembling nightly to look at Jesus in a sycamore tree. So I went up to check it out.

At Erdrick and Barnett Streets, I asked a boy whether he knew where I could find the famous tree.

"The eighth tree down on that side," he said, pointing to the 4100 block of Barnett Street. "But you can't see Him until it gets dark."

I bumped into a woman named Terry, who took me the rest of the way. It turned out that Jesus was in a tree one block from Frankford Avenue and Levick Street, where the Devon Theater was showing *Rambo III*.

The tree is next to a street light, and Terry explained that, when the light goes on and the sky grows dark, the image of Jesus appears.

"It's a real phenomenon," Terry said. "The city sent a crew out to trim the trees about a month ago, and after the tree was trimmed, that's when you could see it."

Terry said Susan O'Mara, who works in ladies' apparel at K mart, was across the street on her front porch about four weeks ago and looked up in the tree. She saw the image of the crucifixion about 20 feet off the ground, where the trunk forks into limbs that look like arms. The image comes from shadows cast by the contours and knots of the tree.

Susan O'Mara told her husband, Chuck, who told a neighbor, and pretty soon word spread through the neighborhood and beyond. Chuck estimates that a few hundred people have come by for the nightly show, some of them staying until 4 a.m.

Some people make the sign of the cross. Some just gasp.

It was only 8 p.m., and Jesus doesn't begin forming until about 8:30, so Terry took me to the home of her sister, Carol Kirwin, to look at photos of Jesus in the sycamore. Carol had 50 copies made and is selling them at cost—26 cents a print.

"It's not a miracle or anything," said Carol's husband, Wayne. "It's like an image. It's art, is what it is."

In the photo, it's easy to see the image of Jesus on the cross. There's even a knot for his knee and a couple of bumps for feet. His head, in a shadow, is slightly cocked.

"It's actually more impressive than you can tell by the picture," said Wayne's brother, Al Kirwin. "The sinews of the body are outlined."

And Carol Kirwin said: "We'd really like the Fairmount Parks crew to come back and look at what they've done for us. They got laid off right after they trimmed the tree."

Some people take it more seriously than others. Mrs. McCann thinks it's a sign that Jesus is watching over a street that has had more than its share of tragedy. Recent auto accidents have taken the life of one girl and seriously injured three kids. And the Kirwins' home was badly damaged by an arsonist.

At 8:30, the Kirwins introduced me to Chuck O'Mara. He was sitting on his porch, which offers the best angle. Susan was still at K mart. A 1972 Chevy Nova, with three hubcaps missing, was parked under Jesus in the Sycamore.

About 8:35, Jesus's head took shape and people began to gather. By 8:45, the torso was complete, the feet coming in. The advantage over the tortilla and the soybean oil tank was that this one was 3-D.

"If you walk up the street," Chuck said, "you can see a knot that looks like His left hand."

At 9 p.m., as the crowd let out from the early showing of *Rambo III*, the sycamore was a sight to behold, its quiet majesty interrupted only by the sound of bugs being zapped by Chuck O'Mara's electric bug killer.

About 20 people were on Chuck's porch and steps. An elderly woman told Chuck he was lucky, because Jesus could have chosen anyone to look down on, but chose Chuck and Susan and their six children.

Chuck, who has been to Lourdes, said he doesn't see this as a miracle or a sign. But he says it's special because it has made people of all ages think about God, and that's especially nice on a block that has had such bad luck.

At 10 p.m., it was discovered that, if you held the 26-cent photograph up to Chuck's black-light bug zapper, the purplish image of Jesus was even more eerie.

Suddenly, the street light went out. Barnett Street fell dark and a gust rustled the leaves. Everyone turned to Chuck, who went: "Oooohhhh!"

You never know.

TAKE A BIT OFF THE SIDES

August 2, 1988

Every once in a while you'll hear people say that nothing exciting ever happens in Northeast Philadelphia. They were silent, of course, when it was discovered that Jesus was in a sycamore tree near Levick and Frankford.

Every night, as I reported a few weeks ago, people visited the 4100 block of Barnett Street to see for themselves. And sure enough, they would go away gasping, shaking their heads, crossing themselves.

At nightfall, shadows cast by a street light illuminated select branches, forming the image of the crucifixion. It was so good, you wanted to stand in the street and confess to the tree.

Some felt it was the work of the Lord. Actually it was the work of a chain-saw.

The Fairmount Park Commission had recently trimmed the tree. Susan and Chuck O'Mara were the first to notice that the way it was cut, it looked like Jesus on the cross. Some people saw it as a sign that their block, which had suffered an uncommon number of tragedies, was now being watched over.

All of which I offer as background, so that I may now inform you of a devilish development regarding the sacred sycamore.

The publicity drew more people to the shrine—as many as 300 or 500 some nights, according to residents. Which was fine with most of the neighbors, who say the visitors were quiet, even reverential. But not everyone liked all the attention.

A few people called police, complaining that they couldn't park on their own street and couldn't sleep, because some of the worshipers gathered under the sycamore almost until the sun took away the night.

"From what I understand," says Lt. Edward Kachigian of civil affairs, "some of the people were taking pieces of bark and stuff like that."

At one point, police barricaded the street. And then someone called the park commission and requested the lopping off of limbs, the very desecration of Jesus incarnate.

And so, on the morning of Friday, July 22, residents braced themselves as two parks vehicles and several police cars, a dark cloud over them, arrived on the scene.

Convoy from hell.

I wasn't there, because I had to watch Democrats hold hands in Atlanta. But I've talked to witnesses, including Nancy E. Herrmann, a reporter for the Northeast Times.

Herrmann wrote that one of the residents asked a crew member: "What are you doing? Are you going to touch that tree?"

After being reminded who was up the tree, one tree cutter said: "I'm not going to be the one who does it. I don't want to touch the tree."

Herrmann reported that a group of children held a sign that read: "Keep our light bright for our Lord."

But the crew proceeded. Or at least tried to.

They couldn't get the cherry-picker basket to work. They tried for 15 minutes. If that is not a sign, the Pope doesn't wear funny hats.

Finally they got it. And then the chainsaw wouldn't work. It was smoking as if enveloped in tongues of fire.

I can think of only one explanation.

"Our mechanical failures are so frequent, we hardly attribute them to a source like that," Park Commission director Alexander Hoskins told me yesterday. "The kind of miracle we're looking for is for all the equipment to start working."

Eventually both the chainsaw and the cherry-picker were working. Some residents averted their eyes, others hugged, others cried, as the basket rose to the heavens.

"They're trimming the arms off our Lord," one resident said as Jesus became an amputee, and then a double amputee.

The branches were dumped into a shredder.

"They tampered with something that was sacred," one resident said. "He might be gone, but He's still there."

I went back to Barnett Street the other night to inspect the damage. And I'm sorry to report that with the trim, Jesus looks like Gumby.

"I wouldn't mind if there were 100 people a night looking at it, 200, 300," Chuck O'Mara said.

As he spoke, visitors still came by, horrified at the fate of the tree.

"Maybe we were meant to have it only a short time," Susan O'Mara said.

That's probably the best way to look at it—philosophically. I think there's a lesson in this, a lesson that can help us in our daily lives.

Next time they don't pick up your trash, call the city and say Jesus is in your garbage can.

THE GREAT CLEANUP CAPER

July 23, 1989

And so we return now to that vacation wonderland, the Jersey Shore, proud home of last year's fecal coliform rebate plan: If the water smells, it's free motels.

It was 5 a.m. Wednesday, before dawn on the Atlantic Ocean. Five businessmen gathered on the beach at Wildwood Crest.

A pizza maker, a pharmacist, three motel owners.

And 300 pounds of chlorine tablets.

They probably assumed they were alone at that hour, which happened to be exactly one hour before the daily water sample is taken.

The bacteria readings had been high. Beaches had been closed. And the people who make their living two months out of the year had begun to panic. They knew what another day of dirty water would do to tourism. Tuesday night, the public works commissioner had gotten calls from 70 or 80 nervous merchants.

Just a year ago, then-mayor Frank McCall had announced: "As of today, we will begin the concept of the Jersey Cape. We will no longer refer to ourselves as being on the Jersey Shore, but as the Jersey Cape."

The idea—I probably should say concept—was to distinguish southern communities from polluted beach communities to the north.

But that was last year. This year, the fecal coliform nightmare is visiting Wildwood Crest.

And so the pizza man, the pharmacist, and the three motel owners put their heads together—a bouquet of unbearable weightlessness—and came up with a plan to save the town.

I reached two of the guys, but they refused to talk. I didn't even get to ask if they do pool service.

Also, as much as I would like to know, I have no idea who threw first.

I'm assuming it was the pizza maker, who is used to throwing things.

They could have skipped the chlorine over the water, since the tablets were about the size of hockey pucks.

I'm wondering whether this was their first time. Year before last, hundreds of dead dolphins washed ashore. Nobody ever figured out why.

And who cooked up the idea, anyway? You have to put your money on the motel owners. I mean, they must have swimming pools. And chlorine.

I can understand the pizza maker going for it. But would you want your prescriptions filled by a pharmacist who thinks a few chlorine tablets will clean the Atlantic Ocean?

"It's like having a building fully involved in a fire and trying to put it out with a beer can," said Rick Fulton, spokesman for the state Department of Environmental Protection.

But that was the least of the troubles for the Wildwood Five. They were not alone on the beach.

Cape May County health inspectors watched the men winging tablets into the ocean and called New Jersey Marine Police. For their efforts to clean the ocean, the men were charged with polluting it. The civil citations could cost them $6,000 each.

"They admitted they were trying to lower the bacteria count because of the pending ocean test," said Officer Thomas. T. Mellon. "In their mind, if the bacterial level was down and the test passed, the water was safe."

For 5 minutes, if that long. After that, who would ever know?

I suppose we could spend the rest of this space considering the flight of those tablets, sailing along, as they did, on the wings of the Jersey Shore's entrepreneurial conscience. But it might be more fun to visit the story of how the men got to the beach.

It should be understood, for starters, that along the Jersey Shore there is virtually no difference between public officials, real estate developers, and merchants. They are in the same business, which is reason number one for the pollution problem. Building applications are approved at a 90 percent clip.

And so it is no surprise to learn that city officials come out of this thing reeking of Clorox. Wildwood Crest Mayor Joyce Gould issued this statement:

"Five Wildwood Crest residents offered to work as volunteers and were granted permission by the borough's Public Works Department to use swimming pool purifier in an effort to assist in an environmental program designed to aid in the purification of ocean waters. This program was carried out to insure that the borough would continue to maintain the high standards of providing visitors with safe and clean beaches."

But in a comment that suggests that the city's "environmental program" is in some jeopardy, Gould said chlorinating the Atlantic Ocean was futile and ridiculous.

"It wasn't a coverup or a façade. They felt they could help keep the environment clean. They genuinely felt a concern for the beach."

A concern for something, anyway.

THE BIG TOP SPRINGS A LEAK

November 29, 1988

As leaks go, the one on the seventh floor of City Hall would have to be considered world class.

Everybody who sees it is impressed. Yesterday, while I watched people slosh by, they said things like: "I don't believe this" and "This is incredible."

Another thing that makes it world class, in my opinion, is how long it has been leaking. Estimates from longtime leak watchers range from four years to 25 years. Of course, they point out, it only leaks when it rains.

Yesterday it rained.

The leak begins on the ninth floor and trickles—some people would substitute gushes for trickles—down to the seventh floor. Not that the city is ignoring the problem. Yesterday, building maintenance brought out six buckets, a mop, two mop pails, and two garbage can lids.

The leak was winning.

"It's raining more in here than it is outside," said a woman as she splashed through the puddle.

As court clerk Delores Mitchell tiptoed through the gantlet of buckets, puddles, and indoor rain, someone warned, "You better get your bathing suit."

You can tell who the employees are, because through years of experience, they know where the water is shallowest and the drips are fewest.

First-timers approach the treacherous falls with obvious naïveté. Some of them wade into the puddle before realizing it's deeper and slicker than they expected. And then, when they slow up, they are like sitting ducks for the merciless cascade.

If you would like to watch the leak next time it rains, here's how you find it. Go to the southeast side of the seventh floor and look for the chair with the stuffing ripped out of it.

Then go north, past the disconnected soda machine with two inches of dust on it. When you get to the stacks of important records from the Prothonotary's Office, which have been heaved against a wall, turn right.

Right about now, you will begin to hear the symphony of the leak. Different tones are created depending on the depth of water in each bucket, and whether the bucket is made of plastic or metal. The trash can lids are like cymbals.

At lunchtime yesterday, the song was the Merv Griffin hit, "I Got a Lovely Bunch of Coconuts," which was written by a Philadelphian in a polling booth.

The leak is at the entrance to the City Hall tower, which is closed for remodeling. Just look for the place where 17 ceiling panels have been washed out. Or for the wall bearing the words of William Penn:

"I have led the greatest colony into America ..."

He should have brought a plumber.

The best seat for the water show is on the stairway landing outside Room 800, where police keep evidence for upcoming criminal trials. Room 800 is no Sahara Desert itself.

Yesterday, the cops had five buckets going. In addition, a garbage bag was wrapped around a drippy pipe to protect officers below. The garbage bag looked like a huge water balloon.

"I'm waiting for the whole roof to cave in," said one officer, who smoked a fat stogie and sat behind a photo of Pope John Paul II.

Fortunately, one side of the evidence room was dry. The room is sort of the Aggravated Assault Hall of Fame—loaded to the rafters with sledgehammers, rakes, screwdrivers, and other holiday gift ideas. They have enough baseball bats in there to supply the National League East.

On the ninth floor, however, water rushes through the room where police keep hundreds of confiscated drug scales and numbers game cards.

This is also where the courts keep records on legal judgments —in newspaper-size bindings. Yesterday, the entire year of 1979, plus the "M" file for 1981, sat in a puddle.

"I think the water just soaks through the floor to the eighth and then the seventh," an officer said.

The guy in Public Property who is in charge of the leak did not return my calls. But people around City Hall said various efforts to repair the roof have died because of the cost.

"They get their new cherry paneling down in City Council offices, no problem," said one cop.

"They probably won't do anything until somebody falls and gets hurt and sues the city," said clerk Delores Mitchell.

This is just a suggestion. What I would do is drill a hole where the seventh-floor puddle collects. Then I would go down to the sixth floor and do the same. And then, at exactly 10 a.m. on Thursday, I would drill a hole on the fifth floor.

The way I figure, the moment City Council President Joe Coleman pounds his gavel on the fourth floor, the whole gang is washed out to sea.

IT'S GOOD TO BE HOME

The idea was to stay a couple of years, see what Philadelphia was about, then go back home.

Someone at the office said to take a train, the Chestnut Hill West line, all the way to the top and wander around up there. Find out what a Philadelphia neighborhood was like.

A light snow fell on cobblestone streets, stolen from a postcard, and I walked down Germantown Avenue, the trolley lugging by, thinking this was a typical neighborhood. When I got to Mount Airy, I knew that was where I wanted to live.

It didn't take long to realize that Mount Airy, despite my notions, was not a typical place. The job took me to every corner of Philadelphia, and the more I traveled the more I realized how lucky I was.

The trees, the architecture, the feel of spring, the smell of fall. The way the stone colonials sit back from the street, solemn elegance, the Wissahickon carving the woods.

And one night my father, visiting, sat with me on my porch in Mount Airy and looked out at his grandsons, playing with 15 or 20 kids as they did all night, every night, that summer. Boy, girl. Every age, every color.

That's the way it was when he grew up, he said. Grownups on their steps, kids playing Kick the Can or some kind of ballgame. And it all got lost somehow, what with color television and corner 7-Elevens and expressways to shopping malls.

The two years came and went. California seemed more distant. Philadelphia felt more like home.

There were times, I suppose, when I told myself I'd never leave Mount Airy. I may even have believed it. But even then, I could see the possibility of a change.

It had to do, in part, with my boys. Their school is in Center City, a public school, and each morning began with a commute we all grew weary of.

People ask me about them, by the way. How come I never write about them as I used to. And I would love to; the material is even better now. Now that they date and tie up the phone with girls and wear their pants down low on their butts, against parental guidance.

I tell my boys that in every generation, there are fashion trends we later regret, and this will be theirs. I have even threatened to hang my own trousers just as low, in their presence, in public. And even that hasn't scared their pants back up.

But I can't write about these things because teenagers occasionally read the paper disapprovingly. And one of these teenagers, the one I once tried to comfort in the presence of Pooh Bear, before a piano recital, is now taller than I am.

As they got older, we did more and more things together in Center City. Movies, bookstores, restaurants, concerts, general browsing, and aimless strolling. They are hypnotized, like their father, by the weight of history, the mysteries of people, the endless motion and drama of the city.

Two years ago, we thought about moving. One year ago, we almost did.

Earlier this year, we were certain one month that we had to do it, certain the next that we couldn't.

Last month, with mixed feelings, we left Mount Airy for Center City.

Above all else, there is something to be said for parking your car for days at a time and being able to walk everywhere. The store, the office, the movies.

Provided, first, that you can find a parking place. Second, that you can remember where you parked. And third, that you don't get a ticket.

There are, so far, no regrets. I've always been amazed by people who think that to merely visit the city is an act either of insanity or heroism.

And although we've known the city, we have the sense, now, of rediscovering it, a thousand possibilities, a million histories, outside our door.

The shadows dressing the buildings and tracing over the streets all day, forever repainting. The horse carved into the mast of a red brick carriage house. The wind dying at sunset, and the high-rises melting to a liquid silver.

We sat on the roof the other night and watched the city light up and I asked my boys if they realized how unusual this was in America, a city with a Mount Airy and with a downtown like this, a mix of places to work, places to live, places to go.

On one hand, you could name those cities. Nine years into a two-year stay, this one is home.

CELEBRATING THE SOUND OF HAMMERING

September 25, 1994

It didn't matter whether it was hot and sticky or cool and drizzly. It didn't matter what inning it was. All summer, while watching kids play baseball in South Camden, I heard hammering in the neighborhood.

It would start every Saturday morning and echo into the afternoon. And I learned, as summer wore on, that it was the sound of volunteers who come in from the suburbs to rebuild crumbling houses.

The idea of regionalism—breaking down walls between city and suburb to fix what's wrong—scares those who think it means taking from haves to give to have-nots. But what's happening in Camden illustrates how small acts of kindness can make a difference.

The baseball program wouldn't have happened without donations from all over the region. The bats and gloves collected by ninth graders at Radnor High, and delivered to the children of Camden, have touched lives at both ends.

And the same is true of the rebuilding of South Camden houses that began nine years ago, when the very notion of it seemed impossible.

"Anybody can announce the possible," says the Rev. Michael Doyle of Sacred Heart. "A church is basically there to announce the impossible."

In nearly a decade, Father Doyle's Heart of Camden has bought 68 houses, some in such bad shape that they cost just $1. When they were rehabbed, the keys were turned over to people who otherwise couldn't afford a home.

Heart of Camden holds the mortgage and collects no-interest payments from owners, who must do community service. All this is done at minimal cost, with just a handful of employees and a horde of volunteers.

"There is something in all our hearts to give back, and we're a channel for that," says Sister Peg Hynes, who runs Heart of Camden.

John Donnelly, a board member and longtime volunteer, says part of it is the appeal of Father Doyle. "He sees poetry in these streets."

One house was adopted and repaired by a Baptist church group, another by a Presbyterian group. One was rebuilt by the Camden County Board of Realtors, another by a group from Echelon Mall.

Sister Peg boasts about the work done by 16- to 18-year-old boys from a Camden detention center and students from Camden and Cherry Hill.

In all, hundreds of people have contributed in ways big and small. An elderly Philadelphia couple bring lunches to the workers.

"Yes, it helps the people of Camden, but there's another side to it. It breaks

137

down the apartheid, the walls that exist around the Camdens of this world," Father Doyle says.

"Camden, with the jobs gone, is the best visual aid in America as to what went wrong. All the trash, the sewage, the prisons come here. The broken bits of things. Everything that would impinge on real-estate values. . . . It's against that backdrop that you have to hammer 2-by-4s."

A block from the church, a small cluster of rehabbed houses surrounds what used to be a dump site and a hangout for pushers and prostitutes. The neat houses have fresh paint, flowers, and vegetable gardens.

Vi Vu, a 12-year-old Vietnamese girl, watches her grandfather create a sand sculpture in her back yard. When the grandfather sees Sister Peg, he stands in prideful respect and thanks her for this visit.

Near the ballfield at Fourth and Emerald, four volunteers who met at Sacred Heart and knew nothing about carpentry four years ago are working on their fourth rehab. They are halfway done turning a bar, bought for $1 in January, into a youth center.

Rich Callahan is the Cherry Hill Township administrator. Jim Delaney of Moorestown is a counselor at Cherry Hill West. Janice Lynch of Moorestown is a human resources director. Bill Wisely of Norristown runs a communications company.

"You have to give something back," Callahan says, even if it means not being with family on a day off. "It's an investment in people, and my wife is very understanding."

Wisely says a Vietnamese boat family, reunited after eight years, moved into one of the rehabs. The crew joined the family in prayer when Father Doyle blessed the house.

The problems are great, Father Doyle says, "and you must celebrate little things. Like the sound of hammering on a Saturday afternoon."

FIGHTING BACK

January 16, 1994

It was 1954, and the neighborhood at 12th and Columbia was turning. Gil Fuller, with a wife and two young children, decided it was time to go.

Some of the neighbors had moved west to Strawberry Mansion in one of those great waves that changed the color of Philadelphia, the way the seasons do. But Fuller, a safety officer for the city, feared that Strawberry Mansion would soon go the way of 12th and Columbia.

Germantown, he thought. That would be solid well into the future.

"I'd been coming up here to visit, and man, I thought it was paradise. It was clean, there were trees, serenity. I loved it."

And now here he sits, 40 years later, in paradise lost.

With him are six other black middle-class men who made the same move Fuller did, at roughly the same time. They're grandfathers now. Retired. And frustrated.

"You heard that song 'Movin' On Up?' " Gil's friend Willie Witherspoon asks. "That's what we thought we were doing."

But some of the things they ran away from in the 1950s have followed them up the hill. Drug-peddling is too blatant, gunfire too constant, murder too frequent. A painful playback for family men who worked for something better.

But this time they're not packing up and moving to higher ground. This time they're fighting back.

They march, they lecture, they make life miserable—as much as any gang of grandfathers can—for drug dealers. And every Monday night, they meet around a Ping Pong table in a back room at the Mallery rec center and talk it over.

"We have got to put down roots somewhere in this city and make a stand," Fuller says, hammering the Ping Pong table with an index finger.

In the circle are Spoon, Rick "Smitty" Smith, James "Dean" Wall, Reese "Not North, Not South" Carolina, Ernie White, and Obie Snyder. Charter members of four-year-old East Germantown Against Drugs (EGAD).

Everyone has a story. One man's daughter was shot in a drive-by. Several men have struggled to understand, and respond to, drug abuse among their children.

They talk about the irony of finding themselves, once more, in a neighborhood on the edge. And it's even more tragic, they say, if you look back at the neighborhood Fuller and Spoon moved from.

"It's nicer there now than it is here," Spoon says. All that new housing, and a sense of rebirth, rather than decline. If only they could get Germantown back to 85 percent of what it used to be, one of the guys says. And the thought hangs in the room, a painful concession.

"It's sad we have to come out two or three times a week, at 3 a.m. or 3 p.m.," Spoon says. "We're all retired and we're supposed to be enjoying life, and this is what we have to do."

They have a gripe with neighbors—especially younger ones—who don't join their fight. And they have an occasional beef with police, too. Not enough support, they say.

Capt. Jeanette Dooley of the 14th District says her force does the best it can. EGAD has been too aggressive at times, she says, occasionally reporting people for merely standing on corners and also inadvertently scaring off prospective volunteers.

But she thinks they don't give themselves enough credit. They have been so effective, she says, crime has dropped in the 10-block area they patrol, and police have been able to focus on tougher areas.

"I was talking to Mr. Witherspoon about the difference they've made," she said, "and he said, `Look, . . . we've lost our children to drugs. We don't want to lose our grandchildren.' "

The men have different opinions about problems—the causes and the cures. But there is common ground.

First and foremost, they still love Germantown. And they know this is a time in Philadelphia when, if private citizens don't fight for what's worth saving, it'll be lost. "As homeowners, we have an economic investment," says Smith, "and an investment in the security of our families."

Although they understand social and economic explanations for criminal behavior, they accept no excuses. And while they can appreciate someone not finding work, they can't tolerate not looking.

"And don't tell us there are no role models," Reese Carolina says.

In this room, there are seven.

WHADDYA MEAN
WE'RE HOSTILE?

===== *May 15, 1994* =====

Y ou saw the story. You saw it, you heard about it, whatever.

Some guy from Duke University, calling himself a doctor, says Philadelphia is the most hostile city in the United States. Which would be fine, of course. Except that when you learn more about it, you realize it was not meant as a compliment.

According to a Gallup Poll commissioned by Dr. Redford Williams, we're the most hostile and mistrustful people around. We even beat New York in something called the "hostility index."

We also take first place dropping dead of heart disease, according to Dr. Williams, who believes there's a connection.

OK. While it is not my intention to stand in the way of pioneering science, I have a problem or two here, and so I called Duke. A woman calling herself Linda, Dr. Williams' assistant, said the boss was not in. She told me he was on a book tour.

A book tour?

Yes, she said.

Tell him he can skip Philadelphia, I said. What's the book title, anyway?

Anger Kills, she said.

Well now isn't that nice. The world really needed one more egghead professor to lean back at his desk, stare at the ceiling, and think up another reason to rank American cities.

But not just any egghead. It had to be somebody at the forefront of medical research. Somebody sharp enough to make a connection between stress and health.

I asked Linda if Dr. Williams ever got out from behind his desk.

"He has a high reputation," she said.

"It's a small town," I said.

She told me to call New York and try to track him down.

No, I'll tell you what, I said.

You tell him to call me, so I can straighten him out. Capeesh?

Linda sensed hostility on my part. Dr. Williams' book can actually help a person like me, she said. Let's say you're in a supermarket checkout line, and it's 10 items or less, but someone in front of you has more than 10 items. What do you do?

That's easy, I said. You say, "What're you, stupid? You can't count, pal, or what?"

This would be wrong, she said.

You could just smack them, I said.

"Wouldn't it be better," Linda asked, "to just stand there and count to 10," until the anger passed?

Higher education in America.

"Here's the problem," I said. "Philadelphia is not a count-to-10 city. And you know what? We're proud of it."

Moments later, I found myself speaking to Dr. Williams himself. And if we didn't quite click in the course of our conversation, I suppose it might have gone wrong right at the top, when I said:

Duke University. I thought it was just a basketball program. I didn't know they had classes or anything.

Or it could have been when I said:

Wha'd you come out of a tree or what?

Dr. Williams was not amused. In fact, he seemed to have no sense of humor whatsoever. And my feeling, based on my own personal research, is that this type of pent-up behavior can lead to serious health problems.

Not to shoot holes in Dr. Williams' hypothesis, I did ask if, in the course of his research, he gave any thought to lifelong consumption of cheesesteaks and hoagies as factors in our dropping dead.

Myself, I would have given cheesesteaks to one group of laboratory rats, and made the second group of rats wear Duke uniforms and watch a tape of their basketball team folding in the NCAA tournament.

Sure, the cheesesteak rats might have died. But before keeling over, they would have beaten the point spread, blown the winnings on a drunken brawl, and blissfully yelled across to the Duke rats, "You talkin' to me?"

We die young, but we live large.

And thanks for the medical advice, I told Dr. Williams, but Philadelphia is not a count-to-10 city.

"The question is whether it can become one," he said.

"No," I said. "The question is whether it wants to become one, and the answer is no."

And another thing.

"I'll tell you what we're hostile about. We're hostile about some professor capitalizing on our natural resources to sell his book."

He had nothing to say. He just did a slow burn, I guess. Frankly, I'm concerned about his health.

THEY ALWAYS GET THEIR VAN

June 1, 1989

All up and down Fifth Street, in the Bloco de Oro strip above Lehigh, people will tell you about a supernatural thing that happens every day.

They say the Parking Authority, working with sonar, radar, maybe Shirley MacLaine, has an uncanny ability to appear out of nowhere within five seconds after the red flag goes up on your meter.

It is legend.

"Oh, forget it," says Gloria Izquierdo, manager of the New Bohio Restaurant. "I got $600 in tickets working here."

"Let me tell you about it," says Amador Rolon, who runs a photo studio. "Once they booted my van, once they booted my car, and they're about to boot my van again."

There's another thing that happens every day on the street. Drugs are sold almost as openly as you'd sell pretzels and hot dogs.

"It happens every 10 minutes," a merchant says of the biggest business on Fifth Street. Though some of the sales are made right in front of shops, they say, most of the activity is confined to bordering corners.

There is nothing startling about the nagging efficiency of the Parking Authority or the open sale of drugs. But as you stand out there and watch the two together, you find yourself making a simple observation.

If you park five seconds too long, the city is on the spot with a ticket. For selling drugs, more often than not, nothing happens.

What that suggests, I think, is crystal clear. It's time to enlist the Parking Authority in the war on drugs.

Give them handcuffs, guns, turn them loose. Nothing else has worked. Nobody is a bigger pain.

Let them write tickets for every customer who double-parks to do business. Dealers will not like this.

"Oh, forget it," they'll say to each other. "I lost half my business last night. They're everywhere, these meter readers, like mosquitoes. Did I tell you they booted my BMW?"

Some of the people on Fifth Street liked this idea. The Parking Authority did not.

"Would you want them to be writing down a license number while a drug transaction is happening?" said spokeswoman Linda Miller.

Actually I would just boot the car right there. I don't really care. I just think that you always go with your best, and no agency in this city is more efficient, relentless, and infuriating than the Parking Authority.

Plus, you send dealers to Traffic Court, they may give it up.

While I tried to find a parking space on Fifth Street, several of the street-corner businessmen made pitches to me. These consisted of winks, nods, and snorts. At one intersection, some guy shooting for "Salesman of the Month" stepped in front of my moving car while shouting, "What do you want?"

I wanted to tell him I was sending the Parking Authority after him, and his life would never be the same.

People on Fifth Street find it interesting that they see more meter readers than police officers. They say they don't mind paying legitimate parking tickets, but they think the Parking Authority could be less zealous. Like it is, say, in South Philadelphia, where you could commit 400 parking violations a day and go without tickets for months.

Bill Salas of the Hispanic Association of Contractors and Enterprises says business has been lost because people can't afford the tickets.

Gloria Izquierdo says many customers and merchants either forget about the meter or they're tied up longer than expected. She says they don't like to park off Fifth Street, where there are no meters, "because you get ripped off."

"You can't find parking places anyway. They got this big hole in the street over here, the city put it in about two months ago, I don't know why. It takes up three parking places. Plus there's beat-up abandoned cars taking up places."

When I went to investigate these problems, a young man asked what I wanted. I figured he was another dealer until a woman, apparently an associate of his, appeared.

She was smiling at me. And pointing to her heaving breasts.

I wanted to tell them I was reporting them to the Parking Authority. I chickened out.

Drugs, prostitution, abandoned cars, street craters. Inefficiency and lawlessness everywhere. Except one place.

Amador Rolon has just told me about the time his wife got ticketed, while in her car, when she pulled up to pick him up from work.

Now we're watching from his shop as a Parking Authority officer works the street. "He'll ticket somebody," Rolon says.

"Hey," he says, his voice rising as the officer approaches a silver and maroon van. "That's mine."

THE STEPS OF SOUTH PHILLY

June 12, 1987

It was the kind of night where they didn't have to use the burner to melt the Cheez Whiz at the steak shops.

A stretch limo was parked at 10th and Federal in South Philadelphia, next to the ball field. Its tail end was in North Philadelphia. Around here, you don't ask why somebody came to a Little League game in a limo.

When it was over, every member of the Capitol Cowboys climbed in and stuck their heads through the sunroof. The car took off on a victory lap, horn honking, a bouquet of noggins poking out of the top.

Other cars honked, and it was as if the Flyers had won the Cup. The limo flashed by Pat's and Geno's and cruised out to Broad, kids waving to people sitting out on their steps, the people waving back and cheering.

I happened to see this because I was in search of the best stoop-sitting block in the city. The 900 block of Hoffman Street was a candidate, especially after Beatrice Rybicki claimed she could have every resident on their stairs in two minutes flat.

Beatrice went up and down the street, knocking on doors. Some people weren't home, and others didn't want to leave air-conditioned living rooms. Beatrice said it used to be a better block. She also told me never to say stoop. It's step.

I think I was meant to be a step-sitter, but where I come from, nobody sat on steps, which were called stoops. Where I live now, nobody has the right kind of steps, because the houses were built by stoops.

I ended up on the 2000 block of Cleveland Street, which runs into Snyder. It had what I was looking for—a good crowd of people on their steps talking back and forth across the street.

It's a street where Vince Cifelli blows a whistle when he sees a car coming, so kids know to watch out. Where the kids spend hours at Chuck's Italian Ice on the corner. And where Ronald Everett, the mayor of Cleveland Street, circles the block at 3 every morning on a security check before he goes off to drive a Stroehmann's bread truck.

When Everett gets home, he walks across the street and sits for 20 minutes on Joe and Viola Conte's steps to get some sun. Then he goes back to his side for the shade, where he spends the rest of the evening.

He sits facing south, always south, with a TV tray that holds a cordless phone, his Piels beer, and a bag of Herr's Potato Chips.

"All he has to get up for is to go to the bathroom," says Cathy, who grew up around the corner and had to indoctrinate her husband, a Chicagoan.

I had always thought that sitting on your steps was a simple thing, but it turns out that it's a science. For instance, on a hot evening, it is best to sit on the east side of Cleveland Street. On the west side, parked cars block the cooling breezes.

"If you see papers blowing to the east side of the street," Joseph Conte says, "it means it's going to rain. Also that it's going to be just a shower."

So at the first sign of east-side paper, Joe moves to the west side, under the Mottos' awning, to wait out the storm. If papers blow west, you might as well go indoors because it's going to rain all day.

Conte is 69 and can sit for hours. His son Mark, 18, who plays for a softball team called The Mob—which is big on the hit-and-run—can't handle more than 15 minutes without suffering lower back pain.

Through years of experience, you learn to shift weight and to use the top step, so the house serves as a backrest. You also should occasionally use a beach chair or pillow, but a young guy playing for The Mob is not likely to sit outdoors on a pillow.

I asked Joe Conte when he went to the pillow.

"When I had the first hemorrhoids," he said. The condition can be accelerated, he warns, "by a cold marble step." Other than that, marble is the way to go.

"It lasts the longest, and it stays cleaner," says Janet Mirigliani. "My steps are concrete, and they hold all the dirt" and dampness.

Kathy Aruffo and Tina Castelli, who recommend Ivory dish detergent for scrubbing steps, say that steps can be used to measure a child's growth and development. If a kid can't leap to the sidewalk from a higher step each year, the family physician should be consulted.

Cleveland Street has a nice mix of young and old, so veteran step-sitters can pass on their wisdom to future generations. You get the feeling that 50 years from now, somebody on this street will be able to tell you how Joe Conte forecast the weather or how Ronald Everett always set up his TV tray.

"I enjoy this immensely," Everett says, surveying the block from his perch. Porch. Steps. "There's nothing like South Philly."

THE GAME OF THE NAME

February 10, 1986

I don't know if you have ever thought about changing your name, but the thought has crossed my mind a time or two.

Every once in a while I get mail from someone telling me to go back to Puerto Rico or some such place, which happens to be impossible, as I have never been there.

People see a name and they develop certain assumptions, frequently in error. For example, I note that Judge William Marutani scored particularly well in South Philadelphia when he ran for office, and so did Henry DeBernardo in an unsuccessful campaign for City Council.

Not that they didn't deserve support, but I believe it is possible that some voters don't yank the lever until they see a name ending in a vowel.

Marutani is Asian. DeBernardo is black.

The reason I bring up this subject is that on Friday I went to Room 395 in City Hall, which is where you go to change your name.

Outside Room 395, a guy was sprawled on a chair, head back, snoring. He may have been a judge, so I tiptoed to avoid rousing him.

Inside 395 was Frank E. Checkovage. He's in charge of name changes, and obviously hasn't taken advantage of the chance to change his own name.

People change their names for professional or personal reasons, Checkovage said. Seven name changes were on the docket Friday, but nobody had arrived yet.

One of the cases involved Herman Dexter Whiteside, who wanted to become Tracci Quartermaine. It seemed the most interesting of the lot. Checkovage said Whiteside's attorney was Stokes E. Mott, who hadn't shown up yet.

So I took a seat in the waiting room, next to a person with a blue purse, a blue-gray overcoat, powder-blue sweat pants, and brown boots. And as I sat there, I thought to myself that Stokes E. Mott is the one who ought to be changing his name, not Herman Dexter Whiteside.

After a long silence, the person next to me said:

"I wonder where Mr. Mott is."

I just sat there for a while, trying to add things up. Excuse me, I said. But what is your name?

"Herman Dexter Whiteside, but not for long," was the answer.

"The name makes me sick. I just went for an interview at SEPTA, and when the supervisor saw me, he said, 'Is that your name? Herman Dexter Whiteside?' And I said yes. So he says, 'Oh, you're a male,' and I could see the reaction in his eyes. And I didn't get the job."

Whiteside, 30, said the same thing had happened at Wanamakers, Strawbridge & Clothier, and Gimbels.

"I'm on public assistance," he said. "Altogether, I've tried 15 jobs or more. They put it real nice, but I know what the real reason is."

Whiteside said he is gay and that people sometimes assume he is a woman, partly because he frequently wears outfits that either sex might wear. He said he has experienced rejection for years, even though he seems quite intelligent and articulate.

People's expectations have been a burden, Whiteside said, and he wants the public to know about this injustice.

"I see a friend in a store and he says, 'Hi, Herman, how you doin', man?' And everybody looks at you."

About a year ago, Whiteside came up with an idea to improve his luck in the job market. If he were a Pat, a Chris, or a Lynn, people might not even inquire about his sex. He settled on Tracci, and decided to change his last name as well.

"I look at General Hospital, and four or five years ago, one of the characters on there was Tracci Quartermaine. She was evil and dastardly and I liked her so much."

The character is no longer on the show. "She ran off with Mitch to Albany, N.Y.," Whiteside said.

Whiteside called an attorney, found out it would cost $395 to change his name, and looked forward to "a fresh start." He said his family approved of the change. "I'm so happy today has come," he said.

But Stokes E. Mott hadn't come. So while we waited, I asked Whiteside what he thought of my name.

"I'd change the last name," he said. "The first name, too. I like Stevie. Steve sounds too macho. I like Stevie Quartermaine."

Whiteside had to leave before his attorney arrived. So he wasn't there when Mott officially transformed Herman into Tracci. I hope the change opens doors for him, because it's not fair that a name or appearance should hold him back.

As for me, I've given this some serious thought. Stevie Quartermaine kind of grows on you. And chances are, nobody would ever tell me to go back to Puerto Rico.

'WE CAN SNEAK YOU IN AT 10'

=========== *March 11, 1992* ===========

The first call came about three years ago, right after I moved and got a new phone number.

I think it was a Saturday morning. I think I was asleep. It rang a long time before I rolled over to it.

"Hello?"

"Is this Fred's Heads?"

I rubbed my eyes. Shook my head.

"Fred who?"

"Fred's Heads?"

"No, this is not Fred's Heads."

Maybe a week passed. I got another call or two. And I wondered what Fred's Heads might be.

There had been a story about a Philadelphia doctor who, for the purpose of medical research, sold heads by mail. So it might have been that people were calling my house to order craniums. This made it hard to get back to sleep.

Then some more calls came. Then some more. All for Fred's Heads.

One day, being an investigative journalist, I looked in the phone book. Fred's Heads was listed at 1505 Wadsworth in Mount Airy. The phone number was one digit off from mine.

I drove by and looked at the sign.

Fred's Heads.

Full service hair care and design for progressive men and women.

And so, with eight zillion phone numbers in Philadelphia, it turns out mine was one slip of the finger away from a unisex hair palace.

I thought about changing my number, but assumed the calls would stop when enough people learned by their mistake.

They didn't. A lot of times the phone would ring, I'd answer, and they'd hang up. I'm assuming a lot of those were Fred's customers.

On more than one occasion, a caller insisted that I was wrong, that I was actually Fred's Heads.

For these people, I made appointments.

"All right," I'd say. "We can see you at 11."

More often, I gave people the correct number. But if they woke me up, or got rude, I made appointments.

Months passed, followed by years. My boys are now at that age where kids

149

make calls without touching the phone. The numbers are dialed hormonally. And so here is the current breakdown of calls to Casa Lopez:

Roughly 22 percent of the calls are for B-Flat Brother No. 2.

Roughly 18 percent are for B-Flat Brother No. 1.

Roughly 2 percent are for me.

And roughly 58 percent are for Fred's Heads.

So let's say I'm waiting for a call from a loved one or a potential loved one. Imagine the disappointment when the phone rings and I hear:

"Hello, is B-Flat Brother No. 2 there?"

I hand him the phone. And for the next 90 minutes, I hear this cycle:

"I don't know . . . Because . . . I don't know . . . Because . . . She said she likes Jess, but Jess said he was liking, like, her sister, and then she sent me a note folded up like a football . . . I don't know . . . Because . . ."

Then he hangs up. The phone rings again. It's for B Flat No. 1, whose 90-minute conversation begins:

"I don't know . . . Because . . ."

He hangs up. The phone rings.

"Is this Fred's Heads?"

"Yes. We can sneak you in Friday at 10."

Last week I finally decided to do something about it. I called Fred's Heads to explain the situation.

Fred got on the phone. He listened to my story. He sounded nice. And now I was feeling guilty about making those appointments. So I went over there.

His name is Fred E. Roney. He seemed like a decent, hard-working guy. I apologized for making appointments. Fred said it was OK.

And then it occurred to me that if I get Fred's calls, maybe he gets some of mine. But he said nobody who called sounded like a teed-off councilman, a bookie, a roofer, a mobster, or Kim Basinger.

In fairness, I have to say Fred got his phone number first. Like 12 years ahead of me. So if anybody should change, it's me. Especially since, as it turns out, Fred is no common haircutter. He has done Muhammad Ali, Marvin Gaye, former Rep. Bill Gray, and Police Commissioner Willie Williams.

(I'd like to publicly apologize to Commissioner Williams if I was ever rude to you or signed you up for a bogus hair appointment.)

For future reference, Fred gave me a card listing his hours and phone number. Please clip and save.

Fred's Heads is open from 9 a.m. to 7 p.m. Tuesday through Friday and from 8 a.m. to 6 p.m. Saturday. The number is:

TWO, FOUR, TWO, FIVE, SIX, FIVE, OH.

Anyone who misdials early on a Saturday will be subject to arrest and prosecution.

DOPE, HOPE, AND REALITY

April 24, 1988

Thursday was a big day on the block because of who was expected to drop by, and so Edgar Jones and his family of six waited on their front steps to see a little bit of light come dare the dark.

Jones, a maintenance man, bought the house for $11,000 in 1973. He would like to sell it now, but he says it would be difficult to give it away. It used to be a nice neighborhood, but now it is one of Philadelphia's worst. A half block away is Eighth and Butler, an intersection famous for drug trafficking.

"We put it for sale twice; no offers," Jones said.

Just then Jesse Jackson walked by.

Here was the presidential candidate who has made drugs one of his key issues, standing tall on the very corner owned by the cut-throat peddlers who keep Edgar Jones's house from appreciating.

And the people cheered, because it was nice to know that someone this big realized they are trapped.

Jackson walked east on Butler and 10-year-old Linda Washington stood on the bumper of a Plymouth Gran Fury to catch a glimpse. She had come home from school and couldn't believe Jesse Jackson would be here.

He walked past where 11-year-old Magdalena Ramos pointed to her steps and told about the time she heard a shot, ran outside, and found a man bleeding to death.

He walked past Edgar Jones's $11,000 investment, where Jones's daughters say they do not let their kids outside alone, and where Mom and Dad say nobody in the hunt, nobody but Jackson, can know their despair.

"He's trying to help," said Mom Jones. "I don't know if anybody can do anything about this situation, but I'll vote for him because the others can't understand the way he can."

Jackson turned left on Seventh Street and walked four blocks to Hunting Park, where he stepped onto a porch next to the Ogrodnek Funeral Home and sang out his plan to appoint a drug czar and establish a foreign policy that chokes the flow of drugs into this country.

And then he began his chant, "down with dope, up with hope," which is roughly as naïve as "just say no." But you get the sense Jackson can take his slogan to places and people whose existence is unknown to Ron and Nancy Reagan.

The speech ended about 6:15 p.m. and Jackson got on a bus headed for a fund-raiser at the Hershey Hotel.

At 6:45 p.m., a man in his 20s moved back to the corner of Seventh and Butler, his place of employment, across from Edgar Jones's house.

At 6:55 p.m., a man pulled up in a Pinto. The employee pulled down the zipper of his jeans, took out a small bag and handed it over.

So it took 40 minutes for business to return to normal. And it appeared, in a single transaction, that Jesse Jackson had lost two votes.

By 7:30 p.m., as a cook at the Hershey Hotel put chicken and broccoli on a plate for Jesse Jackson, five street corners in the vicinity of Eighth and Butler were manned by people who seemed to have mixed up the sequence of Jackson's "down with, up with" message.

None of the dealers was in the mood to talk about Jackson or business trends. They thought they were dealing with an undercover cop.

"Good evening officer," said the man whose dope is in his zipper.

"But I'm not a cop."

"Then you want some of this?" he said, grabbing either his stash of drugs or some other small instrument of destruction.

Later in the evening, while Jackson spoke at the hotel event, a more informal but equally well-organized fund-raiser picked up steady attendance in the neighborhood of his "down with dope" speech.

Virtually every corner in a four-block area was manned, the only exception being Eighth and Butler, where police were parked. When the cops moved, the dealers moved. Cat and mouse all night.

Shortly after 10 p.m., a gunshot rang out and a teenaged kid pulled up to Eighth and Butler in a panic. He said he had just fled a robbery attempt two blocks away.

Dope dealers scattered as a half-dozen police cars raced through the area in search of two suspects. The commotion cleared the streets, except for a man who had spent most of the evening standing outside the Sing Wah Kitchen, three blocks from where Jackson called drugs the number one threat to national security.

He walked with a cane and held up a poster for passers-by. It said "Jesse Jackson for President." He said he had missed Jackson's speech.

But you're for Jackson?

"He's my man," he said, flashing the poster.

A minute later he said:

"You wanna buy some cocaine?"

MOB BULLY AND POET LAUREATE

============ *May 4, 1989* ============

The floor show continued yesterday in Room 15-B of the federal courthouse, where Ralph Staino Jr., mob bully and poet laureate, wept like a child, and Tiger Lil, his ex-showgirl companion of some 35 years, cried a river over her man's sentencing.

The handsome and marvelously tan "Junior" Staino, looking a little like Marlon Brando before Brando bought a banana farm and let himself go, went into court 57 years old. Two hours later he was 90.

U.S. District Judge Franklin S. Van Antwerpen sentenced Staino to 33 years in prison for his supporting roles in two attempted mob hits—they struck out both times—and five cases of extortion.

Lillian "Tiger Lil" Reis, who has some experience of her own in the area of criminal law, offered an appraisal of Van Antwerpen's work.

"I think this guy's name should be hangman judge," she said outside the courtroom in a building dedicated to destroying the mob. "I think his name should be Roy Bean."

Moments later, in an encore performance before another judge on a drug conviction, Staino was relieved of $200,000 in the way of a fine.

The burden of the loss was perhaps lightened by the fact that, according to cops, the walls of Junior's home were insulated with $100,000 in cash. Also mitigating the loss was Staino's diary notation indicating that, without benefit of employment, his net insulation was in the neighborhood of $2 million.

Still, he fell hard yesterday, and now much of the Nicky Scarfo gang is off to a federal housing project because of business operations that fell under the government definition of racketeering.

Staino's sayonara was perhaps the end of the Hollywoodesque relationship between the mob soldier and the still dangerously lovely Tiger Lil, former nightclub owner, former movie star, former accused and exonerated mastermind of a half-million-dollar Pottsville heist that had Staino chipping rock for years.

Her brushes with the law, many stemming from her operation of the Celebrity Room in town, were legendary. In 1963 she won a $1.8 million libel suit against The Saturday Evening Post for an article entitled "They Call Me Tiger Lil." Her attorney was Bobby Simone.

"I'm still living off that," says Simone, who was in court yesterday. He's one of Junior Staino's attorneys.

The blond Reis, done up in purple and tossing glances around the courtroom like lassos, sat no more than 25 feet from her man yesterday. When it came time for Junior to read a statement about his commendable citizenship, he lost his grip after saying he'd been with one woman for 35 years. Lil cried, and so did he.

First he's writing poetry. Next thing you know, he's blubbering in public. They don't make men like they used to.

Junior slumped down in his chair, dabbing at his eyes, and an attorney finished the statement for him, a statement with no poetry but plenty of remorse and love of family and I-never-harmed-anyone warmth and goodness.

Prosecutor David Fritchey, choked with emotion, thought it should be mentioned that Mr. Good Citizen threatened to rip out somebody's eye. Fritchey offered a reading of Staino's secretly recorded pep talk to a client.

"If you don't have that [blanking] money, I personally will put your [blanking] other eye out. You hear what I'm tellin' you?"

Staino, after that conversation, turned to a colleague and said, "Ooh, I loved it."

Later, when the murder indictments came down, the fugitive Staino cooled off in the Dominican Republic, where he filled his diary with love notes.

"I miss you terribly Lillian," he wrote. "I'm getting very bored. I just miss everything about my family, and also the United States. There's no place like home."

Fritchey could not help but recall, however, that when federal agents tracked down Staino, they did not find a lonely coconut in a grass hut.

"We love each other today," Lil said yesterday, "I believe as much as we did 35 years ago. In spite of his one indiscretion."

Her hope is that Junior will do closer to 10 than 33. Whatever, there's plenty of time to polish the prose. Last year Staino wrote:

The man assigned to hear our case
Is fair and just I'm certain.
Should we fail and they prevail
We'll go bye-bye via Judge Van Antwerpen.
So long Junior, see you later
Say hello to Nicky and Phil.
Stop the sobbing, get your pen
And write to Tiger Lil.

I REST MY CRANKCASE

November 15, 1988

In our continuing search for those who go beyond the call of duty, today we visit three public officials who drank motor oil in the name of truth and justice.

Actually only one of them drank motor oil. The two others gargled it.

First, some background.

Dr. Thomas F. McGarry, chief of cardiology at Lower Bucks Hospital, is tooling along in Solebury Township on September 11, 1987, when he wraps his truck around a car. Miraculously, no serious injuries.

A police officer invites McGarry to try his luck at the Breathalyzer, and the doctor hits the jackpot, winning a trip for one to Bucks County Court.

The doctor says he can explain. He says a container of motor oil was cracked open in the collision and splashed all over, and the car was upside down.

And oil went in his mouth.

And so, to get rid of the taste, he took about 12 blasts of Binaca.

Which contains alcohol.

"He said he was spewing oil for the next 2 1/2 to three days," his attorney has said.

Here, a couple of thoughts.

First, while remaining completely objective, I would suggest that you could strap yourself to the underside of your car, have a loved one drive you through JiffyLube with your mouth open, and take on, at most, only a 1 1/2 to two-day supply of oil.

Second, let's hope that, during those 2 1/2 to three days of spewing, the doctor did not perform open-heart surgery.

Anyhow, although I remain completely objective, district attorneys, by nature, are very skeptical. And so there was some joking about a new cocktail: two parts gin, one part Pennzoil, with a splash of Binaca.

The doctor took his gusher story to trial in February, and a jury of his peers said, legally speaking, get out of here. But the conviction was thrown out on a technicality.

For the second trial, defense attorney William Eastburn and Bucks County prosecutor Cheryl Wonderly turned to science. Eastburn got a chemist to mix motor oil and breath spray in a laboratory dish, and the chemist said 99 percent of the alcohol lingered for 30 minutes.

Wonderly saw a flaw in the relevance of that. Dr. McGarry's mouth is not a laboratory dish.

She called Hilltown police Sgt. Ashby Watts, a Breathalyzer expert, and asked how he felt about filling his mouth with motor oil.

"I guess I'm kind of crazy," says Watts, who agreed to do it and recruited another expert, Officer Tom Piatek of Lower Salford police in Montgomery County.

And so the two officers, along with assistant D.A. Lou Busico, met with Wonderly one morning to re-enact the events of September 11, 1987.

"We met at the McDonald's in Solebury," says Watts, "because the doctor had stopped to have a salad with oil and vinegar. The thing is, it was 7:45 in the morning, because that's the only time we could all meet. I don't think the salad bar is open that early, but Cheryl called ahead to ask McDonald's to make some salads."

Please continue, officer.

"Then we went over to Solebury Township, to their police station."

And what happened next, to the best of your recollection?

"We went in and had some motor oil."

Wait a minute, you can't just say it like that. Let's slow it down.

All right, so they go inside and Wonderly—who, by some accounts, was smiling throughout this thing—pulls a quart of oil out of a bag and pours it into three Dixie cups.

"I think we said something like here's looking at you, or bottoms up," Busico says.

"We were talking about who would go first, and I decided to go," says Piatek.

A significant error on his part.

"I didn't know you weren't supposed to drink it."

He found out by watching the two others swish it around and then, to his horror, spit it out.

The three then overdosed on Binaca and took Breathalyzer tests every 10 minutes or so for an hour.

The highest reading was .022 percent blood alcohol, for Watts. Most of the readings were .000.

The legal limit is .100. The doctor's two readings, the night of the accident, had been .128 and .141.

A second trial ended in a hung jury. But last week, with testimony from Watts regarding the work of the Pennzoil team, McGarry was found guilty of drunken driving. He is free pending appeal.

Our heroes say the oil wasn't as bad as they had expected. It was 10W-30, like the doctor had used.

Heavier viscosity this time of year can cause knocks and pings.

IN SECTION 314

October 23, 1993

"These are great seats," said Louie the Barber. And he was right. The fans in the same row looked familiar. There was a Moe, a Larry ... and a Joe? "Actually, I think John is the least talented of the four of us. Wouldn't you say, Larry?" said brother Joe Kruk.

It can be a small town, Philadelphia.

I call the number in the paper and the man with the World Series tickets tells me he's Louie the Barber. The very man who once gave me a mob-do, as he has so many wiseguys.

"These are great seats," he says.

And so they are.

Row 3. Section 314. Behind first base. How Louie the Barber got them, I don't want to know.

So I'm settling in for Game 3 and I look to my left, same row, and there's a familiar face.

You're thinking Jimmy Hoffa? Maybe Nicky Scarfo?

Better than that.

It's John Kruk, the Phillies' first baseman.

Actually, it's not quite John. The belly's too small, the hair too short. But it looks like him.

An older man is next to this guy, and there's a resemblance there, too. He looks as if he could be John Kruk's father. And now the man is motioning down to a woman on my right. John Kruk's mother?

But you don't want to be an idiot. What if it's not them? And even if it is, do they want to be bothered?

More important, is the John Kruk family in the Mafia?

After a while, I can't take it. Yes, says the John Kruk look-alike. His name is Larry Kruk. John, the all-star first-baseman, one-liner specialist, and Philadelphia folk hero, is his brother.

Next to Larry is his dad, Frank, who goes by Moe. And that's Mom down there, Lena, with her sisters, and with John's former baseball coach back home in Keyser, W. Va.

As for the seats, they got them from John Kruk, not Vito Corleone. Larry can't explain how I ended up in the middle of all those Kruks.

Moe tips his cap, a country hello. It has a blue West Virginia pin next to the P.

I tell the Kruks that John is my all-time favorite ballplayer, and that I spent my summer beefing up, perfecting the John Kruk batting stance, and patterning my life after his.

And now Moe and Larry are looking at me as if I'm from the hills.

Wait a minute. Moe and Larry?

There's a Joe, too, Larry says. But not Curly Joe, just Joe.

Larry, a machinist in Hanover, Pa., says Joe is driving up for Game 4 from North Carolina, where he's a high school P.E. teacher.

"There's four boys," says Larry. "Joe, then Tom, me, I'm 33, and then John. John's the baby."

The whole thing got started in 1948, when Moe Kruk worked at Owens Glass and coached the company's women's basketball team. One of his players shot the ball so well he married her, and Mrs. Kruk spent the next 20 years trying to keep enough food on the table, knowing one thing full well.

If she cooked it, they would come.

Out on the field now at the Vet, the baby, who weighs 215, likes his beer, and occasionally shows up on David Letterman, rips a hard single his first at-bat.

I ask Larry if it's true, the story about how John developed such a sharp eye at the plate.

Sure enough, he says. Mom and Dad had three or four acres, and the boys built a ballfield out there, complete with a backstop. Only problem was, Mom had a garden in right field.

"It was some corn, tomatoes, all kind of stuff," Larry says.

The first three Kruk boys swung right-handed and were natural pull hitters, which was fine with Mrs. Kruk. Her garden was safe.

Then comes John. A lefty.

If that boy grows up pulling the ball to right, chopping up the garden, it means less food on the table.

So the older boys made right field an automatic out. And John, who had to develop better bat control than his brothers, grew up keeping his eye on the ball and spraying line shots over the inedible portions of the Kruk property.

"We always say that if Mom's garden was in left field, she might have three Major League sons," says Larry. And John wouldn't be one of them.

"I'll tell you what," says Lena Kruk. "The ball went to right field enough that they ended up wrecking my garden anyway."

Lena and Moe say they're as proud as parents can be. Proud, too, that their millionaire son is the same good-natured, burger-eatin', dirty-gettin', story-tellin' homeboy he was before he became the national posterboy for every couch potato Major League wannabe.

"He hasn't changed a bit," Larry says. "Johnny'll never change."

His hair, though. Mom and Dad have a problem with the long hair.

"It sucks," says Moe. "But Dave Hollins and Lenny Dykstra won't let him cut it. They're superstitious or somethin'."

Some other fans have noticed the resemblance now, and they've come by Section 314 for autographs. Larry gets a chuckle over it. How many machinists are asked for an autograph?

But Moe Kruk has taken to it like a duck to water.

"We're gonna get writer's cramp," Moe says, nudging Larry.

In his second at-bat against the Blue Jays in Game 3, John Kruk shoots a double into the corn and tomatoes area of Veterans Stadium. He is now hitting .636 in his first World Series.

"We could all play ball," says Larry. "But we got to where we stopped at a certain level and John just kept going. In Legion ball one year, I hit 4-something and was third or fourth in the league. Johnny hit .620."

Moe Kruk looks up and sees his son's .636 on the board.

"That's pretty fair," Moe says.

I ask where John got it. Moe gives it some thought, but not much. This is the fall classic. It's no time for modesty.

"I could hit pretty well myself," says Moe, a high school star.

You think you're a better hitter than John?

"Oh, man," Larry says. "Now you're going to hear some . . . "

Not just a better hitter, Moe Kruk says. A better shooter, too, in basketball.

"I could shoot better than all four of 'em," Moe says. And now he leans in real close, as if he's got a secret. "You know what? So could their mother."

Out on the field now, as the game begins slipping away from the Phillies, the first-base umpire blows a call.

"I umped the boys' games," Moe says, shaking his head. "Forty years I umpired, and I never missed a call. Not one."

The Phillies lose Game 3, 10-3.

Game 4, Phillies down two games to one. Brother Joe shows up.

"I didn't drive all the way up here to lose," he announces, scanning the sold-out stadium. "We're proud of John, and I know he'd love a World Series ring. It's been great. The people of Philadelphia have been great. We were down 2-1 to Atlanta, so I think we're fine here tonight."

Hey, Joe. Are you a better hitter than John, too?

Joe turns to Larry.

"Actually, I think John is the least talented of the four of us. Wouldn't you say, Larry?"

John chews a lot of gum, sometimes a new stick every inning. Joe chews a lot of tobacco, sometimes a new chaw every inning.

Joe sets a beer cup down in front of him in Section 242. A portable spitoon. The hairier the game, the more he chews and spits.

He chews through 32 hits, he chews through 29 runs. By the time the Phillies blow a five-run lead in the eighth and lose 15-14, all of Section 242 has a nicotine high.

"It ain't over yet," Moe Kruk says.

Game 5. Brother Tom shows up. The whole family's in the park now.

In the first inning, Joe and Tom and Larry and Mom and Dad watch the baby hit a sharp one toward the produce section of the Vet.

What would have been an out, back in Keyser, turns out to be the game-winning RBI, the second in the series for John Kruk.

"I knew it," Moe Kruk says when the Phillies have won, 2-0, extending the World Series to tonight's sixth game. "I knew we was goin' back to Toronto."

THE JOY OF CYCLING

Being a man of standards, I decided when I took up cycling that I would never buy a pair of those tight little black pants.

The bike shop talked me into the pants.

But there's only so much of yourself you can compromise, and so I decided I'd never wear one of those helmets that look like spaghetti strainers.

They talked me into one.

You have to draw the line somewhere, and I drew the line at the shoes. Cycling shoes make bowling shoes look good.

My cycling shoes are powder blue. I even have a riding jersey.

And so Mr. Cool now rides along the streets of your town looking like an ice cream cone.

I'm not proud of it.

But hey, I'm a little healthier, maybe even happier. The sport does have its benefits. One of which was mentioned in the news recently.

It seems that Bicycling magazine conducted a reader survey. The largest reader survey in the magazine's history. The questions had to do with thoughts regarding the connection between cycling and sex.

Of course, I read the results with some interest.

Among other things, 66 percent of all respondents say cycling has made them better lovers, 43 percent have postponed a bike ride to have sex, 28 percent have met a partner through cycling, 81 percent report an increase in vigor, and 22 percent of all recreational riders claim to have had a roadside encounter.

You ever go to a party and not get any cake?

The only thing worse is being there in your party hat and somehow not even knowing they served cake.

Maybe I'm on the wrong roads or something. I should have known all those rides to Dairymead Farm were a waste of time.

At least there were a couple things in the survey I could identify with. It said 84 percent of all riders think about sex while cycling, and 62 percent suffered genital numbness.

I like to think that at one time some hotshot veered into the bushes to join the 22-percent roadside encounter group, only to find himself in the 62-percent group of losers.

While riding, men are more likely than women to think about sex, the survey said. During sex, women are more likely to think about cycling.

Allegedly, 88 percent of all riders are heterosexual, 8 percent are homosexual, 3 percent have an open mind, and 1 percent are unsure.

161

Fine. But why design cycling outfits for the 1 percent?

Actually I have had a little action on the streets. I don't want to boast or anything, but once a week or so, just because I happen to be on a bike and in the right place at the right time, somebody talks dirty to me.

Just Sunday, for instance, I'm cruising Norristown high in the saddle because it's that kind of town, and here comes some car from behind. A woman leans out and says:

"Get out of the way, a—."

So I get to Valley Forge National Historic Park and here's some woman ahead of me on a bike. The survey says I've got a 22-percent chance. All of a sudden I start thinking about the 62-percent thing. You can talk yourself into that, you know.

I start pedaling faster to catch up. I don't know why. The magazine says there's a better chance I'm thinking about love than she is. Even assuming she's on the same wavelength, and we end up getting intimate, chances are she'll start thinking about cycling.

As soon as I get close, she speeds up. I pedal faster, she gets farther away. I can't catch her.

I hate her.

The woman in Norristown was more my type anyway.

Actually, the way you have to dress, it never struck me that women could find cyclists sexy. But the survey said 68 percent of the women find cyclists more attractive than non-cyclists and 83 percent actually think the clothes are sexy.

To understand why, the article suggests that you go for a ride, "glance at your shadow's sleek form," and, "Heck, just look in the mirror when you get home. Admit it. You've never been sexier."

I've looked at the shadow and it isn't mine. I get some guy with a gut.

I get home and, when nobody's looking, I look in the mirror.

Mel Gibson is not in there.

Through the steam I can see Mr. Fruit Stripe with bowling shoes and a spaghetti strainer on his head.

The doorbell rings.

Kim Basinger is not there.

I think I need different routes or something.

IT'S COME TO THIS, BEN

August 16, 1990

A̲s the city slid deeper into the hole this week, and nobody seemed to know how to get us out, I happened to find myself in the neighborhood of Philadelphia's greatest politician.

It suddenly occurred to me that if anybody could straighten us out, he would be the one.

In case you've ignored the news, so as to avoid ripping your hair out, Philadelphia city officials are making the S&Ls look well-managed.

A budget that was supposedly balanced six weeks ago now has a projected deficit of $200 million, the city is looking for some sucker to lend us $450 million, the mayor was wearing a hardhat and referring calls to the finance director, and the finance director was hiding in a closet.

All this was running through my head as I visited Philadelphia's alltime great leader. To be honest, he might be working at a disadvantage these days to Mayor Goode, Betsy "Don't" Reveal, and City Council.

I mean, he's dead.

But it's too close to call.

Ben Franklin was laid in the ground in 1790. He sleeps at Christ Church Cemetery, Fifth and Arch. In the two centuries he's been dead, you could fit Philadelphia's good mayors in a phone booth.

I found myself talking to Franklin as if he were alive. At first it was strange, but it soon got comfortable, probably because many of the contemporary politicians I talk to share the company of worms and don't have a pulse.

Here's a man, Ben Franklin, who brought countries together. In today's Philadelphia, nobody can even bring the neighborhoods together.

That's one of the reasons for this mess. Sure, Washington has mugged us, Harrisburg is an accomplice, times are tough. But for six years this city has made moves to get us into the next week instead of the next year. Budgets are phony and decisions are based more on the next election than anything else.

As I stood there, wondering how we're ever going to solve our problems, hoping for inspiration from Ben Franklin, I heard a voice.

"No money."

I looked up, startled. No one was there. Maybe I was hearing things.

I looked at the grave, and then . . .

"Try later. No money."

It was eerie. Was Franklin trying to tell me something?

And then I saw two street people pass the iron fence outside Franklin's grave. As they disappeared, one said to the other:

"Man, I got $4 yesterday."

Next thing I knew, eight tourists came in and stood over Franklin. Before they left, they tossed coins on the grave. It was mid-morning now and tourists were coming in steadily. A lot of them left coins.

Six feet under, Ben Franklin is a better fund-raiser than the mayor.

"It's a tradition," said Michael Arrington, a National Park Service ranger. "It's supposed to be good luck to toss a coin. And Franklin said a penny saved is a penny earned."

It all began to make sense. Street people are pinching money from the grave of Benjamin Franklin.

"All the time," Arrington said.

Just like the city treasury. One minute there's money in the kitty. You turn your back, it's gone.

"They usually wait for tourists to leave, but one guy was taking coins right off the grave in front of a bunch of tourists," Arrington said. "I made him empty his pockets. I've had them climbing the fence after hours and using brooms through the fence to sweep up the coins."

At Christ Church, two sextons said they visit the grave twice a day to beat others to the money. The coins, up to $12 worth each day, go into the general fund at the church.

"I think the vendors steal it, too," said one sexton. "The guys who sell balloons and souvenirs on Independence Mall."

I went back to Franklin's grave, embarrassed for the city. A man, waiting for more coins, had trapped a pigeon and tied its legs together. He was dangling it upside down.

I think he was an assistant city finance director.

In his will, Franklin left $4,000 to Philadelphia. It was to be spent wisely, with interest, exactly 200 years after his death.

Early this year, with a fund grown to $520,000, the city decided to blow the whole thing on carnival events and hire Ben Vereen and Aretha Franklin for entertainment. They changed their mind after the outcry.

And now a city run by yo-yos is about broke, Franklin's legacy of investing in the future has been trampled even as the city celebrates the anniversary of his passing, and Dickensian birdmen rob his grave.

Happy 200th, Ben.

SIMPLE AND COMPLEX:
ART IS IDEAS

December 19, 1993

It hangs on the wall where I work at home, and when things aren't going well—meaning every 10 minutes or so—I glance over at the print.

It's the Gulf of Marseilles, as seen by French post-impressionist Paul Cézanne, and that's what intrigues me. That nobody saw it as he saw it.

I have no training in art, and so I can't begin to describe the painting in a technical way. I can only tell you what happens when I look at it.

The bay, soft in blue, goes silent, and the town floats at the water's edge, red rooftops bleached by the sun and washed by sea breezes.

It's not a frozen moment, but a history of time. A story told in colors that are emotions more than colors.

Cézanne was the first painter I thought I might ever understand. As with every painting of his—of landscapes and people alike —I feel as though I've been let in on a secret. He has found the undiscovered view and built a window, and the subject reveals itself as never before.

Two weeks ago, city officials announced that the Philadelphia Museum of Art, in 1996, will host an exclusive three-month show of Cézanne paintings pulled together from London, Paris, and Philadelphia. More than 300,000 people are expected to see the show, called by one expert "one of the most important art exhibitions of the second half of the 20th century."

I was on the train from New York to Philadelphia a day or two after the announcement, and a woman near me opened the newspaper to a copy of Cézanne's Large Bathers, which hangs on a wall in Philadelphia and is considered a masterpiece.

The woman turned to her friend.

"Large Bathers," she said, snickering.

She brushed off the story and moved on to an item that said "Zsa Zsa Gabor and her husband have been ordered by a jury to pay Elke Sommer $2 million for saying that Sommer was a broke has-been."

Until recently, I'd have gone the same way, choosing a Zsa Zsa or an Elke over a Cézanne. But now I move on to Cézanne immediately after reading about Zsa Zsa, Elke, and last night's basketball games.

In 16 years of public and Catholic education, nobody said anything to me about art that made it sound nearly as interesting as my Mad magazine or the next episode of Dick Van Dyke. In the American culture, few people know enough about it to know what to say.

In America, billions of tax dollars are spent on an experimental and crash-prone military aircraft with tilt-rotor engines, and nobody asks questions. But the first time a work of art challenges mainstream sensibilities, the nation screams for an end to public funding.

When I was younger, it would have been easy to get my attention on the subject of art. All anyone had to say was this: Art is ideas, and we can always use new ones.

It's as simple and as complex as that. But I didn't really understand it until I saw Cézanne's pain in trying to explain himself. And then a trip to Russia made it even more clear.

In snowy Leningrad at the dawn of glasnost, a line of people snaked for blocks, their breath visible in the January air. They were waiting to get into the Hermitage Museum, which, until that time, had been a prison for ideas.

Inside were all the masters, their work hidden from a public for whom free thought had been forbidden. And now here they were, walking through Rembrandt's shadows and into Monet's dreams.

I visited a Russian school on that trip and saw no art on the walls, except for one room, where the class paintings, of a building, were neatly taped to a door.

Every one was exactly the same, as if art were a doctrine, a science.

It is not. It is a search.

"I am working doggedly, for I see the promised land before me," Cézanne once wrote. "Shall I be like the great Hebrew leader or shall I be able to enter? I have made some progress. Why so late and with such difficulty? Is art a priesthood that demands the pure in heart who must belong to it entirely?"

Cézanne died at the beginning of this century. At the end of this century, people will come to Philadelphia from afar, stand on the hill above the Gulf of Marseilles, and peer through the window he gave the world.

A CULTURAL EVENT

December 23, 1987

T here's a good reason why I've bolted out of the office and am driving like Mario Andretti along the river, down School House Lane and into Germantown.

I'm running late for the cultural event of 1987. Of course, the Maplewood Music Studio Student Recital.

I promised I wouldn't miss it, because it just so happens that I have a special relationship with two of the featured pianists. The three of us are close enough for me to tell you that in the last week, they haven't once put their dirty socks in the hamper.

Folks, meet the B-Flat Brothers.

The younger of the B-Flats, who is 7, believes that life is a never-ending joy ride, and a music recital is just a drive-through concert. He is looser than Gumby after a couple of drinks.

The elder B-Flat, who is 9, contemplates things such as how the planets ended up in their current alignment. He has been experiencing a touch of stage fright. This manifests itself in subtle ways, and only an astute observer can pick up the clues.

When he refused to eat or sleep, I sensed that something was wrong.

So we went to his room, closed the door, and sat down for a man-to-man talk next to Winnie the Pooh. Turns out the kid had a concern shared by many artists at his level.

"I'm afraid I'll mess up."

Well, I said, life is full of challenges, not all of them pleasant, but you can learn from them. Just give it your best, and if you mess up, it really doesn't matter.

Here, the parent is lying.

I get to Yarnall Auditorium just in time. At least 50 spectators are here for an afternoon of first-rate entertainment, including renditions of "Here Come the Chimpanzees" and "Twinkle Twinkle Little Star."

Much to my surprise and relief, the elder B-Flat Brother has had a few practice runs and is relaxed. He is smiling at me as if to say, "Look, we both know your little speech was a lot of bull, but thanks anyway."

It is a quality moment.

His little brother, however, Mr. Party Pants, is falling apart. What an ironic turn of events.

The little B-Flat has involuntarily tied his body around a chair and the color

167

has drained from his face. Today, he has matured to the point where he realizes life is unfair.

It'll be a while before the moment of truth. The B-Flats are near the end of a list of 30 performers.

The way a recital works, the entire audience pulls for every performer, hoping that this collective energy results in a harmonic convergence.

This is especially nice at Maplewood because of the cross-section of people. The performers go from about 4 to 54 and come in all flavors and levels of experience. Some of them dress in their Sunday best, unlike the B-Flat Brothers, whose idea of formal wear is clean tennis shoes.

And now, for our next performance, says Maplewood owner Rich Rudin, Emily Dowdall will play "Mary Had a Little Lamb" and "Jingle Bells." On violin.

Emily, barely as tall as the violin, is decked out in a nice plaid Christmas skirt. She struts up to center stage and flawlessly fiddles away.

I think it's fair to say the songs have not been played quite like this before. Emily, now bowing before a wildly appreciative audience, has a million-dollar smile.

The recital continues smoothly, moving through works by Beethoven and Mozart. And now it's time.

The little B-Flat is called up to play "Lightly Row," sort of his life story to this point. He could actually just stay in his seat and strum his nerves, but he somehow manages to walk up without moving his feet and play the song without moving his fingers.

The parents are actually more nervous than the children at this time, and there's a very good reason for that. You don't want your child to get up there and embarrass you.

Just kidding. You're nervous because you know *they* are, and you want them to do well and possibly go on to make tremendous amounts of money some day so you can retire.

The little guy plays it perfectly and walks back looking like he has just won a year's supply of junk food.

Rudin now calls for the big guy.

I wish, as he walks up there, that he hadn't chosen such a sophisticated piece.

So he's about three-fourths of the way through "Auld Lang Syne," he's playing it perfectly, and then all of a sudden he misses a note, gets off track, and it sounds like something by the Moody Blues.

He pauses. He makes a face indicating that he deeply resents my speech. And then he starts over and plays like Van Cliburn. Perfection.

After the show, the B-Flat Brothers and I do high-fives.

Now, if we could just get them to pick up their socks.

LETTING GO OF A BEST FRIEND

August 2, 1992

The moment her Uncle John invited her to his Center City condo Thursday night, Amanda knew what he wanted to talk about. She didn't want to hear it, but knew she had to.

John Kelly has been calling in family and friends, one by one. He takes them into his bedroom and lies down on the bed to rest his aching body. Through the window, the Ben Franklin Bridge arches gently over the Delaware. And John, 33, his voice slow, talks about where he's going.

Amanda, who's 18 and lives in Cherry Hill, brought chicken, rice, and salad for dinner. They ate and talked and laughed. They could always have a laugh.

She'll be on her way to Trenton State College soon, majoring in history, so they had lots to talk about. John told her he's concerned about her generation, with all its anger and violence. Politically and philosophically, they always hit it off.

"He's only 15 years older than me," says Amanda, who began getting close to her uncle four years ago, "and we had a lot of the same interests. We went to a couple of concerts together, and we were interested in the same movies, and he'd take me down to South Street."

He bought her two rings. She wears the amethyst every day, because it's her birthstone. The pearl ring she saves for special occasions.

Amanda says her uncle is one of her best pals, and she's told him stuff she's told nobody else.

She suspected he was gay, but he didn't say anything and she didn't ask. It didn't matter. Then about two years ago her parents told her he was gay. And he had AIDS.

"I felt like I was hit with a brick," Amanda says. "I was numb for days."

They became even closer. She once visited him in the hospital, and over hoagies, he talked about his lifestyle, about his fight to accept himself and to be respected by others.

John has a way about him, a way of taking away a person's discomfort at the door, the way you might take a coat. A way of making a person free to talk, free to listen.

Amanda knew that's how it would be Thursday night. She knew he'd be more concerned about her than about himself.

"After dinner, we went into his bedroom. He said, 'Listen, there's an ulterior motive for you to be here tonight.'"

She braced.

"He said, 'It's coming to the end now and I just want you to know it and not have to hear it from anybody else.' He said he wanted to make sure I was OK with it, and if I was angry, I could talk to him about it.

"I guess we sat there about a half hour, and he kept telling me how much he loved me, and he held my hand and we both cried."

John was at peace with it, and that made it a bit easier for Amanda. He said he was going to a place where he'd be able to keep growing, spiritually, and learn things he couldn't learn on this planet. He said he looked forward to seeing his lover, Tom, and other friends.

When you live with AIDS, John had once said, courage and fear become indistinguishable. You wake up each day and bargain with the universe.

In his case, he bargained for a little more time with people he loved. He bargained for time to help other people with AIDS, and time to make speeches in which he took down the fences people like to build.

"I got very upset when somebody made a gay joke or an AIDS joke," Amanda says. "And I let people know I wasn't happy. I tried to make people understand there's nothing wrong with being gay."

Amanda was once at a religious retreat where people took turns telling about the person they most admired. She told of her Uncle John, and the strength he gave her. She said she admired him for his choices, for his intolerance of hatred and hypocrisy, and for his courage.

But she knows he's too tired now, and hurting too much, to bargain any longer.

"When Tom was dying, I know John kept telling him to let go and go toward that light," Amanda says. "I almost wanted to say to John Thursday night that he should do the same thing now."

On a wall near his bed, John has taped this verse:

All goes onward and outward
. . . And nothing collapses.
And to die is different
from what anyone supposed.
And luckier.
— Walt Whitman

John and Amanda hugged a lot before she left.

"He said he wanted to dance at my wedding and he wanted to hold my children and he knows it's not possible physically, but that he'll be at my wedding, and he'll see my children. And I don't doubt that at all."

YOUNG ROBERTO GETS
HIS GLOVE

===== *August 14, 1994* =====

Roberto, 11, wasn't supposed to leave the house Saturday. He was in trouble for misbehaving when he got upset about his Friday night Little League game getting rained out.

So what he did, he got up early and put on the old gray baseball uniform he loves, the one Father Sal gave him so he wouldn't go completely crazy waiting for the new ones. And while his family slept, he snuck out the back and went to the ballpark at Fourth and Jasper in South Camden.

Maybe his team would play the washed-out game. If not, maybe he could get into a pickup game. Along the way, he ran into three friends.

It was a good day at the ballpark because the wind was blowing away from the sewage treatment plant. A team of 6- to 8-year-olds, the Central Music House Sluggers, was warming up, waiting for their opponents.

The guys couldn't stand it.

"Hey," Roberto says to me, "you wanna play with us?"

Roberto is skinny, with copper skin and light eyes.

Sure, I say, and we walk to the outfield.

"Two against two, you be steady pitcher."

All right, Roberto.

"Hey, how you know my name?"

You're lefthanded, right?

"Yeah."

I remember one game where you didn't have a glove for your right hand so you kept taking the glove off your left hand to throw the ball.

"You put that in the paper?"

Yeah, and people called to offer gloves. You didn't get one?

"No. You put me in the paper another time, too. I got jumped on my bike on the way to practice."

You're the same Roberto?

"Yeah."

Roberto shows me his wrong-hand glove, and for the first time, I see that all the fingers of his right hand are cut off at the first knuckle.

"My father burned my fingers off," Roberto says. "He stuck my hand on a burner when I was 2. He's in jail."

He interrupts my next question.

"Come on, let's play."

171

Roberto's team is getting killed. But he's all hustle on every play, and each at-bat is a chance to show off his Major League batting stance.

We're in the top of the fourth when a 1974 Dodge wagon drives onto the field containing the Catelli Brothers Hurricanes. The doors fly open and coach Alex Perez lines up his 11 players single-file and leads them on a warmup jog, each kid doing the same high knee-kick as the coach.

"It took me two hours to pick them all up," Perez says. Transportation has been one of the biggest hassles in the new league, because many parents have no cars. "At one house, I had to shake the kid awake."

It turns out that while the Hurricanes are at full force, the Sluggers are short. Sluggers coach Jerry Cruz, wearing a "Rodeo Drive, Beverly Hills" T-shirt, asks if he can borrow my four players.

Roberto doubled to left in the first. A couple of innings later, a parent asks Jerry Cruz who's winning.

"Everybody's winning," the coach says. "Out here, nobody loses."

While the game is on, I drive out to meet with Roberto's mother. She says she had gone to the store that day, leaving Roberto with her husband, and when she got back Roberto was on his way to the hospital.

She says her husband denied hurting Roberto, but she didn't believe him. She left him and has remarried.

Roberto is a good boy who acts up sometimes, she says. He has a gift when it comes to fixing things. He'll pick up discarded bicycle parts here and there and make a working bike. Maybe that will be his living one day.

Back at the park, the game is over.

How many hits you get, Roberto?

"Five or six," he says. "Can we have a ride home?"

First he wants to show me something. A glove for a lefthander has been donated to the league.

"Father Bruce gave it to me," Roberto says. "You like it?"

Roberto sat on the steps of the church Saturday afternoon, opposite the wooden cross planted by parishioners to discourage a drug operation. He said he was going to wait there until he found out if the new uniforms, ordered for South Camden's first Little League season in years, had come in yet.

ON THE CUTTING EDGE

November 5, 1986

All my life I've been two steps behind the fashion trends.

When bell-bottoms were in, I had peg legs. When peg legs came in, I had bell-bottoms. I didn't even throw out my leisure suit until last year.

The last couple of days, I noticed another trend that passed me by. I'm talking about the latest hairdo.

You may have seen it in the newspapers and on television. In the last 11 days, 45 people have been indicted in the Philadelphia area, and 90 percent of them had the same haircut.

You know the look I'm talking about. Let's call it the mob do. (Just so I don't get sued, not all 45 indictees are mobsters. Some of them have less reputable professions. Judge and councilman, for instance.)

The mob hairdo is combed straight back, neat as a brush, and is kept fairly short. A miniature pompadour is acceptable, but it has to have that blow-dried look, like you've been riding shotgun in a rumble seat.

Take Little Nicky Scarfo, grand poobah of some local goombahs and one of 17 reputed mobsters—including one reputed mobette —rounded up Monday. Think what you will of the man, but when he got pinched, Scarfo was making a fashion statement.

For his arraignment, a formal affair, Scarfo was resplendent in a pin-striped sharkskin suit with a sharp cut and a good shine to it. He also wore a wide print tie and, of course, the mob hairdo.

He ought to be on the cover of GQ.

Just once, I thought, I should get in step. I don't know if I can afford a sharkskin suit, but I can get a mob haircut. So I made some calls to see if there's a barber who specializes.

"I thought I had been asked every detail," said a South Jersey prosecutor. "Nobody ever asked me that."

I suggested he find out. You tell everything to your barber. If cops had dropped a microphone into the ceiling of a mob barber shop, Nicky might already be up the river.

A South Jersey stylist said she knew exactly the type of hairdo I was talking about. "Styled and bouffant," she said, "every hair in place, with a rounded, high look." But she has no mob customers, and she asked that I not use her name.

"I don't want to have a horse head in my bed," she explained.

I called attorney Bobby Simone, who not only represents an occasional thug, but also wears the hairdo in question. I asked him why everybody has the same haircut.

"Where'd you come, out of a tree or what?" Simone asked.

Geez, what a wise guy.

I thought he was going to hang up, but instead he cited case history like a pro. Which came as no surprise, because I figured if he weren't a good attorney he might be a dead attorney.

"Chickie Narducci had no hair," he argued. "Frank Sindone had totally different hair." He also mentioned "Nicky Crow" Caramandi. But he was intrigued by the hair connection.

"Maybe that's the strength of the government case to establish a conspiracy," he laughed.

I asked Simone who does his hair. Louie the barber, he said. Louie works at Rocco and Elmer's, Seventh near Bainbridge.

My appointment was for 12:30 yesterday.

"How do you want it?" Louie asked.

I asked if he had seen the morning paper. He said he had.

"You notice how the mob guys all had the same haircut?" I asked.

"Yeah, I noticed that," Louie said.

"That's what I want."

Louie needed no further instructions. He grabbed his scissors and went to work.

We had a pleasant chat. Louie said he was an aide to former councilman Jimmy Tayoun. In some of those patronage jobs, Louie said, you don't really have any "official duties." Except that if they were against something, Louie had to go to the meetings. If they were for, Tayoun was the front man.

"Ever see the mobsters come in here?" I asked.

"Nah," Louie said. "Couple of times."

He said Simone comes in every two weeks, which is why his hair always looks great. He came even more often during a recent trial, Louie said, so I asked who he was defending.

"No, when he was on trial," Louie explained. "It's like a good-luck charm for him to come in here. . . . But I saw his picture in the paper the other day and he looked bad. He looked like Willie the Worm."

Probably needs a trim.

Louie finished my cut and for once in my life I was in fashion.

I didn't realize how good a job he had done until I put on my trenchcoat and sunglasses. I didn't feel different, really.

But I had the urge to start a concrete business.

MR. TEMPLE AND THE RIVER

The priest first saw Sean Brennan on a summer day in 1976, when he signed up to go to Father Judge High. It wasn't an easy day for Sean.

A scrawny little guy walks through unfamiliar hallways with his mother, sees unfamiliar faces, and figures he's going to be the only kid in school who isn't part of something. Sean's blood cells were doing about 200 knots.

Charlotte Brennan said a prayer, right then and there, that her son would find his niche at Judge.

The priest spotted Sean.

"I've been looking for somebody like you," he said.

Charlotte wasn't expecting special delivery. She asked the priest his name.

"Father Brennan," he said.

Another good omen.

What Father John Brennan had in mind for Sean Brennan was to fold him into the back of a boat. He needed a coxswain for the school crew team.

The priest didn't know Sean was pint-size because of a brain tumor that was removed when he was 10. He didn't know the doctors figured Sean wouldn't be around past 12.

He didn't know what he'd started.

Sean Brennan became one of the best coxswains around. Of the colleges that wanted him, Temple University had the inside track because Temple and Father Judge share a boat shed on the Schuylkill below Strawberry Mansion Bridge.

"This is his home," Temple coach Gavin White said at the shed.

Sean—the youngest of seven children born to Charlotte and Thomas Brennan—had three goals after high school. A gold medal in the Dad Vail Regatta, a college degree, and a job. Temple already had a varsity coxswain, so Sean started with the JVs.

The job looks easy, getting a free ride while eight other guys do the work. But a coxswain controls the tempo, steers the ship and decides when to light fires. Sean Brennan was an incendiary device.

"He found out the names of the kids in another boat one time and he's calling to them during the race, by name," giving them the business, Gavin White says.

One time on the river he gave hell to an opposing coach for coaching during a race, which is illegal.

Sean became the varsity coxswain his junior year. Two weeks before the first meet, he went to White.

"I can't make practice Thursday," he said. He felt lousy and wanted to see a doctor. "I'll be back Friday."

A brain tumor was removed three days later. The team went to the hospital before going to Georgia for the first meet.

"Get out of here," he told them. He allowed no one to fuss over him.

White put Rob Plotnick, a kid with no experience, in the coxswain's seat. In the middle of a tight race in Georgia, Plotnick told his crew:

"Let's do 20 strokes for Sean."

The Temple boat responded as if a Mercury outboard had been fired up. Temple breezed, and 20 strokes for Sean became a ritual.

When Temple won the Dad Vail that summer, Sean greeted his pals on the shore, his head scarred from the operation. There were tears when he put the gold medals on his teammates.

Sean told them he'd be back. One year later, in the same spot, they put a gold medal on him. He had won his job back and won the Dad Vail.

Earning a B.A. wasn't enough for Sean. He went for a master's and worked as a graduate assistant in the Temple athletic department to pay for his education and his rent.

Around Christmastime he felt ill. He claimed it was the flu.

They operated again in February. His speech was slurred, his vision blurred, he limped. He told friends he'd be at school before they knew it.

Two weekends ago, Sean went to the Schuylkill with friends. It was a gorgeous day and he looked out on the river, feeling its current in him, seeing more than any man can see.

He called his mother from work the next morning at 7:30 and said it was great to be back.

His boss, Earl Cleghorn, got in and saw coffee on his desk, meaning Sean was back. When he asked how he felt, Sean didn't answer. He wrote on a pad that he was having a seizure.

After six days on life support, Sean Brennan, 24, whose friends called him Mr. Temple, died at 11 p.m. Saturday at Temple Hospital.

Those who knew him have trouble expressing what he taught them, how he changed them. They talk about perseverance, love, courage, and then they apologize for not explaining it better.

About 300 of them went to the funeral Tuesday and heard Father Brennan tell about that summer day in 1976.

Charlotte Brennan told Sean's friends she'd like his name on one of the Temple boats. She'd like for him to always be on the river.

THE NATION AND THE WORLD

GRAVEYARD OF THE VERY YOUNG

April 19, 1991

ISIKVEREN, Turkey—He died at noon yesterday in his tent, and while his wife and six children grieved, other relatives loaded the man onto a stretcher and carried him to a cemetery.

His body was wrapped in a heavy gray blanket, but you could tell from the form beneath it that he was a small man. His blue plastic shoes poked out and looked like about a size 7.

They picked a spot close to the grave of his 3-year-old daughter, who died 10 days ago. But so many have died since then, they couldn't remember exactly which grave was hers.

"It is either this one or that one," a man said.

It was especially difficult to tell because among the 14 graves in the immediate area, all but one was 3 feet long or less. Six were about two feet long.

After settling on a place 10 feet from where they thought his daughter was buried, a man turned the first shovel of dirt for 45-year-old Abrahim Jalal, who would become the 261st Kurdish refugee put in the ground here in the last three weeks.

The 259th and 260th were still being buried within about 50 feet of where Jalal's body lay, but their bodies already had been dropped in and dirt was being thrown over them.

This camp also has two other cemeteries. This one, which sits at the edge of a cliff, is the biggest.

The graves used to be several feet apart, and you could walk between them easily. Now bodies are buried between other bodies, and you can barely move through the cemetery without stepping on someone's grave.

The graves are shaped like half loaves of bread, sloped a foot or two above ground level, and they all point the same way.

The Muslim custom is to point the feet toward the sunrise and the head toward the sunset. So all the dead here are angled toward the edge of the cliff, as if their spirits are preparing for takeoff.

Of the 261 graves, 167 are 3 1/2 feet long or less, like the grave of Abrahim Jalal's little girl, Hozan.

And 51 of those are about two feet long.

If you place one foot in front of the other, they cover the length of the child below.

When you stand in the center of the cemetery, fallen children are all

179

around. Four over there, six down that way, and a dozen on the other side of a tree. One of those stark, ghostly trees that is common here. A tree without leaves or flowers, just a harsh trunk topped by a skeletal thicket, like a vulture's hand raised to the sky.

Many children walk through the cemetery on their way from one place to another, and you find yourself visually measuring them against the graves to imagine what lies below.

Some of the kids who walk by have facial burns from chemical weapons that were used against them in Iraq. To stand in this cemetery is to see both the durability and fragility of human life.

The men were about two feet down now for Abrahim Jalal. Halfway there. He had been a clerk at an elementary school back home. He got sick in the camp here, and was gone quickly.

The lack of food, the lack of water, the unsanitary conditions. It was all of those things.

At least half the camp has diarrhea, which is on the ground everywhere because there are no toilets. Many children walk barefoot. And many have a cough that sounds like a small explosion in their chests.

At the hospital tent, the lines were long. A relief worker said there was a shortage of safe water and some people were drinking from mud puddles. Many more will die soon.

At the grave of Abrahim Jalal, the men stopped to discuss whether they had dug deep enough. As they did, a man of about 20 walked slowly to the edge of the cliff.

He sat down next to a grave and then lay his upper body over it as if to hug the person inside. And then, while sobbing softly, he talked to whoever was in there.

After a few minutes he sat up again and reached under the neck of his sweater. From his shirt pocket he pulled out a piece of white cloth and carefully began to unravel it. Inside was a color photograph of a wedding. He pointed to himself in a picture wearing a handsome black suit. And then he pointed to the young, pretty woman next to him in the picture. She wore a bridal gown, and on that day she became his wife.

After pointing to his picture he pointed to the grave. And then he lay over it again, hugging his wife.

After two hours of digging, the relatives of Abrahim Jalal had created a perfect rectangular hole about four feet deep. At the bottom was a narrower recession about a foot wide and a foot deep for the body.

They picked up the stretcher and carefully slid the body into the grave. It fit perfectly into the groove at the bottom. They turned the body to the right, toward Mecca, and then opened the blanket to place the arms and hands in a comfortable position.

The dead man's hands were caked with dirt, but they still looked soft, as if there still were life in them.

They fell into place in a peaceful way, one hand over the other, on his stomach.

They pulled the blanket over him again and then covered him with flat pieces of cardboard from boxes. The boxes had English printing on them.

"Meal, Ready to Eat. Mullins, S.C."

Abrahim Jalal was covered with boxes that held food intended for American soldiers who fought in the Persian Gulf war. A war that ended with Saddam Hussein still in power, still free to slaughter the Kurds.

They began throwing dirt on the boxes now, as Jalal's brother sat and cried. It took only a few minutes to cover him up. The 261st grave was finished.

An hour later, as the sun slipped low in the sky, it streamed softly through clouds of camp fire smoke. Through the filtered light, those trees grew even more stark.

And down in the cemetery, the 262d and 263d graves were being dug, each one no more than 2 1/2 feet long.

POETRY ON THE MOUNTAIN

April 22, 1991

ISIKVEREN, Turkey—Under the light of the moon and stars, and the glow of a thousand campfires, Hassan Solivany opens his books and begins to read poetry.

Don't speak
Don't search for reason.
This night
Every night
In the towns and villages
Death is the gift to those who search.

So begins a poem about Saddam Hussein's imprisonment of the mind. Hassan Solivany, a 34-year-old accountant married to a teacher, wrote it in 1988 and brought it with him to this mountain camp of 200,000 Kurdish refugees.

He brought his poems, his short stories, his novel. All of them are meticulously hand-printed in soft-back tablets.

He keeps them under blankets in the corner of his tent, and has protected them for a month from all the rain and snow. He handles them as if they are treasures.

This camp is a mile or so beyond the border of Iraq, where his work was never published. He was a lowly Kurd whose thoughts did not reflect those of Saddam Hussein, and so they were silent screams.

In that regard, he was not alone back home. And he is not alone here.

Solivany and about 50 other writers and artists, who met regularly to share forbidden thoughts, now meet here in the camp.

Back home, they would go to the university in Mosul and meet over lunch once a week. One of them would do a reading. They were people of ideas in a society that controlled thought.

Here their gatherings are less formal, but more frequent. And there is so much more to talk about. Sometimes they meet as night falls over the camp, and they have made it through another day of watching human beings stripped of every emotion but fear, every instinct but survival.

They're still in a prison. A horrible kind of prison, fenced by the rifles of Turkish soldiers. But here there is less repression of ideas, and the General Union of Writers in Mosul has found a strange kind of freedom as refugees.

"Sometimes we meet by the helicopters, or maybe by a campfire. Not the whole group. Maybe a few, maybe more," Solivany says.

"From this experience, we all have the inspiration to write. So when we get together, we discuss our ideas, and we discuss the situation. I don't think any-one has written while in camp, but we will all write about this when we are gone from here."

In this camp and others, the night is the only time for reflection. The day is busy with the chores of survival. Finding food. Finding water. Making sure the kids are OK. Solivany and his wife, Shermen, a teacher, have four children.

But when it isn't cold, the night is kind to the camp. It is kind because it hides so much filth and misery, and frees the mind to imagine something better.

Maybe a modern metropolitan city on a hill. The glow of the campfires are street lights. The faint forms of the tents are houses.

It's a pleasant night. A night for dreams.

The air is still. Smoke stings the eyes and quiet creeps over the camp as it grows later. Fewer babies cry. Few voices are heard. Fewer people are cough-ing that cough of death.

In mythology, it is said that the mountains are the only friends of the Kurds. For the first time, with darkness hiding the graves, it seems true.

Solivany leans back on a blanket under the open sky and flips through his unpublished novel—*Guldstan in the Night*. It's about an Iraqi woman who pre-pares for the return of her husband, a soldier, from the war with Iran.

In meticulous detail, the book describes her tragic preparation.

"She does not know her husband has been killed," Solivany says.

"I did not agree with the war against Iran. Saddam Hussein's people of-fered me money and cars to write positive things about the war. I would not do it. I did not like the war for Kuwait, either. He is a crazy man, Saddam Hus-sein."

Solivany says he appreciates the U.S. war against Hussein. But Solivany and other writers believe that after the war the people of Iraq were deceived into thinking they would have U.S. support in their attempts to overthrow Hussein.

This night, Solivany has company. The rising star of the General Union of Writers has dropped by his tent. His name is Kawa Hassan. He is a poet of 25. His home—they do not call them tents—is past the hospital and across the cemetery.

Two days earlier, Hassan could be seen by the cemetery, pleading for help for his sick children. He wore the dirt of these mountains, which is the camou-flage of teachers and artists and engineers and writers. He did not tell the stranger he was a writer; he only said he needed help.

Now, by the fire, he says his kids are holding up.

Now, darkness has removed his camouflage and he is a writer, the pride of the General Union.

"We are filled with sadness about our situation," Hassan says, realizing that sadness does not begin to describe what he feels inside. He says that he has seen refugees shot dead by Turkish soldiers while fighting for food.

These images have become a passion in this young poet. He will write about them, he says, when they get to wherever they are going. He doesn't really care if it is Iraq or somewhere else, as long as it is a place where he can enjoy the simple freedoms of going where he pleases and writing what he feels.

"I love his poems very much," Solivany says, the light of the fire flickering over his face. He says Hassan's poems are about the only things that exist. Love, hate, suffering, politics, and death. "They are beautiful. We are all so proud of him. One day, maybe you will hear his name again. Maybe you will buy his books."

Solivany and Hassan begin discussing their favorite writers. Solivany likes Hemingway, Tolstoy, and Keats.

"The Old Man and the Sea is my best," Solivany says.

Hassan likes Hugo, Hemingway, and Jack London.

Theirs are among the few books translated into Kurdish. In his spare time, Solivany gets Arabic versions, translates them into Kurdish, and makes them available through the General Union of Writers.

"I do not like houses, money, or cars," Solivany says. "Books are my life, and I love them as I love my wife."

Dawn will come at 5 a.m. The camp will awaken slowly, and the day will bring death to some. Hassan Solivany and Kawa Hassan will begin the daily struggle to survive. Solivany will take his 5-year-old son to the doctor. He will do nothing for the tightness in his own chest, except hope it gets better.

But that will be tomorrow. Now there is the night.

And although they have taken almost everything from Solivany, he still has his books. He still has his ideas, and a passion that burns like all the fires flickering over the camp.

Under the light of the moon and stars, in the company of 200,000 others who have made it through another day, Hassan Solivany the refugee is reading poetry on the mountain.

THE O.J. FEEDING FRENZY

June 19, 1994

With so many options, it's hard to decide who comes out of the O.J. Simpson affair looking the best and the brightest.

Could it be O.J. himself?

Here he is, reeling in the aftermath of the horrible murders of his wife and her friend, he's the prime suspect, and yet, he has the selfless compassion and wherewithal to write a note in which he says that although he felt like a battered husband, he still loves his wife, and he's going to miss his golfing buddies.

But it's not that simple.

You could go with the loyal supporters, 300 strong, who surrounded Simpson's house and chanted "Free O.J." Friday night when the nationally televised chase finally came to an end. One fan said she had seen O.J. in the movie *Naked Gun*, and he didn't seem capable of murder.

I was hoping they'd do the wave.

But if you're going to be fair about choosing heroes, what about the Los Angeles Police?

Working with perhaps the most physical evidence in a murder since Jack Ruby shot Lee Harvey Oswald on national TV, police considerately waited, waited, waited, and then, when they were finally ready to arrest the most-watched man on the planet, they couldn't find him.

Which brings us to the media.

Not only was footage of the freeway chase so real that it brought back memories of "One-Adam Twelve," but to diffuse the nation's tension, we got endless banter and speculation from TV anchors, despite their having nothing to say about a man they knew nothing about.

A fitting climax to a week in which every newspaper and every 40-watt TV station in America seemed to have somebody planted outside the gate to O.J.'s mansion.

Frankly, I couldn't get enough of the suspense. Not over whether O.J. did it—but over whether anyone would have the humility or decency to keep his or her mouth shut or, better yet, take a poke at the next reporter who asked what they thought of the whole thing.

Maybe *Larry King Live* can still set up shop outside O.J.'s house or the jail and interview additional people who might at one time in their lives have seen O.J., or his ex-wife Nicole, or one of the children, or possibly all of them, get into a vehicle, exit a vehicle, or motor by in a vehicle.

With any luck, the source will recall if it was the Rolls Royce, the Mercedes, the Bronco, or the Ferrari. Then we'll be onto something.

Much as we were when self-described friends of O.J., his ex-wife, or Ron Goldman, who was once on the TV show *Studs* and was killed with Nicole, provided reporters the inside dope—or at least, their best guess—as to the exact nature of O.J.'s relationship with Nicole, Nicole's relationship with Goldman, or whether O.J., whom they last saw in 1986, was capable of violence.

As for the seven or eight people in Los Angeles who have not yet found a way to get in front of a camera on the subject of O.J. Simpson, a thought occurs. I think they should have their say on a special edition of the hit television show *Frasier*.

Frasier Crane is a radio-show psychiatrist adept at soothing all manner of angst, grief, and depression. So it seems perfect. Except that it's been done, sort of. Before Nicole Simpson's body was cold, in fact, her therapist was spilling her guts about the victim's private life.

Speaking of TV, it remained unclear at my publication time whether the TV movie on the life and times of O.J. Simpson would be produced by, say, today. (Please check local listings.) It was clear, however, that a book would be out "within days." St. Martin's Press said the author was Don Davis, whose previous subjects were Jeffrey Dahmer and the Menendez brothers.

I just hope Davis understands that unlike the others, Simpson is a true American hero, having become (A) a great football player, (B) a sportscaster, (C) an actor in several bad movies, and (D) the spokesperson for a car-rental agency.

Not to mention that he had a gorgeous blond wife. Speaking of which, I don't think anyone put this horrible tragedy in better perspective than Nicole's pal Amy Goodfriend (I swear it) who said of her murder:

"She's blond. She's tanned. She's absolutely beautiful. I'm in shock. I can't believe this."

And they say we've lost our way and live in a cultural vacuum.

AN ELECTION POST-MORTEM

November 6, 1991

Good morning, Philadelphia.

How's it going?

Maybe you already know. But if you didn't hear about the Second District, go to your bathroom, right now, and look in the mirror.

Now slap yourself.

Lucien Blackwell is a congressman.

He may be in the car as you read this, on his way down to Washington.

He's yelling at passing motorists, for practice.

Go ahead. Slap yourself again.

U.S. Rep. Lucien Blackwell.

But before you begin to seriously injure yourself, the hacks didn't make a clean sweep.

It looks like Dick Thornburgh is history, buried by Sen. Harris Wofford. Of course, Wofford didn't play fairly. He talked about issues. But I think another factor helped him.

I don't know if you saw it, but the five living presidents got together the other day in California.

Personally, I think it was a public service that they gathered so close to Election Day, reminding the nation that a vote is a terrible thing to waste. The caption, to borrow a popular theme, could have been:

America: What Went Wrong?

The occasion was the opening of the $60 million Ronald Reagan Presidential Library. The library has 47 million documents, 46.93 million of which Reagan doesn't remember seeing. The remainder were receipts from astrologers. Instead of a metal detector, the entrance has an electronic zapper that temporarily gives visitors the IQ of crash-test dummies.

This way, they don't come out wondering why there isn't much mention of tax breaks for the rich or the Iran-Contra boondoggle. Or the fact that Reagan spent approximately three-fourths of his presidency asking Nancy if they'd had lunch yet.

In a speech, Reagan said the library contains "a great jagged chunk of the Berlin Wall, hated symbol of, yes, an evil empire, that spied on and lied to all its citizens ..."

At this point, Richard Nixon began choking.

Gerald Ford, attempting to pat Nixon on the back, knocked him unconscious with a blow to the head.

Carter, mistaking Ford for a rabbit, beat him with an oar.

"Certainly," Reagan said, "it is my hope that the Reagan library will become a dynamic intellectual forum ..."

At this point, Jimmy Carter began choking.

Ford, attempting to pat Carter on the back, instead hit George Bush, who broke into speech:

"Ronald Reagan was unmoved by the vagaries of intellectual fashion," Bush said, which was a nice choice of words, since you don't want to show up at a guy's library opening and call him a complete bozo.

"He treasured values that last, values that endure," Bush continued. "And I speak of patriotism and civility and generosity and kindness and voodoo economics."

I made up the voodoo economics.

But let's say you're George Bush. Several years ago, you had the sense to realize Reagan's economic program was a giant zero. Next thing you know, he asks you to be vice president, and, being a man of conviction, you leap into his lap.

Now you're standing next to the guy in California, not sure whether he's awake at his own party. They're giving him a $60 million library and you're supposed to say nice things about him while your own popularity is taking a nose dive.

Because of voodoo economics.

And the whole nation is on the verge of switching lanes.

The interesting thing is that with roughly the same domestic and economic problems, Bush's popularity was higher than ever just several months ago. Before, during, and after the war, which had the same effect on most Americans as the electronic zapper at the Reagan library.

So I predict it won't be long before we go to war somewhere. I say it should be a place larger than Grenada but smaller than Kuwait, or roughly the size of the grounds where Reagan's new library sits.

Experts tell us the Senate race between Wofford and Thornburgh is a barometer of the nation. And it's nice to live in the place where the country begins to shake the cobwebs out of its head.

But having traveled through the state a little bit, and having noticed that there's nothing between Pittsburgh and Philadelphia but pecan logs and goat farmers, I'm a little concerned about our national role.

Nothing personal to folks in the sticks. I just don't know if people in the hinterland are as sophisticated as those of us in the big city.

Where we sent Lucien Blackwell to Congress.

THE NEW GOD AND GUNS AMERICA

November 13, 1994

If I have a single regret about Tuesday's election results, it's that we have to wait until January before we take that first step toward a new and improved United States.

But that doesn't mean I don't already feel warm all over about the prospects for change. And change, of course, to a more virtuous and moral America, is what we all wanted.

I guess since it was the victorious Republicans who recently killed campaign finance reform, and also buried the bill to restrict gift-giving lobbyists, the first change we can look forward to is an end to this type of annoying legislation.

Or, to put it another way:

"I don't think we need any more legislation regulating tobacco," said Rep. Thomas Bliley, a Virginia Republican who pocketed $93,790 from tobacco interests from 1987 to 1992, and who figures to head the House Health and Environment Committee.

This will free us to go about the task of lowering taxes by $190 billion and beefing up our bazillion-dollar military, the kind of revolutionary change that hasn't been tried in at least two or three of the last 14 years.

I just wish I could decide what to do first—go shopping with my freed-up capital gains, or apply for a defense contract.

I'm thinking of calling New York Sen. Alfonse D'Amato for advice. Not only is the proud prince of patronage expected to be the new chief of the Senate Banking Committee, but his brother Armand was accused of accepting $32,500 from a defense contractor for lobbying Alfonse.

That aside, I'd have to say that my favorite part of the new God and Guns America is the prospect for more peacetime military spending while Strom Thurmond, who is unintelligible, heads the Senate Armed Services Committee, and Jesse Helms, the popular segregationist, is in charge of Foreign Relations.

It's like putting global security and international brotherhood in the hands of Bartles & Jaymes, though I mean no disrespect to the wine-cooler guys.

I actually like the image of Strom and Jesse going abroad on a fact-finding mission because, if nothing else, it explains the need for school prayer. And although such a mission is liable to set human understanding back a hundred years, and could also result in our declaring war on the entire continent of Africa, that wouldn't be such a bad thing.

What good is a stronger military if you don't trot it out now and then?

One thing I don't quite understand is how an expansion of peacetime military spending and the construction of umpteen new prisons fit into the concept of less government.

Another thing I don't get is how you spend more money on those things, cut taxes by nearly $200 billion, and deliver a balanced budget.

I thought the answer was to dismantle welfare, an important goal in the newer and more Christian America. But then I saw the tax plan by Texas Republican Bill Archer, incoming chief of House Ways and Means. Under Archer's proposal, welfare doesn't end. It just shifts to a different income group.

The plan includes a $500-per-child tax credit for families earning up to $250,000 a year, for a total of $107 billion. Three-fourths of the capital gains cut would go to families with a six-figure minimum income, and 95 percent of the new benefits on Individual Retirement Accounts would go to the wealthiest 20 percent.

Archer, using a proven campaign tactic, didn't explain how he'd pay for this. But I'm sure we'll get a full accounting from House Speaker-to-be Newt Gingrich of Georgia, soon as he's done explaining how Democrats were responsible in the case of the South Carolina woman who admitted, after first blaming a black man, to killing her two sons.

Gingrich promised to pass on the details of America's new agenda to us through radio talk show host Rush Limbaugh, assuming he doesn't become chief of civil rights, and various Christian Coalition broadcasts.

In times like these, as America recaptures what it stands for, you have to feel good about not being a Buddhist or a Jew, let alone gay. Or, for that matter, Ollie North, the one candidate I pulled for all the way. Not so much because he deserved it, but because the country deserved him.

Let's not let it get us down, though, as we go about the task of setting America straight. In two years, he could be defense secretary.

THEY'LL FIX EVERYTHING

I know we're less than a week down the road to light and wonderment. But already, I'm enjoying the spirit and glow of the New America.

Like six or eight others nationwide, I have a few nagging doubts, which I'll get to. But only because the undertaking is so ambitious.

The Republican "Contract With America" pledges to lay the groundwork in just 100 days to fix whatever might have bothered you the last 40 years, whether it was taxes, bureaucracy, or Negroes on welfare. And if it all gets taken care of before the 100-day warranty runs out, they're going to fix everybody's oven clock.

The Republicans gave their goals snappy names like the Taking Back Our Streets Act and the American Dream Restoration Act and promised to remain eternally baffled as to why someone raised in an urban wasteland doesn't behave more like them.

Wednesday, of course, was Day One of fiscal and personal responsibility, as well as an end to free rides. It began when House Speaker Newt Gingrich, who restructured his $4.5 million book deal for the occasion, made a stirring speech about everyone working together.

Roughly eight seconds later, Republicans shot down a Democratic proposal to ban gifts from lobbyists. Then they all tripped over themselves trying to leave the room at the same time, so they'd get a good seat at wingdings hosted, laid out, and paid for by lobbyists.

The reassuring thing here is that, Republican or Democrat, new plan or old, one thing never changes.

These are some funny people.

Take the part of Gingrich's speech when, disoriented by the heat of TV lights, Rush Limbaugh's chief Doberman appeared ready to toast Kwanzaa and pass out hams to the poor.

Here's a man who has led the most conservative revolution in 40 years, largely on a promise to heap more misery on the dregs of society. He was going to snatch babies from freeloading moms and put them in homes run by Spencer Tracy.

He had everyone believing that in Philadelphia, for example, where the poverty rate is 20 percent, 320,000 people might be pulling into the two-car garage after work and tossing another log onto the fire if welfare and poverty weren't so damn cushy.

And then, in the middle of his speech, he became Jesse Jackson.

My guess is that the night before the inauguration, Newt, a movie buff, saw

Brother From Another Planet. That's why he asked us not to forget the plight of those who don't find a seat on the party wagon.

We won't. Not when they start piling up at the doors of newly elected Republican governors and legislators who, ironically, will be getting it put to them six ways by Washington.

Not that we shouldn't finally get serious in America about slaying and reshaping government, discouraging free rides, encouraging initiative, and demanding that people take responsibility for themselves. There's just one small question.

Where are they supposed to work?

Maybe on the multibillion-dollar Star Wars program being dusted off by the GOP. Or maybe they'll become servants for the big winners in the New America—those pulling in $200,000 and up. Welfare isn't erased; it's written over to the wealthy.

The Job Creation and Wage Enhancement Act calls for a 50-percent cut in the capital-gains tax, which should give us six or eight new jobs, and maybe four raises. Then there's a gargantuan tax break, oddly enough, for the corporations that lubricated legislators at Wednesday's Beef and Brew. Maybe they'll hire more waiters for the next feed show.

If the scenery looks familiar, it's because this train already left the station once. It's one of the reasons the deficit and debt are now larger than the space between planets.

Ronald Reagan, unfortunately, isn't the only one who's forgotten. So it's no surprise that the numbers don't add up this time, either. If Republicans balance the budget, as promised, they'll have to chop billions from programs and services they haven't told you about yet.

They will, make no mistake, dismantle welfare. But that won't take the edge off debt, crime, fear, and suffering. The only way to do that is to devote the nation's energies and resources to educating and employing people who either can't get ahead or never even got started.

Thoughts for another contract, and another America.

'HOW DO THEY SLEEP AT NIGHT?'

November 21, 1993

I was out of commission most of the week, and passed the time reading the papers. And after a while, I realized that as I completed each story, the same question occurred.

How do they sleep at night?

Pick a story. Any story.

The Osprey?

This is the multibillion-dollar experimental aircraft that takes off like a helicopter, flies like a plane, and crashes like a clay pigeon.

Allow me to summarize reporter Nathan Gorenstein's story.

July 20, 1992.

The Osprey isn't ready to fly, but it has to. About 100 big shots from the military and from Boeing and Bell are waiting near Washington to celebrate the landing. If all goes well, it could mean billions more in sales.

So despite safety concerns, and despite the fact that the cockpit is aglow with warning lights as the engines are fired, the Osprey takes off from Florida.

"We were pushing it," a program manager later said. "Nobody thought the aircraft would actually fly that day. It needed more local test flying."

But the dignitaries need a show. And they get one.

With the guys in party hats looking on, the Osprey crashes into the Potomac, killing all seven crew members.

Had it happened 2,000 years ago, it would have made the Bible.

Today, we don't need parables.

We have Washington.

And we have Oregon Sen. Bob Packwood.

Bob, a Republican bon vivant, likes women.

Bob likes tongue-kissing, groping, and grabbing women.

Bob is a pig.

And not very bright. He keeps a diary.

This makes two recent scandals in which the existence of a little black book has sent people diving for cover. One, as you know, is kept by someone who works with a team of whores for hire, and whose clients include the rich and powerful.

Then there's Heidi Fleiss.

In Packwood's case, 28 women allege sexual harassment, and Bob's diary, which covers his years on Capitol Hill, could be his undoing.

In addition to sordid details about innumerable cheap rolls, late-night rendezvous, and back-room quickies, the diary is believed to contain information about Packwood's sex life.

As well as love letters to Laura Petrie.

One more thing about Bob. He's the ranking GOP guy on the Senate Finance Committee, which writes corporate tax laws.

And this brings us to the "How Do They Sleep?" portion of the story.

Bob's pals in politics and business, confronted with the sad details of his private life at a time when they are establishing corporate codes against sexual harassment, have had to make a difficult decision.

How much money do they give Bob for his defense?

The answer, so far, is $275,000. Or roughly $10,000 per French kiss. A crude way of putting it, but hey, it's all about money.

As long as Packwood takes care of his friends in big business, he could show up for work with his pants around his ankles and a garter belt on his head, and they would stand behind him with their checkbooks.

Thanks, Arco. Way to go, Amoco, Cigna, and Bell Atlantic.

By comparison, the Packwood 28, the women who say Bob intimidated, harassed, or humiliated them, have raised $26,000.

America the beautiful.

And now for a "How Do They Sleep?" item from the fair city of Philadelphia.

Ordinarily, you don't see political hacks knocking on doors in Hispanic neighborhoods, asking residents if they need help with anything. But 100 people told Inquirer reporters that visitors informed them of a "new way of voting" that didn't require them to leave the house or even fill out a ballot.

Some said they didn't even know whom they were voting for. But in most cases, it was Democrat Bill Stinson, who had nearly 1,400 absentee ballots to fewer than 400 for Republican Bruce Marks, who lost by 478 votes in the Second Senate District.

When will we ever learn to appoint the special prosecutors before, rather than after, the election?

This is a city where the dead have voted, the dead have won.

And the pols have always slept like babies.

THE SPECTER OF DALLAS

January 8, 1992

Outside the theater Saturday, on the way to the car, my son had a question:

"Dad, why did everybody laugh when they said that thing about an ambitious junior counselor?"

Well, I said, they laughed because the ambitious junior counselor is now a United States senator from our very own Philadelphia. His name is Arlen Specter.

The movie, of course, was *JFK*. And my son, intrigued by the film, had another question.

"What did they mean when they talked about the magic bullet?"

This, of course, is why you keep children around.

To illustrate what was meant by Specter's bullet trajectory theory, which helped the Warren Commission conclude that Lee Harvey Oswald acted alone, I chose not to enter my car the conventional way.

Noticing that another car was parked directly behind my own, I walked maybe 20 yards behind the second car, began running at full speed, and hurled myself through the back window.

I exited, of course, through the front window of that car, and my momentum then carried me through the trunk of my own car. I then exploded out through the right rear passenger window, pivoted in mid-air, shot back into the car through the roof, exited the front passenger window, turned and re-entered through the windshield, and came to rest in the driver's seat.

And I didn't have a scratch.

With this, I think my son had a better appreciation of Specter's work, and a better understanding of why, 28 years later, many people still consider the government's investigation of JFK's assassination a joke at best, and a coverup at worst.

And let me suggest that you don't have to believe director Oliver Stone's far-reaching and paranoid conspiracy theory in order to get something out of *JFK*. The movie's most compelling argument is that the Warren Commission, either through incompetence or to protect someone, botched the investigation of the most spectacular and important murder of the century.

Specter, of course, does not agree, and said as much in an op-ed piece that ran in Sunday's Inquirer. Unfortunately, the article was largely unresponsive to the magic bullet charge, although Specter did say that his colleagues shot an "anesthetized goat" to help nail down the theory.

Because Specter's writing was somewhat obtuse, you couldn't always determine the entrance or exit point of a particular argument. And he used quotations from Thomas Jefferson and Winston Churchill, among others, who until now were not known to have been in Dallas. So in the end, it was impossible to know whether the article was the work of a conspiracy, or Arlen acted alone.

But not bad for an ambitious junior columnist. Maybe it's because Specter is getting lots of practice defending himself, thanks in part to his performance last year in the Anita Hill case, where he again represented the Washington establishment as Chief Doberman.

My personal favorite part was when Specter, in one of his smoother moments during the sexual harassment hearing, chuckled over his own mention of large hooters, or was it big boobs?

Whatever, I don't think it was a very nice way to refer to Senators Alan Simpson and Strom Thurmond, especially since they were sitting right next to Specter on that grassy knoll of a panel.

Talk about snakes in the grass.

Talk about a conspiracy.

Actually, I kept thinking that somewhere in his argument to prove that Clarence Thomas wasn't a pervert, Specter was going to shoot another goat. Either that, or start giving us trajectory theories on the Coke can.

Instead he spent roughly 400 hours asking questions 12,000 different ways, until he found an answer that didn't match up perfectly, and then he told the nation that he'd caught Anita Hill in an act of perjury.

You'd think that in 28 years, a man would graduate from the league of ambitious junior counselors.

But hey, justice prevailed. Anita Hill said she was sexually harassed, a panel of stand-up guys with bad hair decided she was either a liar or a delusional scorned female, and a man with less than two years of experience as a judge, traveling a route nearly as remarkable as the magic bullet, became a Supreme Court justice.

As Specter runs for re-election, one more thought on that magic bullet. You get the feeling it's still whizzing along after all these years. And you wonder if its next target is Arlen's foot.

RIGHT THEME, WRONG MOVES

January 17, 1993

They've come up with a name for President-elect Bill Clinton's inaugural wingding. Actually, it's more than a name. It's a theme.

An American Reunion, New Beginnings, New Hope.

And I guess it's pretty good because it sends the right message. That after 12 years, we're starting over. And it's going to be different.

And with that pledge in mind, you can't help but notice that as the Clinton team members come out of the huddle, they've got their pants down around their ankles.

Yes. I know it's early. Maybe too early to know anything for sure.

But if I had to guess, I'd say these guys are going to be a lot more fun than anybody expected.

For instance, there's already a report of a rift between Clinton and Vice President-elect Al Gore.

And at the rate he's going, William Jefferson Clinton could have more policy reversals than any president in history.

Before even taking office.

Clinton on Haitians during the campaign: The Bush policy "is another sad example of the administration's callous response to a terrible tragedy. I ... would give them temporary asylum."

Clinton on Haitians now: "Boat departure is a terrible and dangerous choice. For this reason, the practice of returning those who fled Haiti by boat will continue."

In the campaign, Clinton put a tax break in your middle-class pocket. Now he's picked it.

In the campaign, he talked of an executive order supporting gays in the military. Now, he's in favor of having someone explore a directive.

In a story, he said he favored normalizing relations with Iraq instead of blasting away to no end. Now, he says he was misunderstood.

On those issues, if you're looking for a silver lining, the main difference between President Bush and Clinton is that Clinton has the good sense not to say "Read my lips" before turning flips.

Not to mention, he has an eye for talent. And I'm talking here about building the New Beginnings, New Hope team of professionals.

Such as Attorney General-elect Zoe Baird, who hired illegal immigrants as servants two years ago. And didn't pay Social Security taxes on them until, coincidentally, this month.

Attorney general.

Stop me before I'm forced to say I'm not making this up.

Because I might recall that Clinton's secretary of state-designate has been accused of lying about Army spying. Or that the People President's first hire, for chief of staff, is a millionaire gas man.

Then you have Commerce Secretary-designate Ron Brown, whose law firm represented the corrupt Haitians. That was nothing. Last week, Brown couldn't figure out why he had to cancel the "Friends of Ron Brown" gala that would have been bankrolled by the corporate giants his decisions will affect.

Clinton had to pull him aside and explain. Afterward, a Clinton flack praised Brown for doing "the admirable thing by removing even the appearance of a conflict." And then, presumably, she went back to helping plan Bill Clinton's $30 million, corporate-sponsored inaugural bash.

General Electric. Merrill Lynch. Shell. Coca-Cola. Nearly 200 corporations put up $100,000 apiece.

They're crazy about politics.

Clinton rewarded the man who collected their money by naming him White House political director.

Organizers are charging $15,000 a ticket for dinner, $25,000 for the entertainment. The Ritz-Carlton offered a four-day, $23,000 Premiere Presidential Package that included use of a Bentley. It sold out.

It's nothing but high rollers and stretch limos all over town.

Hillary Clinton, keeping the memory of Nancy Reagan alive, found a designer who's making her a special gown for the ball.

Hillary's brothers, meanwhile, asked the likes of Ford and Chevron for $10,000 a pop for skybox seats at one of the soirées. One of them told The Wall Street Journal, "I don't see any conflict. It's no big deal."

All Billy Carter did was drink beer.

New Beginnings. New Hope.

This is reform?

Like I say, it's too early to judge Clinton. About 500,000 people, 400,000 of them band members, will party in Washington this week. I say we watch and we wait.

If they all hold hands on the Mall and sing "We Are the World," or if anybody films a soft drink or car commercial, I say we start with the impeachment.

IT'S A WHOPPER OF
ANOTHER KIND

January 22, 1992

As busy as we all are, especially in these tough times, it's hard to stay on top of the news. And so every once in a while, an important development slips by without much notice.

That appears to have been the case with a story that broke Friday, so I thought I'd go back over it. Especially since it was about a possible turnaround in the sluggish economy.

As it happens, Vice President Dan Quayle was in Southern California to play golf in the Bob Hope Desert Classic. But there's more to the job of being vice president than official business night and day.

So Quayle was just driving around to kill time before the celebrity phase of the tournament. And there he was, cruising down the highway in his vice presidential motorcade, when he alertly spotted a "Help Wanted" sign in the window of a Burger King.

According to the Associated Press, Quayle took swift action, ordering the motorcade to a halt. That sign tells you something, he explained. It tells you the economy may be ready to make a comeback.

The vice president then walked into the Burger King to see if it was true. And indeed, it was. There's work, after all, for America.

At four bucks an hour.

"Don't give up hope," Quayle later advised the nation's millions of unemployed.

Outside the Burger King, Quayle hopped back into his limo and went to a Lockheed Corp. plant, where he criticized Democratic proposals to slash the Pentagon budget.

And, bright and early the next day, he fired a few missiles off the tee at the Bermuda Dunes Country Club, where his partners were a couple of whoppers from way back. Bob Hope and former President Gerald Ford.

Well, that would be the end of the story, except that I made a few calls out West, encouraged as I was by evidence of the economic recovery.

And sure enough, it turns out Quayle's prediction was right on the money. Terie Roeder, manager of the Norco Burger King, said business was booming because people were coming in to ask if Quayle had really been there.

While speaking to Roeder, I recalled that Quayle visited a Burger King in

New Hampshire a week earlier. And so it could be that President Bush's economic recovery plan is to send Quayle to a different junk-food restaurant each week.

If he doesn't mind some personal advice, I'd like to suggest the Taco Bell chain next, in the interest of diversity, although they don't give out those little cardboard crowns like Burger King.

Roeder, by the way, said she would have given Quayle a free burger, but her flame broiler was broken.

"I told the vice president the positions started at $4.25, and there's room to grow," Roeder said.

In a couple of years, you could be up to five, six bucks an hour.

Or maybe get into management, although Roeder says you still can't buy a house "or feed a family of five," even on a manager's salary.

Holly Smith, 23, was one of the lucky employees who met Quayle at the Burger King in California.

"He shook my hand."

Flipping burgers, Smith said, helps her squeak by. Her husband, a carpenter, got hurt on the job and has a few more weeks of disability pay. But after that, it looks bleak. Her husband's dad, also a carpenter, just got laid off.

"We've never been well off, but we've really had to cut back," said Smith, who has a 16-month-old son. "We've eliminated going out, and just try to pay the bills."

I'm not sure, but it could simply be a matter of location. Down the road a ways, in the direction of Palm Springs, people seem to be living a bit more comfortably. For instance, a single round of golf at Bermuda Dunes, according to clubhouse staffer Cheryl Blatt, costs $65.

I'm not sure if Holly Smith likes to tee it up, but if so, that's about three days of work at Burger King, after taxes. Or, figuring she serves maybe 50 burgers an hour, a round of golf costs 1,200 whoppers.

But that's if she plays as the guest of a member. If she wants to join, that's another sandwich altogether.

"The monthly dues are $300," Blatt says. But that's only after you buy a membership.

And the going rate is $42,000.

If Holly Smith worked full-time at $4.25 an hour, she'd make $8,840 a year. And so in just five years, she could be closing in on the American Dream.

But the best part is, as a personal acquaintance of Dan Quayle, Smith would probably be knocking it around with the likes of Gerald Ford, George Bush, maybe even Pat Sajak.

Is this a great country or what?

TEATIME IN IRAQ

May 1, 1991

Amadiyah, Iraq—Nobody said it would be easy to get to Saddam Hussein's summer palace.

The directions go pretty much like this:

Go into Iraq from Turkey, head east past the American military camp, keep going when you get to the British marines, turn right at the *peshmerga* rebel checkpoint, and then try to talk your way past the Iraqi soldiers.

Maybe they'll be in a good mood.

If so, you'll see Hussein's Hideaway past his private airport, up on a bluff overlooking a beautiful valley.

OK. So you get in the car and go.

Heading out of Zakho, you see the American camp. And about 20 miles later, you see the British marines. They tell you they are the last line of the coalition forces, but it should be safe to continue.

They say the Iraqi army seemed to have retreated south of the area of the palace, as it has agreed to do. And they say they doubt that the Iraqis left many land mines in the area.

OK.

Now the road isn't so good all of a sudden. It's dirt and rocks much of the way. But it winds through a velvety green stretch of rolling hills that are framed for miles by sharp mountain peaks. Saddam has pretty good taste in real estate.

You cross a bridge, veer right, and there are the *peshmergas*.

Five of them.

Its hard to believe that this ragtag gang of Kurds fought the Iraqi army. The *peshmergas* don't have uniforms, so they all show up for work with whatever they happen to be wearing. Three of these guys are wearing sneakers.

Their machine guns are a collection of used parts. Grenades are clipped to their belts. One man of about 50 has a rocket launcher strapped to his back, and it looks like a spear.

For their checkpoint station, the *peshmergas* are using a white and orange car that's been stripped and gutted. They're out here in the middle of nowhere, guarding a road that few people seem to have any interest in using.

And they seem pretty happy to see you. The road is OK up ahead, they say, waving goodbye.

Now you're 50 miles or so down the road. No Iraqi soldiers yet.

You pass little Kurdish villages that are deserted. Saddam Hussein has turned northern Iraq into one big ghost town.

You pass a field where heavy artillery shells are stacked on the ground like fat loaves of bologna at the deli counter. They're just sitting out there, without explaining themselves, available to anyone who gets an urge to blow up something.

The road is a little better now and you're zipping along, anxious to see the palace.

And there it is.

A hilltop chateau, with red tile roof and a view of the private landing strip. It's not a castle. But it's at least a mansion.

At the bottom of the hill, the villa is surrounded by a concrete security wall. It's about 12 feet high.

You drive around looking for the gate, wondering what kind of opulence you're going to find when you rummage through Saddam Hussein's personal belongings. And just when you come upon the gate, you have company.

Three Iraqi soldiers are guarding the entrance. The British must have missed these guys.

The Iraqis are holding machine guns. They motion for you to stop. They walk toward your car.

Now a couple more soldiers appear. And a few more.

You step out of the car to talk to them. Ten Iraqi soldiers are now facing you in a semicircle. They are armed. Up on the grounds of the chateau, you notice many more soldiers.

Your country was just at war with these people and practically annihilated them. And now they're asking you where you're from.

You look down and kind of mumble into your chest.

Amrca.

Ahhhhh, they say, looking at each other.

AMERICA.

They don't seem upset. They just seem curious about the whole thing. And they don't appear to have been ready for company.

Two of them are wearing flip-flops. Even the *peshmerga* had sneakers. One guy's shirt isn't tucked in. This doesn't look like the elite Republican Guard.

They're repeating the word to each other. America.

The guy who seems to be in charge steps forward. A question forms on his lips.

"CIA?" he asks.

Nononono. CIA? No way. You laugh.

They laugh.

Then they say:

"Saddam Hussein good?"

Right about now you notice the clinking noise under your feet. You're standing on hundreds of empty shells from machine gun bullets. You notice that the building across the street has been shot up pretty good.

You pretend you don't understand their English. They repeat the question.

"Saddam Hussein good?"

Well, you know, Saddam is, well, he's probably misunderstood, but yeah, in general, well, of course he's good. Yeah. Certainly.

Saddam Hussein good.

Correct answer.

They offer you Monte Carlo cigarettes. They want to shake your hand.

They seem to realize they lost the war in a big way and are now at the mercy of outside forces. They say they'll probably be leaving this area soon, and moving south.

But they still seem to have a fair amount of pride left, and they're holding on dearly to their last shreds of authority before they're forced to retreat from their own land.

They say you cannot go up to the palace. It's not Hussein's summer palace anyway, they say, getting a little firmer now. It's owned by some rich guy who just happened to throw up a concrete wall around it and hire a bunch of soldiers.

OK.

One guy says, well, yeah, it sorta is Hussein's hideaway. But Saddam is in Baghdad and these housesitters are not taking in guests.

Come back in a week or so, they say, and we'll probably be gone.

So you get back in the car, give them a wave and a smile, and drive around a little. Actually, there are a few more mansions around here. Some other Iraqi soldiers tell you that all of them belong to Saddam Hussein. One soldier pointed out a mansion high on a mountaintop that looked even more spectacular than the first one. But they wouldn't let you near the place.

On the way back to Turkey, you pass the gate of the first mansion. The same soldiers are out there, and they actually seem glad to see you again. So glad that they invite you in for a spot of tea.

OK. These are not guys you want to turn down.

They lead you into a trailer. It looks like a college dorm room. There's a sign on the door in Arabic. It says for Kurds to keep out, one soldier translates.

There are two beds. The soldiers want you to sit down on them. Seven of them have pushed into this small room. Just to watch this meeting with the Americans.

The Iraqis proudly hand over glasses of fresh-brewed tea. They want to know how you like it.

Damn good tea.

Over one bed, a photo of Saddam Hussein is taped to the headboard. Next to it is a photo of a blond starlet.

"I want to go to Hollywood," one soldier says.

Another one says he likes Madonna.

You mean her music or her looks? "Her looks," he says.

Another soldier says:

"I like Jackson Michael."

His buddies laugh.

"Oh," he says. "Michael Jackson."

You decide not to ask whether he means music or looks.

While this international summit continues, two American jets fly overhead.

Through the open door, you can see them streak by. The Iraqi soldiers say they can identify them now by the sound. F-16s, A-10s, whatever.

"Americans killed many Iraqis in the war," one soldier says.

They want to know if George Bush is finished politically because of the slaughter.

He seems to be doing OK in the opinion polls, you answer. They ask whatever happened to Jimmy Carter. You have a little trouble explaining that now he builds houses for the poor.

"Iraqi people have good hearts. They love everybody," one soldier says.

The warm feelings do not appear to extend to the Kurds. Kurds are cockroaches, one soldier says.

"If *peshmerga* come here now, I would kill them," he says.

One soldier now pulls the photo of Saddam Hussein off the wall.

He kisses it.

"Saddam Hussein good," he says, looking into the eyes of his visitors.

"Saddam hero," says another, doing the same.

They appear to be waiting for nods of approval.

Saddam good, you say. Iraqi tea, very good.

ANOTHER VIEW OF A WAR

June 11, 1991

"**M**y TV is on the fritz," Marjorie Zaun was saying from her home in Cherry Hill.

And so, no, she didn't watch yesterday's ticker-tape parade in New York honoring veterans of the Persian Gulf war. Nor did she catch coverage of Saturday's parade in Washington, in which military hardware took the place of traditional floats. No TV then, either.

But even if it were working, she doubts she would have tuned in.

The mother of Lt. Jeffrey Zaun, a Navy flier who was shot down and captured in Iraq and became a reluctant national celebrity, isn't sure we ought to be celebrating.

"I think we're glorifying war," she said.

Marjorie Zaun makes it clear that she has nothing but respect for those who put their lives on the line. And she has nothing against anyone who wants to celebrate, especially if they do so out of support for the troops.

She just says that for her, it's not as simple as good and bad, right and wrong, winning and losing.

"It's much more complex."

She says that as America celebrates, she can't help but think of all the Iraqis who were killed, and the suffering that continues to this day. Who knows how many? One hundred thousand? Two hundred thousand?

"I know there are Iraqi mothers who loved their child as much as I love Jeff, and it's painful. A lot of innocent people who weren't for Saddam Hussein had to pay a price for what he did."

Marjorie Zaun was speaking on the same day a story was published out of Nevada, where her son is in training. Jeffrey Zaun, who earlier had said he wore his hero badge uncomfortably, now had this to say:

"I don't ever want to kill anybody again. This country didn't get to see the cost of the war. I did. People think, `Hey, we went in there and just kicked ass,' but they didn't see the Iraqi mothers get killed."

The parade in New York was said to be the largest in the city's history. An estimated 4.7 million people watched 24,000 marchers. This was much larger than the parade in Washington, which cost the Pentagon about $7 million.

Though it was reminiscent of World War II glory, the majority of gulf soldiers never fired a shot or even saw the enemy in the 100-hour ground war. It wasn't a contest of bravery or will, but of technology.

In all the jubilation and flag-waving, there did not seem to be much concern about the fact that Saddam Hussein remains in power. Or that he may still have nuclear bombs. Or that the Middle East is no more stable than it was before the war.

In fact, even as America threw itself a party in New York, Saddam Hussein's army reportedly launched raids on hundreds of thousands of fugitives trapped in southeast Iraq.

At roughly the same time, there was news in Kuwait, the country America liberated. A martial-law court handed out a 15-year prison sentence to a man suspected of transporting explosives, even though there were no witnesses against him.

Human-rights groups say hundreds of suspected Iraqi collaborators are being sentenced in Kuwait without ever seeing their accusers.

In Cherry Hill, Marjorie Zaun said she isn't so sure the Kuwaiti treatment of Iraqis is any better than was the Iraqi treatment of Kuwaitis. And she said that she and her son were troubled by the fate of Iraqi Kurds.

The Kurds, who seem a more democratic people than the Kuwaitis, were encouraged by President Bush to rebel against Hussein.

But it was suicide. They were bombed out of their villages, and, while the United States looked the other way, forced to run.

Thousands did not make it.

Lots of children, for instance. On the Turkish border was a camp called Isikveren. Every morning, tiny graves were dug.

One day a 45-year-old man died in his tent, his wife and six children at his side. He was taken to the cemetery and buried next to his 3-year-old daughter. When he was laid in the hole, his family covered him with flattened-out boxes that once held pre-fab meals made for American soldiers who fought in the gulf war.

Marjorie Zaun said she is proud of her son for being torn by this war and being honest with his feelings.

She isn't convinced we had to go to war. It bothers her that it was such a mismatch. And she can't celebrate while so much suffering continues.

"There have just been too many people that have died," she was saying as the parade moved through Manhattan, an American spectacle decorated with 12 million pounds of confetti, 200 miles of ticker tape.

And one million yellow ribbons.

THE FAMILY ON THE FOURTH

========= *July 13, 1989* =========

My vacation began with oil gushing into the Delaware and ended with Ronald Reagan announcing baseball's All-Star Game on NBC.

The full damage may not be known for years.

In between I went to California. Attendance is not mandatory at the Lopez Family Annual Fourth of July Picnic, but they talk about you if you're not there. They also talk about you if you are there, but you can at least defend yourself.

This year's picnic presented a couple of moral dilemmas for our family. Two of the rituals violate, or threaten to violate, federal law.

One involves lawn darts. The other involves fireworks and the flag.

Lawn darts are about a foot long, blunt-tipped, with plastic fins. You set white plastic rings on the grass and try to toss the darts into the rings. They're perfectly safe if you're careful. But in 10 years, three people have been killed by lawn darts.

Not at our picnic. In the country.

And so before leaving office, President Reagan, at the behest of the Consumer Product Safety Commission, signed legislation banning the sale of lawn darts.

I don't know whether our lawn darts were purchased prior to the ban and are therefore legal. Or if we're supposed to turn them in immediately to avoid prosecution.

There was some talk at our picnic of switching to another sport. Something approved by the President, Congress, and the Consumer Product Safety Commission. I mean, we could have shot up some targets with semiautomatic rifles.

But only if they were made in this country. President Bush banned the foreign ones. As far as I know, Reagan's lawn-dart ban applies to both domestic and imported lawn darts.

We decided to take our chances with the lawn darts and scheduled a tournament for immediately after the fireworks display, which was our other problem.

My father always flies a flag in his back yard for the picnic. He also puts on a fireworks display.

Fireworks are illegal, I confess. On top of that, my father has a little problem with fire. I mean, you wouldn't want him and Mayor Goode at the same barbecue.

It's not that fire always gets out of control. It's that whatever my dad wants fire to do, fire does the opposite. My brother says that to snuff out the annual forest fires that scorch California, "They should send Dad there to barbecue hamburgers."

On the Fourth of July, my dad frequently holds a firework in one hand and a garden hose in the other. And I think it should be noted that the fireworks display takes place not far from the flag.

Being on vacation, I didn't follow the news carefully. But I gathered that President Bush—to beat back a tide of anti-patriotism that involved I think two flag burnings—wanted to make it illegal to burn the flag, despite the Supreme Court ruling. Support for that idea swept the nation.

So there we were. Independence Day. Stars and stripes. And Dad with several dozen small explosives.

Like I say, I wasn't following the news closely, so maybe I was confusing Supreme Court stories. But I feared that my dad could be executed for burning the flag if he happened to be a minor and/or retarded.

Fortunately, the fireworks display proceeded without major incident, though there was one scary moment. One firework was supposed to dance around, dangling from a tree by a string, and spin a happy rainbow of colorful sparks. Instead it sort of fizzed and spit lazy embers in the direction of, yes, the flag.

"Mr. Lopez," I imagined the prosecutor barking at my dad in court, "isn't it true that on Independence Day, you not only torched the American flag with illegal fireworks, but you later played lawn darts?"

Fortunately, the flag was unharmed, and nobody died playing lawn darts.

Later in the week we spent a day on San Francisco Bay, which is being polluted because the federal government has thousands of troops stationed all over the world, but not a single federal agent enforcing pollution laws on one of the most beautiful waterways in this country.

I was a little hot about that as I flew home, reading of the $2 billion Reagan administration HUD scandal that took place about the time of the Iran-Contra scandal, while Reagan was signing lawn-dart legislation.

Well, baseball has always been an escape for me. So I turned on the All-Star Game. The guest announcer—I have no idea why—was Reagan. He wanted to know how to pronounce the J in Julio Franco.

And I felt good for having played lawn darts.

DECADES OF MURDER

September 19, 1991

M OSCOW—She is 64 and wears wire-rim glasses low on her nose. She walks anonymously, with shoulders rounded and white hair pulled back.

And she takes the subway to the KGB.

Tamara Popova has lost count of the number of times she's made this trip from home. In the six weeks since she started the routine, it has to be 15, maybe 20 visits.

Popova doesn't go in the front door, from where you can see the stump that was left when the statue of the KGB's founder was ripped from its pedestal in a forever-frozen moment of history.

She enters from a less imposing back street, lined by markets. It is the door known to Muscovites as the place you could always go, 24 hours a day, to dump on your neighbor, rat on your boss, earn someone a ticket to Siberia.

But not anymore. The door you once walked through to give people up is now the door you walk through to find out what the KGB did with them.

Though the disappearances of people in the Stalin era were never who-dunits, nobody expected this.

The KGB isn't just confessing to decades of murder. It's providing the evidence.

The man who runs the reception office, Colonel Edward Kucheryavenko, says it now exists to clear the names of "those persons who were unlawfully persecuted." And to provide access to "those who want to find the graves of their relatives."

And that is why Tamara Popova and all the others come. They come to pore over record books brought up from the archives and retrace the steps of loved ones swept away in the night.

You have to arrange these meetings by written request, and sometimes the KGB is not all that cooperative, Popova says. But it seems to be getting easier. When you come in, they direct you to a small room and leave you there with the records.

Popova comes often because 20 of her relatives were arrested between 1917 and 1937. Her family was hounded because her grandfather's brother, Yuli Martov, one of Lenin's revolutionary allies, left the country after a split with Lenin.

As Popova begins to tell her story, a woman's cries can be heard down the hallway. Popova ignores it. She says she has heard others cry before.

The woman's wailing is closer now, and she appears in the lobby. Still weeping, she is escorted out of the office and into the falling rain.

A lot of people come in knowing nothing, Popova says, and leave knowing a loved one was shot.

"Maybe she just found out," she says.

Popova already had the outline of her family's story, and began coming here just to confirm hunches and fill in gaps.

"I had no precise information about who was killed and how," she says.

She didn't know the details, for instance, of her father's fate. It used to be that if the KGB provided a death certificate, a dash would be in the place where the cause of death should be. Not long ago, she found out about her father.

"He was shot," she says.

"He was 30."

It was just several weeks ago that she found the details. She says he was shot very close to where she now sits.

Under the KGB buildings are underground cells, where the air still holds the cries and gasps of countless victims. Her father's last breath is down there.

She has seen the statement, she says, of the man who shot her father and then signed the file.

The last time she saw him was 1935. She was 7 when they took him one night. She is told that the next morning she had a streak of gray hair, and it stayed through her childhood.

She smiles at the memory of her father, who read books, played chess, and took her skiing and skating.

That same year, she saw her mother for the last time. She later died in exile. Popova remembers her mother as more serious, but singing a lot. Both parents were economists.

Popova says her own life was saved by the wife of Lenin, who was loyal to the Martov family. Lenin's wife arranged for her to be raised under an assumed name in Moscow, by a good family.

And it was a good family, she says. She grew up wanting to be a doctor, but Moscow State University would have studied her family history before admitting her. She couldn't risk that, so she became a botanist.

Always, she wanted to know more about her past. It was Mikhail Gorbachev's changes, she says, that make it possible for her to now visit the KGB.

Sometimes, you have to look for hours to find details like those about her father's murder. The information is scattered, and to find records of your own family is like walking through a cemetery in search of a particular gravestone.

But she already knows plenty.

She says 10 of her 20 relatives were murdered.

Her grandfather. Her grandmother. Her grandfather's brother. Two aunts. Two uncles. Two sons of her grandfather's sister.

Her father.

Two more died in camps. The other eight all died in exile.

She knows there were beatings. She knows that an aunt was kept for days

210

in an underground tank so narrow she couldn't sit. The torture squads would then slowly fill the tank with water, up to her throat, drain it, and fill it again. First hot water, then cold, then hot, then cold again.

For all 20 relatives, she has now collected "rehabilitation" certificates. This means the KGB has admitted that the charges against them were trumped up.

She keeps them in a drawer at home.

Only once, while telling this, does Popova lose her grip. She stares at a wall and says it's too hard sometimes, these long sessions at the KGB.

But she knows she has to be here, out of a sense of obligation to her family, and because not knowing is a torture all its own.

"I don't allow myself to let anything happen here," she says.

Not in this office where the sons of the KGB men who might have tortured her family now hand her the evidence. She has already imagined and been told all the worst, anyway, so there are no shocks here.

Not until she gets home does she let her courage soften. Sometimes she will feel it in her chest, and take medicine for her heart. Her husband, who has no such history as this, will comfort her.

As she tells her story, she frequently smiles. It is a crazy smile, given the context, but the craziness is not hers.

It is the mark left by those who would inflict so much suffering and misery on innocent people. The crazed smile of surrender to the world's insanity.

Tamara Popova takes the subway to the KGB, and she takes the subway home, the pain of not knowing replaced by the pain of knowing too much.

ROSS PEROT
DOWN THE SHORE

September 27, 1992

This summer at the Jersey Shore, I played one of those boardwalk games where they give you a padded hammer to whack these little heads that keep popping up out of holes.

Maybe a dozen of these little mutants spring up like bald-headed gophers, and you have to be quick, because they keep ducking back into their holes like cowards.

I don't think it developed into a problem, really, but I would generally play up to six hours at a time.

That's not a problem, is it?

Anyhow, it got more intense when I realized whom the gophers resembled. H. Ross Perot.

A period of therapy followed my trip to the Shore, and I was OK. Until last week. Last week was bad.

Every time I opened a newspaper or turned on the TV, there he was. That little head popping up.

This happened in a crowded restaurant at one point, and I beat Ross senseless with a baguette.

It's nothing personal. I really like the idea of a double-talking billionaire waking up from a nap, pulling the knot on his tie, and volunteering to save us from ourselves.

If Ross gets back into the race, he says it's because George Bush and Bill Clinton aren't dealing honestly with our biggest problem—the economy. And before I reach for the hammer, I'd like to say something.

He's right.

In fact, it's the big lie of the campaign. We've got a federal deficit, folks, of about $350 billion, or roughly the amount that's slipped into the crevices of Perot's sofa. We have a national debt of $4 trillion. We have millions of people in poverty and millions out of work.

And neither candidate has an honest plan to chop the deficit or create jobs, which are related, in part.

Let me put this in perspective. Let's say you make $65,000 a year. This isn't bad, right? Not until you realize that you spent $100,000. Before you know it, you've got to lay off two kids and fire the dog.

The federal government, however, just keeps spending, as if it can print money on machines or something. Then one day one of our great leaders decides there's only one way politicians can control themselves.

By constitutional amendment.

That's right. A law that says they can't spend more than they have. Plus they have to be in bed by 10 and not leave their dirty socks out.

Which they should never have added to the bill because the whole thing went down in flames.

Between Clinton and Bush, Clinton has the better plan. But he still speaks in generalities, exaggerates administrative cost-cutting, and looks bad in running shorts.

In defense of President Bush, he at least has an interesting approach.

Basically, he wings around the country telling everybody he is in favor of that constitutional amendment, because we have to control impulsive spending. And when everybody stops cheering, he opens a big bag and throws money to them.

This makes it easy to understand why the Republican campaign is content to spend so much time (A) talking about draft dodging, and (B) trashing that slut Murphy Brown.

What Bush and Clinton don't have the stones for, of course, is telling people the truth. Not only is the party over, but everyone has to chip in to cover the tab.

Which brings us back to Perot.

You will recall that when he was in the race, Perot had legions of loyal followers, not a one of whom was bent over double with intellect. I mean, I thought everybody was fed up with obscenely self-important politicians who either side-stepped questions or just plain lied, who spoke in generalities, and who were filthy rich and well-connected.

Ross Perot was all of those things, and yet thousands of people were pinning buttons on themselves and slapping bumper stickers on their cars because he babbled about things like balancing the budget without breaking a sweat.

He was a bigger liar than Bush or Clinton. Only after he left the race did he talk about the sacrifices people would have to make, and he said he quit because he didn't think anyone wanted to hear the truth.

Well, they don't. And it's largely because of bozos like him and Ronald Reagan and George Bush telling them only what they want to hear.

If the candidates aren't dealing with the issues, Ross Perot is part of the reason, not part of the solution. And if he wants to do a service, he ought to tell people what dupes they were to blindly support him, and he ought to suggest that they demand more of Bush and Clinton.

And then he ought to duck back into his hole before the hammer drops.

A SUPREME SOAP OPERA

Y ou almost had to remind yourself what was happening.

Here's a nominee for Supreme Court justice of the United States of America, answering allegations that while he was head of the Equal Employment Opportunity Commission he talked about pubic hair on Coke cans, large genitals, and animal sex.

Here's an angry President Bush standing by his man, wondering what happened, as the nation's women circle his can't-miss conservative black candidate.

Here's the all-guy, coat-and-tie U.S. Senate Judiciary Committee, having blown its responsibility to check the allegations thoroughly, trying belatedly and awkwardly now to do the right thing. More for their own political futures than anything else.

This is a committee that includes Sen. Ted Kennedy, who left a woman to drown after plunging off a bridge.

And Sen. Strom Thurmond, who rose to power as a redneck segregationist crocodile.

And Sen. Dennis DeConcini, one of the Keating Five.

And Sen. Joseph Biden, who stole a speech.

And Sens. Alan Simpson and Orrin Hatch, a couple of reptiles from way back.

And Sen. Arlen Specter, moving with a chuckle from the subject of large penises to a subject he said he was sure everyone would be more comfortable with—large breasts.

On national television. With half the country glued to the tube.

Who needs Phil Donahue?

And while it was absurd theater on many levels, almost laughable once or twice, mostly it was sad.

Pathetically sad.

Here was Clarence Thomas, a judge of great pride and poise, defending himself against this X-rated humiliation. His wife looked shattered.

Here was Anita Hill, a law professor of great pride and poise, saying that Thomas harassed her in the weirdest ways in the very office where he allegedly led the fight to overcome such things.

And TV was the perfect forum for reducing two people of great promise to freakish subjects of national gossip, stealing their privacy forever, and leaving the country to wonder which one is lying.

Thomas called it "a high-tech lynching for uppity blacks." And while he is

214

entitled to phrases of exaggeration and drama, I would remind Mr. Thomas that, first of all, his two major accusers are black.

And that the senators you would most naturally associate with figurative lynchings are his chief supporters.

For Thomas to be telling the truth, Anita Hill has to be a complete loon. She didn't strike me that way. I could be wrong, but I saw courage and conviction and a lot of composure as she answered the same painful questions over and over. And I don't think Thomas served himself well by saying he didn't even watch her testimony.

But then, I think he's lying.

I don't think you invent the details Hill testified to. I don't think you put yourself on the line on national television, with your elderly parents sitting behind you, and talk about Coke cans and Long Dong Silver.

And it isn't easy to explain why another woman, Angela Wright, would fabricate a similar story.

So why would Clarence Thomas deny every detail, rather than argue that it was a matter of perception?

Because he's telling the truth. Or because he wants to save himself.

Or because he got so caught up in his own rags-to-Republican myth—even though he was a modest judicial talent with a strange history of contradictions—that he considered himself invincible.

And yes, he was a modest, marginal nominee chosen more for his politics than his record, so it's a little hollow now to hear him lash out against the politics of this hearing.

But regardless of what happens to him, there are some lessons here.

This is not about sex so much as power. President Bush didn't get that, the Senate didn't get it, and most of this country's guys haven't figured it out.

You can't have men control all the power, in government or business, and be fair to women at the same time. There is no woman on the Senate Judiciary Committee. If there were, this circus would not have taken place.

The other thing to understand is that the ground rules in relationships between the sexes keep changing. What used to be tolerated is no longer appropriate.

It's entirely conceivable that 10 years ago, Anita Hill felt she had to keep her mouth shut or get buried professionally. One message of this hearing is that those days are over.

HAITI AND NORTH PHILLY

September 28, 1994

The way I understand it, there were a number of reasons the United States put 15,000 troops on boats, planes, and choppers and sent them on an all-expenses-paid trip to the Caribbean nation of Haiti last week.

First and foremost, to restore the kind of life people are entitled to under a democracy.

Haiti, it seems, is a violent, chaotic place where elections are stolen and the laws on the books mean little or nothing because armed thugs rule the streets like gang members. That's why the very name of the mission is Operation Uphold Democracy.

If you've followed the news at all, you know that many Haitians live in poverty because the economy is a shambles, and they live in fear because of police brutality and the dangers posed by warring factions who are armed to the teeth.

Our military exercise is not meant, however, at least as far as I or President Clinton can tell at the moment, as a shoot-'em-up. It is more of a mercy mission, designed to restore order, put duly elected President Aristide in power, and assist Haiti's poor and oppressed.

All of which is extremely good-hearted, as the $1 billion American tab, so far, will attest. And all of which raises an obvious question.

Why doesn't the U.S. invade North Philadelphia?

Why doesn't it invade the South Bronx, South Central L.A., Miami, Detroit, Washington, and Chicago?

In Philadelphia, the Second State Senate District to be precise, there's even an election parallel that makes you wonder if the Haitians sent their election officials and politicians to Philadelphia for training.

The federal courts, you'll recall, threw the so-called winner out of office because of his party's widespread fraud, which included the hoodwinking of poor Hispanics.

Unfortunately, it took forever to get the job done, whereas if President Clinton had called it Operation Uphold Domestic Democracy and sent in troops, we could have been back in business a lot quicker.

Although the opportunity has been missed, there are still as many reasons to land in Philadelphia as in Haiti. For one thing, I'd like to see a weapons buyback program here like the one the U.S. military is running in Haiti. It didn't work all that well in America, but maybe that's because we didn't offer nearly as much cold cash as we're offering the Haitians.

It's $100 for semis, $200 for automatics and $300 for machine guns.

In America, where guns kill 25,000 people a year, we offered free pizzas.

My thinking is that the U.S. could park the aircraft carrier on the Delaware under the Betsy Ross Bridge, or maybe the Ben Franklin. Then they could bring soldiers ashore at Penn Treaty Park in amphibious vehicles and drop paratroopers directly into the area police call the Badlands.

It is an area where chaos rules, a drug trade is the only economy, the infant-mortality rate ranks with those of Third World nations, and decent people lie trapped, cowering in poverty and fear.

As for warring factions, we've got the gangs killing each other and any-body who happens to get in the way, an occasional case of police brutality, and the kind of ugliness that led Friday to the beating of a deaf black woman and her son by five idiot whites who clubbed their way into her house with base-ball bats.

I say we go in now and we go in strong.

It's true, the Delaware isn't quite as sexy and exotic a locale as the Caribbean. And it's a lot easier to lend a hand to somebody else's problems than to acknowledge your own.

But it's hard to get beyond the parallels. Just take a look at the scene sent back home by The Inquirer's Mike Ruane, who landed in Port-au-Prince with the 3,000 men of Bravo company to find an injured boy:

"From the soccer field, where they would minister to the boy, to the exotic, poverty-stricken boulevards where they were almost engulfed by joyous Haitians, Bravo company set about the business of U.S. foreign policy.

"And things got pretty basic: They treated the little boy, who, it turned out, may have been trampled. They waded through frighteningly huge crowds with a kind of cool apprehension. And they saved a man who was being beaten by a mob, before vanishing in clouds of rotor dust."

Bring Bravo company home. Yes, it's a dangerous mission. But that never stopped us overseas.

DEATH ON A PATIO

August 19, 1992

SLAVONSKI BROD, Croatia—The Manjaric family always had a thing for their backyard patio, where the light played softly off the white-stucco house with the red-tile roof.

Josip, an electrician, and his wife Vdenka, a math teacher, would sit out with their two sons and play cards, have a drink, share a meal. It was walled in by other buildings and had the feel of a miniature plaza, the perfect space for modest lives and simple dreams.

And so when the shelling eased up the other day, the sons, Hrvoje, 20, and Branimir, 18, inseparable from the time they could pronounce each other's names, went out on the patio for some fresh air.

That's what people do all over this town, which has been hammered for more than two weeks with heavy shelling by Serbian forces pressing up from northern Bosnia. Nobody stays out very long or wanders too far, but every so often the spirit has to leave its prison, if only for a moment.

A typical day brings more than 100 mortar shells on the town, which had about 100,000 residents until half of them cleared out. For those who remain, sirens scream over the neighborhoods, and then it's one blast of thunder after another, bombs spinning down randomly on a city of unarmed and defenseless civilians.

"You better come in now," Vdenka called to her sons when the bombs sounded as though they were moving closer to their part of town.

A friend of Hrvoje and Branimir had just been out on the patio with them, saying hello and goodbye. He was on weekend leave from the Croatian army and had to report back.

Hrvoje got out of the army back in May, and had been working as an auto mechanic. He and his father had fought side-by-side, in fact, for the 157th Brigade, going into battle together and returning home within a week of each other. Branimir was planning to join up as soon as he was old enough.

Although Josip and Hrvoje respected the shells that fell on their town, shells that kill and maim more people every day, it was hard for them to imagine that harm could come to them at home after they survived the front line.

And so Hrvoje and Branimir probably felt protected, somehow, in the privacy of their patio, even as the shells fell a few blocks away.

Josip was in the kitchen, watching television. Vdenka, who wasn't feeling well, was lying on the sofa next to her husband, hoping the boys would hurry up and get back inside, where they'd have at least a bit of protection.

Sometimes the bombs give you a warning of maybe one or two seconds. If they're close, you can hear them whistling, and you might have time to dive for cover. Sometimes.

The next mortar shell into Slavonski Brod that day carried over the center of town and to the east. It passed dozens of open fields and hundreds of houses and thousands of people, and finally it caught the top of the garage in the Manjaric family's back yard, 15 feet from where Hrvoje and Branimir sat and chatted as they had countless times before.

The explosion shook the house with a horrible, deafening concussion. Josip and Vdenka jumped up and called for their sons, but there was no answer.

Josip ran to the back of the house and threw the door open. He couldn't see a thing because the patio was a cloud of dust. He called his sons again.

Nothing.

Josip threw himself into the cloud and reached blindly for his sons. When he had felt enough to know what was there, he went into the house and brought out a white bedsheet.

He laid it on the patio and went back into the dust and the rubble and brought out his sons.

Neighbors came to help, but Josip said nobody would do this job but the father of the boys. A doctor came, but he was of no use, except maybe to tend to Vdenka's shock.

Josip was meticulous. He put his sons back together the way they were supposed to be, as much as was possible, on the sheet. And then they were taken to the mortuary.

It is two days later now.

Photos of the brothers are tacked to the front gate of their house. Out back, on the patio, the light is still soft.

Three wreaths lie on the back patio under a brick wall scarred by the spray of shrapnel. Eight candles are placed around the wreaths. Family and friends, including several soldiers, come to the house to pay their respects. No one knows what to say.

The funeral will be in a few hours.

"Sometimes, when they stayed out too late and I got worried, I would go on foot looking for them," Vdenka is saying of her sons.

They liked to be with friends in cafés. If she didn't see them in one, she almost always saw one of her former math students, and they would tell her where to find Hrvoje and Branimir.

She shows pictures of them now. Hrvoje has frizzy, light-brown hair, and he's wearing a denim jacket. His expression is humorless. Branimir, with darker hair that falls over his forehead in bangs, is wearing a light-colored shirt with a dark-blue collar. He is smiling, and there's a twinkle in his eye.

As Vdenka speaks of her sons, the shelling continues, bombs falling within several blocks of their home. She reacts as if each explosion kills Hrvoje and Branimir again. Lying on the sofa and dressed in black, she turns to her side and groans. A niece cradles her head in her arms and blocks her ears.

"Oh God, help me," Vdenka prays.

Josip sits on the sofa and holds his wife's hand. When machine-gun fire erupts, his wife shakes. Don't worry, he tells her, it's antiaircraft fire, Croats shooting at Serbian planes.

"I have my son's army uniform in the closet," Josip says, his eyes red and hot. He repeats the words, speaking to everyone, but mostly to himself.

"I never thought Hrvoje would be killed in our own yard. If he had been killed in Bosnia, in battle, I wouldn't take it so hard. But here? In our back yard?"

He repeats this, too, as if he might be able to make sense of it by hearing it again.

"We didn't talk much in battle," he says. "We are both Croats, and we wanted to fight for our country because we love Croatia. If we were killed there, we would at least have had some chance to defend ourselves. Here, you get no chance. No chance to kill like a man before you are killed."

He raises his voice now.

"The Serbs will not put their feet on Croatian soil."

His tone and his words upset his wife.

"Don't talk like that," she pleads, crying.

"Why not?" he says. "I don't have anything anymore and I'm angry. I'm very angry."

In the chapel at the cemetery, the white caskets sit side by side, covered with wreaths. Branimir is on the left, Hrvoje on the right.

The local radio station warns townsfolk not to attend funerals, because the cemetery is near the Sava, and across the river, less than two miles away, is the front line. The enemy can see people gather, and shells have flown toward the cemetery during funerals past.

But people are coming on foot, on bicycle and by car for the burial of Hrvoje and Branimir Manjaric. More than 150 altogether, gathering in 90-degree heat under a sky that's clear but for a thin haze.

At precisely 4 p.m., a 10-piece municipal band in blue uniform begins playing traditional songs. At 4:01, as six soldiers carry each casket out of the chapel, a bomb hits the town.

At 4:02 another bomb hits, maybe a quarter of a mile away, and the general alert siren cries over the funeral, followed by the sound of machine guns.

Sweat soaks through the back of the saxophone player's shirt as the procession makes its way past dozens of new gravestones toward Hrvoje and Branimir's plots. Behind the caskets, a young couple are dressed as bride and groom, a custom symbolizing that the deceased had everything in front of them.

Halfway to the graves, two more bombs fall, one of them no more than a few hundred yards away, and Vdenka Manjaric collapses. Her husband and another man catch her before she goes all the way down, and they hoist her back up. She drags her feet along, holding on for support, her body drained of strength.

As the priest begins praying over the gravesites, the whistle of an approaching bomb can be heard. One hundred and fifty people duck for cover, some of them behind gravestones. The bomb carries over the cemetery and explodes in a field.

People pick themselves off the ground, disbelieving, assaulted by the limitless cruelty of human beings. Some turn away and head for home, their faces twisted in horror.

But most people stay. In defiance and in respect.

The next bomb whistles an even longer time and the whole assembly ducks for cover again. This one, like the last, carries beyond the cemetery.

Josip convulses, his emotions all knotted. Vdenka groans in pain.

The priest has not let any of the bombs interrupt his prayers. His voice and his bearing are steady.

Hrvoje and Branimir are lowered into the earth as the band plays the Croatian national anthem, and the bombing stops just long enough for Josip and Vdenka Manjaric to return to the home where they held such simple dreams.

ACROSS AN OCEAN,
NOTHING HAS CHANGED

August 6, 1989

LONDON—This is not a complaint or anything. I mean, I'm happy to be here, and looking forward to watching the Philadelphia Eagles play the Cleveland Browns today at Wembley Stadium.

But I started playing with some numbers and realized I made a mistake when I told you that Philadelphia and Pennsylvania public officials, who are lodging at the Ritz here, are paying $180 a night. I apologize for the misleading error.

It's more than $200 a night.

The Ritz, by the way, is across a park from Buckingham Palace.

The elegantly furnished rooms have mini-bars.

My hotel room is about $60 a night, including shower cap. It is across the street from Wimpy Burgers.

Now, for starters, it's not clear to me why 11 officials from the city, state, and Convention and Visitors Bureau need to be here, some of them with wives or husbands. They claim it's to promote tourism and investment.

The question is, in what city? Every time I see one of them they're talking about going to the theater, or Harrods, or the Tower of London.

They do attend an occasional social to sell Philadelphia as the land of heart's content. Ray Christman, Pennsylvania commerce director, says he has developed a dozen leads on businesses that might set up shop in Pennsylvania.

But if the Pennsylvanians were willing to do some investigating, their time could be much more productive.

Eleven-strong as they are, they could send out teams to find out why London, with five times the population of Philadelphia, has cleaner streets and parks and less graffiti. And why the London subway system, much larger than SEPTA's, is far cleaner and more efficient.

It seems to me that the best way to promote tourism in Philadelphia is to address those problems.

But let's get back to the question of why, at taxpayers' expense, the Philadelphia junket battalion should be at one of the world's fanciest hotels.

Tom Muldoon, president of the Philadelphia Convention and Visitors Bureau, said they got a discount through the Four Seasons in Philadelphia. I checked with several London hotels. They all said they offer group discounts.

To be fair, I decided I'd check on how much the Cleveland delegation is spending.

They're not at the Ritz. They're at a Holiday Inn on the outskirts of London. Rooms are $112 a night.

"We heard it was a decent hotel," said Carol Rivchun of the Cleveland Chamber of Commerce.

She said there were 25 people in the group. I asked how many were city or state employees.

"Only one. The mayor. The rest are business VIPs."

So Cleveland taxpayers are paying for only one person to be here?

"Actually they're paying zero. The Cleveland press was very aggressive about saying tax dollars shouldn't be spent here. The mayor's trip was sponsored by the business community."

I see.

On Friday I decided to pay a visit to the Ritz. I'm a resident of Philadelphia and I wanted to see exactly what my tax dollars were buying.

I had to take a subway from my hotel, of course, to get to the centrally located Ritz.

The hotel is an architectural marvel, sitting majestically on vibrant Piccadilly and rising over Green Park. I pushed through the revolving door, got maybe 10 feet inside, and a hotel attendant came after me.

"You can't be in the hotel, sir."

Why not?

"It's not allowed with your attire."

My chance of staying for high tea, $16, didn't look good.

I just stood there, not sure I wanted to leave. A second attendant came to help out the first guy.

"You're not allowed in the hotel wearing jeans," she said.

I wanted to ask her if she had any idea what kind of riff-raff were booked into the hotel.

The woman escorted me to a side room. She told me I could stay in there, but don't come out.

They were my dress jeans.

"You interested in going to the theater tomorrow night?" asked a guy from the Philadelphia Convention and Visitors Bureau. He was going both Friday and Saturday.

Tom Muldoon, president of the bureau, came by and I told him I was thrown out of the hotel.

"It's a class place," he said. "I put your photo up on the doors and told them to keep you out."

I left the country. I crossed an ocean. I landed in a foreign place. Nothing has changed.

ABOUT THE AUTHOR

Steve Lopez has been a columnist for the Philadelphia Inquirer since 1985. He has received the H. L. Mencken Writing Award, the Ernie Pyle Award for Human Interest Writing, and a National Headliners Award for Column Writing. His first novel, *Third and Indiana*, was published in 1994.